JUNGLE COURAGE

W. BLAKE GIBBS

WESTBOW
PRESS*
A DIVISION OF THOMAS NELSON
& ZONDERVAN

WestBow Press books may be ordered through booksellers or by contacting:

WestBow Press
A Division of Thomas Nelson & Zondervan
1663 Liberty Drive
Bloomington, IN 47403
www.westbowpress.com
844-714-3454

Because of the dynamic nature of the Internet, any web addresses or links contained in this book may have changed since publication and may no longer be valid. The views expressed in this work are solely those of the author and do not necessarily reflect the views of the publisher, and the publisher hereby disclaims any responsibility for them.

Scripture quotations are taken from the Holy Bible, New International Version®, NIV®. Copyright © 1973, 1978, 1984 by Biblica, Inc.™ Used by permission of Zondervan. All rights reserved worldwide.

ISBN: 979-8-3850-0167-5 (sc)
ISBN: 979-8-3850-0168-2 (hc)
ISBN: 979-8-3850-0166-8 (e)

Library of Congress Control Number: 2023911910

Print information available on the last page.

WestBow Press rev. date: 8/8/2023

To
Ruth and Esther,

who lived the story,

but especially to Esther,

for your love,

your grace, and your wisdom,

and for making our life together part of the story.

I love you all the numbers!

"Go into all the world and preach the gospel to all creation."
—Mark 16:15 (NIV)

Contents

A Personal Note...

I first learned of the Landrus family when I was a young boy. My family attended Bethany Church in Alhambra, California, and Harold and Ella Landrus were missionaries the church supported.

Every three or four years, the Landruses would come back to the United States on furlough, and we would hear their tales of ministry and adventure in Africa. After about a year of raising financial support and regaining their health, they would leave again for Liberia, West Africa, and another term on the mission field.

Years later, at the close of one of those furloughs, their youngest daughter, Esther, did not return with them to Africa but, instead, remained in California to attend high school. Shortly thereafter, we started dating, and my "education" about the Landrus family, about being a missionary, and about life in Africa began.

In 1965, Esther and I were married, and she asked me to promise I would take her "home," which meant Africa, to visit her parents before they retired.

Four years later, we made our first trip to Africa together. At the time, Harold and Ella were serving at New Hope Town, a leper colony in the deepest, most remote jungle you can imagine. It was an incredible experience for me to see, feel, and understand firsthand what their lives were really like.

I have never written a book before, but as the years have gone by, and I have learned more about the story of Harold and Ella Landrus and their children, Paul, Ruth, and Esther, I knew theirs was a story that had to be told. It is a story of faith and courage, of commitment and love, and of joy and sadness. It is a story of adventure almost defying imagination. My dream is that someday someone like Harrison Ford might learn about their story and make a movie of it. It is beyond any Indiana Jones movie ever made. The difference is it is all true.

The Landruses went to Africa because, in their hearts, they believed God had called them to be missionaries there. It was their choice to go, but they also felt compelled to go. They simply had to do what God had laid on their hearts. They were driven to do so. That is what gave their lives purpose and meaning.

They didn't go to impose Western ways or Western culture on the Liberian people. They didn't go thinking of themselves as superior or "better". They went because they wanted to share Jesus with people who had never had the opportunity to hear about and experience His grace, mercy, forgiveness, and love.

In addition to addressing people's spiritual needs, Harold and Ella wanted to help people with their physical needs. Wherever they served in Liberia, they held daily clinic to treat those who were sick, hurt, or injured. They taught reading and writing. (In English, because the Liberian government wanted everyone to learn English as a means of helping to unite the country with its more than twenty different tribal languages and dialects.) They provided food and clothing to students and workers at their mission stations and to people in surrounding villages.

The Landruses' story takes place in a dramatically different time, place, and culture than exists today. Africa is not the same as it was when Harold and Ella were missionaries. America is not the same. Their story is as they experienced it back then—how they saw it, lived it, and understood it. It reflects their perspective, their beliefs, and their "all in" commitment to serve the Lord and the Liberian people.

Harold and Ella were people of deep, abiding faith. When they were faced with a challenge, they prayed about it. They asked God for His intervention in that particular need, whether it was for physical healing, clear direction as to what they should do next, or anything else. If it related to direction, once they believed they knew what God wanted them to do, they set about doing it. With steadfast purpose. No second-guessing. No turning back. Just get on with it.

God made Harold to be a missionary. I don't think anyone who knew him could imagine him being anything else. He wouldn't have survived normal life in America. There would have been too many rules, too many conventional ways he would have had to try to follow. He just wasn't created for that kind of life.

In Africa, he and his family thrived in circumstances that would have been beyond the rest of us. As a family we used to tease that, when

Harold retired, an entire company of angels collapsed from exhaustion after looking after him through all those years of adventure in the jungles of Liberia.

Nothing seemed to bother Harold. Nothing seemed too great a challenge. He never gave it much thought. He just went about doing what he felt God wanted him to do and did so with an unrelenting single-minded purpose. He did it without fanfare and commotion. Decades before the Nike slogan, "Just do it", came along, he was doing it. A man, his wife, and children, quietly toiling in the jungles of Africa for the cause of Christ. The results were lives of worth and accomplishment we would all be proud to leave as our legacy.

The Landrus family lived their lives to serve and honor Christ. It is my prayer, in some small way, this book serves and honors Him as well.

The story is told chronologically and is told in much the way I think Harold and Ella would tell it—simply, directly, "plain vanilla". The events and episodes presented are all true. In places names and characters have been added, where real names were unknown. Dialogue has been created reflecting as accurately as possible what was happening at the time and the nature, character, and relationships between the people speaking.

As you read their story, I hope you are blessed by it, encouraged by it, and challenged by it. Perhaps it is time we set aside our own agendas, step out of what is comfortable for us, and let go of the pursuit of what we want. Then we can launch out on the grand adventure God has for each of us—doing what He has uniquely equipped us to do for His Kingdom.

Harold and Ella did so, and their lives became the remarkable story you are about to read.

God bless you,

W. Blake Gibbs
November 2022

Chapter 1
Beginning Together

S itting on an uncomfortable wooden bench at the back of a large circus-style tent waiting for the program to begin, Harold was thinking about why he was there. If he was honest with himself, it was because he wanted to escape having to study all afternoon. He was not a particularly good student, and his studies were a challenge.

When he was in his late teens, he felt very deeply in his heart God was calling him to be a missionary. Now in his early twenties, he was enrolled at Southern California Bible College, intent on becoming equipped to serve the Lord as a missionary in some far-off corner of the world.

During the 1920s, traveling preachers, endeavoring to awaken the spiritual consciousness of the nation, were common around the country. They would come into a town and erect giant tents to hold revival or "tent" meetings.

Harold had heard about one in the area and invited Bill, his college roommate, to come along to see what it was all about. Harold reasoned these kinds of events were certainly better than studying. Besides, they were often a good place to meet nice girls. That provided all the incentive either of them needed. Their studies could wait.

As they watched and waited, Harold saw four attractive young women enter from the back of the tent. They were smiling and chatting with one another as they started down the aisle. One of the girls immediately caught Harold's interest. He nudged Bill with his elbow. "Do you see that girl coming down the aisle over there?" he asked.

Bill looked. "Which one?"

"The pretty one. Second one back," Harold responded.

"Uh-huh." Bill wasn't paying much attention. He was looking at one of the other girls.

"That's the woman I'm going to marry!"

Bill almost fell off the bench. Looking at Harold in complete surprise, he asked, "You're going to do what? What are you talking about?" He followed quickly with, "Who is that girl?"

Harold just kept looking at her and repeated very matter-of-factly, "That's the woman I'm going to marry." Pausing, he then added, "I don't know who she is. I've never seen her before in my life."

As they continued to watch, the girl Harold had identified began looking around the tent and happened to glance in his direction. Their eyes met ever so briefly. "She smiled," Harold said with a wide grin. "Did you see that, Bill?" Harold punched Bill's arm. "She smiled."

"You think so, huh?" Bill said, shaking his head in total disbelief and beginning to wonder if his roommate had completely lost his mind.

⌒

When they arrived, Ella and her girlfriends were surprised at the size of the crowd as they walked toward the open entrance to the tent. One of the girls remarked, "There are really a lot of people here. I hope we can find seats together." Entering the tent, she said, "Oh, I see four seats together up near the front. Let's go."

As they walked toward the empty seats up front, down the sawdust-covered aisle between rows of chairs and benches, the girls had no idea their entrance had attracted the attention of the two young men sitting in the back.

Walking forward, Ella glanced around the tent, amazed there were so many people in attendance. For just a moment, her eyes met the gaze of a young man sitting at the back. They were looking directly at one another. The corners of her lips raised in just the hint of a smile. Then she turned away to follow her friends to the seats they had found.

Bill was still shaking his head in disbelief. He and Harold had been roommates for almost two years. He thought he knew Harold pretty well. He knew Harold was planning on becoming a missionary and that he was determined, dedicated, and very much a get-the-job-done kind of guy. He was focused. He did things with purpose and resolve. Yes, Harold could be spontaneous, but Bill had never heard him do or say anything like this.

Harold didn't pay much attention to what the speaker had to say that day. He just wanted the service to end so he could try to meet the girl he'd seen. Once the last hymn was sung, the last prayer was spoken, and the people were dismissed, Harold made his way to the aisle at the end of his row of benches and posted himself there so he could see each person as they exited the tent. Bill immediately saw what Harold was doing and patiently waited to one side.

Then Harold saw her coming up the aisle. His heart started pounding. He wasn't sure whether he should try to speak to her or not. What if she wasn't interested in dating? What if she was already seeing someone? But he knew if he didn't say something to her now, he'd never see her again. He didn't know her name. There'd be no way he could find her. This was his only chance.

Ella was looking in the other direction, talking with her friends, as she got near and hadn't noticed Harold standing there. As she walked past, Harold reached out and touched her arm. She turned quickly to see who it was, and their eyes met for the second time. Harold's determination almost failed him, but it was too late. He had already committed himself. Before he could say anything, she said, "You startled me. Can I help you?"

As far as Harold was concerned, she was just about the prettiest thing he had ever seen. *Those big brown eyes,* he thought. *Wow!* For a moment he considered whether maybe he should just turn and run, but he managed to muster up his courage and said, "Excuse me. I didn't mean to startle you. I would just like to introduce myself. My name is Harold Landrus, and I'm a student at Southern California Bible College."

Ella just stood there quietly looking up at him.

He took a deep breath and, after an awkward pause, managed to blurt out, "I was wondering if I might call on you."

My goodness, she thought. *Right out of the blue, no introduction or anything. But he does seem to be a gentleman. And after all, he is attending Bible school. He must be a pretty good guy if he's doing that. He seems a little awkward, but he is rather nice-looking. What should I say?* Then she thought of a safe response. She said, "We have a Bible study at our house every Friday night. I guess it would be all right for you to come if you'd like." She told him she was Ella Pratt and gave him her address. Then she turned and walked toward her girlfriends, all standing nearby, anxious to hear every detail of Ella's encounter with this stranger.

Now that it was over, Harold's relief was almost as great as his anxiety had been before he'd talked with her. He stood watching her and then felt a little embarrassed as he realized he had to be the topic of the very animated conversation that had begun the moment Ella rejoined her friends.

Bill came up and put an arm on Harold's shoulder. "Well, ole buddy, are you happy now?"

As they walked away, Harold relayed everything about Ella and every word she had spoken.

~

To help earn money for his schooling, Harold had a job driving for Mrs. L. L. Layne, who lived in Alhambra, California. Mrs. Layne was very fond of Harold and not only paid him well to drive her around town but also gave him a small room to live in when he wasn't in his dorm at school.

After meeting Ella and learning about her Bible study, Harold thought the next Friday night would never come. The week seemed to drag on forever. All he wanted was to see her again. When Friday finally did arrive, he put on his best slacks and shirt and asked Mrs. Layne if he could borrow the car for the evening. She agreed without hesitation. She was delighted to loan him the car. This was the first time she could remember Harold expressing an interest in any girl.

Harold drove to the address Ella had given him. He knocked at the door, and Ella answered. "Oh, it's you," she said. "I wasn't sure if you'd come. Come in, and I'll introduce you to the others."

As he stepped into the room, Harold was sure she was even prettier than he remembered.

Ella led him around the room, mistakenly introducing him as Harold Skullins. She had mixed up his name with another Harold she knew. He wasn't sure what to do. He wanted her to know he was Harold Landrus, not Harold Skullins, whoever that was, but he didn't want to embarrass her in front of her friends.

After a couple of introductions, one of Ella's girlfriends came up to her, took her by the arm, and led her into another room. "What's the matter?" Ella wanted to know, a little perturbed she had been interrupted.

"Ella, that's not Harold Skullins," her friend said bluntly. "That's Harold Landrus. You're introducing the poor fellow as the wrong man."

Ella was mortified. All she could do was go back and apologize, but Harold took it with good grace, and they all sat down for the Bible study.

At the close of the evening, as he was about to leave, Harold took Ella aside and asked if she would go out with him. Much to his disappointment, she said "no."

That sort of established a pattern for them. Harold never missed a Friday night Bible study, and he never failed to ask her out on a date. Unfortunately, she never failed to say "no" either.

Harold was nothing if not persistent. He simply would not give up trying to get Ella to go out with him.

After three months of asking, Harold had grown accustomed to getting "no" for an answer. Then one Friday evening after their Bible study, he asked her to go with him to a Christian youth rally in Long Beach.

"I really think you'd enjoy it," he said, trying to persuade her.

Then, much to his surprise and disbelief, with a smile as though this was the first time he'd ever asked, she said, "Why, yes. I'd love to go."

They went to the youth rally the following Saturday night. Harold loved every minute of it. On the way home, they had a flat tire. As far as Harold was concerned, fine with him. All it did was make his time with Ella last longer. When he got home, he told Bill, "That's the only flat tire I ever enjoyed changing."

Once she said "yes" to their first date, Ella continued to say "yes" each time Harold asked, and their three-year courtship began. They enjoyed dating and went to Bible studies and church youth functions regularly.

From the time she had become a Christian, Ella felt she wanted to be a missionary, but she hadn't mentioned it to Harold. They had been going together for some time when she learned he was part of an Africa Missionary Prayer Group, which met regularly to pray for missionaries serving in Africa. It was then they discovered they both shared a desire to be missionaries in Africa.

One evening a few months later, as they sat alone together, Harold had three questions burning in his mind he wanted to ask her, but he was reluctant to do so. They were probably the most important questions he would ever ask her. He was nervous and hesitant.

Sensing his uneasiness, Ella asked, "Harold, is something wrong?"

"No," he answered. "Just got something on my mind."

Marshaling his courage, he looked into Ella's eyes and said, "I have some questions for you about our future."

"OK," Ella responded. "What are they?"

Pausing, he went on, "Are you willing to be a missionary?"

She looked back with a smile, answering, "Yes, you know I am. We both want to be missionaries. We've talked about that."

"Yes, that's true," he said and then continued, "Well, do you want to have children, to raise a family?"

Wondering where he was going with this, she answered, "Yes. Yes, I would like to have children."

Taking a deep breath, Harold pressed on, "If we were facing a serious problem and couldn't agree on the best answer, would you be willing to abide by my decision?"

She paused for a moment, thinking. After what seemed like an eternity to Harold, she responded, "Yes, I would. I believe the man should have the final say in a family because, if he truly loves his wife and children, the decisions he makes will always be motivated by what is best for them."

He smiled and looked at her for several moments. Finally, he said, "Well, then, you're the girl for me. Will you marry me?"

With a broad smile, she answered simply, "Yes, I will."

<hr />

As the *Post Advocate*, the local newspaper, described it, Harold and Ella were married in front of a "host of friends and family" on August 30, 1931, at Bethany Church in Alhambra, California. They had started attending Bethany while they were dating, and it had become their church "home." The ceremony was conducted by Dr. C.E. Britton, the pastor.

Harold and Ella's Wedding Day, August 30, 1931

Dr. Britton had grown up with numerous health problems and was a man of small physical stature, but he was a giant in his Christian faith and in his knowledge and understanding of the Bible. In 1928, he and his mother had come out of the Foursquare Church movement in Los Angeles to hold Bible studies in the Alhambra area. Those Bible study meetings had resulted in a growing group of believers and, ultimately, in the establishment of a church, which they named Bethany Church. The church became well known in the community and attracted many people, including Oscar Pratt, Ella's father.

Oscar; his wife, Anna; and their two girls, Lillian and Ella, had moved to Alhambra from Pocatello, Idaho, in 1920. When they'd first arrived, the family had attended the local Methodist Church. As they grew up, Lillian, two years older, and Ella were both active in the church's youth group and enjoyed a lively social calendar.

Oscar, though, was not content with the rather staid preaching from the Methodist minister. When he heard about Bethany Church, he decided to visit to see what it was all about. He liked it immediately and convinced the family to try it. They, too, liked Bethany and began a lifelong membership there. Later, Dr. Britton's unwavering support and encouragement would be critical in making Harold and Ella's dreams of becoming missionaries to Africa come true.

Chapter 2
Assignment Aguilar

The young couple honeymooned for a week on Catalina Island, off the Southern California coast. As soon as they returned, they sent applications to the General Council of the Assemblies of God in Springfield, Missouri asking to be appointed as missionaries. A few weeks later, the denomination's missions department responded that Harold and Ella first needed to pastor for at least two years in the United States before they could be considered for missionary appointment.

This was a big disappointment for Harold and Ella, but they recognized it was probably for the best. About halfway through their courtship, Harold had left Bible school to work full time. Ella had enrolled in Bible school about a year before they were married. After getting married, they decided she should continue at school and at least complete her second year before they did anything else. Then they would see about pastoring a church in preparation for becoming missionaries.

When Ella completed her studies, Harold suggested they go to Colorado, where he had been born and raised, to see if they could find a church to pastor. In July 1932, they packed their few belongings and headed east.

It was a tradition with many church denominations at the time to hold weeklong regional or district "camp meetings" each summer. These were intended to be times when the denominational leaders and pastors from the area, as well as many of their church members, could meet at a campground or recreational facility for prayer, singing, and fellowship. Harold and Ella arrived in time for the Colorado "Rocky Mountain" District Camp Meeting. It seemed the perfect place for them to talk with the district officials to see about finding a church they could pastor.

At the time, the head of the district, the superintendent, was a man by the name of Woodworth. Harold and Ella looked him up and introduced themselves. "We're here to ask you about finding a church we can pastor for a couple of years so we can be appointed as missionaries," Harold explained.

Brother Woodworth (they were all part of God's family, making them "brothers" and "sisters" in the faith) was a kind man with a warm smile. He looked at the eager young couple standing before him and didn't know what to say or where to send them. The only place he could think might be interested in having a new pastor was a small group of believers in the little mining town of Aguilar, in the southeast corner of the state. It wasn't much of a church, just a few people who tried to meet regularly in a rented storefront, but their pastor had left, so they needed a new one. Brother Woodworth didn't really want to send this bright young couple there. It would be a difficult place for these youngsters to start out. It was likely to be too discouraging for them. And, after all, he did want them to succeed. However, try as he might, he couldn't think of another place.

"Well," he said finally, "you can go to Aguilar if you'd like. But let me tell you, it will be a real challenge for you. Then again, I guess if you can make it in Aguilar, you can make it as missionaries most anyplace."

They looked at each other and then at Superintendent Woodworth. Harold said, "We'll take it. Thank you!" Thrusting his hand out to shake on it.

Known as the "Gateway to the Spanish Peaks" and boasting a population of nearly 2,500 during the height of coal mining in southeast Colorado, Aguilar wasn't much when Harold and Ella arrived. It was just a collection of a few dozen run-down storefront type stone and wooden buildings facing each other across a dirt road. They were surrounded by a number of small houses scattered somewhat haphazardly in the valley below the mountains. Coal mining was Aguilar's primary reason for being there at all, and it had fallen on hard times. Most of those who had moved to Aguilar to work in the mines were now laid off. They didn't have any place else they could go. It was the Great Depression, and there was little work to be found anywhere. Most people in Aguilar were surviving on government assistance.

While the time of what became known as the Great Dust Bowl was still a couple of years away, the area around Aguilar was already feeling the effects of drought. Winds drove fine brown dust and dirt everywhere. All things considered; Aguilar left a great deal to be desired in terms of a place to live.

Despite the conditions, Harold and Ella were excited about being there and about getting started in the ministry. They knew this was a necessary stepping stone to becoming missionaries, so they tackled their assignment with enthusiasm.

They held their meetings (they really couldn't be called church services yet) in a rented storefront along what passed for the town's main street. They lived in a small "apartment" above the main floor meeting space. When they arrived, the apartment was in poor repair. It had a small cooking area, a table with chairs, and enough space for a couple of sitting chairs. There was a small separate bedroom. Unfortunately, the apartment didn't have indoor plumbing. They had to carry water in from outside for cooking and bathing. The outhouse was a trip down the stairs and a short walk to a small wooden cubicle out back.

Their "congregation" consisted mostly of a few women. Some were wives of miners and of local farmers, but most of them were wives of unemployed men who had nowhere to go and no prospects of a job. The women would come in for the meetings. The men would sit on a bench out in front on the porch. They could hear what was going on inside, while pretending they weren't at all interested.

Harold and Ella were paid a salary of fifty dollars a year for pastoring the Aguilar church. The little congregation tried to supplement that with gifts of food, which they could get with their government food stamps, but a little over four dollars a month was all the people could come up with in cash.

It was not an easy life. But Harold and Ella loved the people and were happy to be doing God's work. The people loved and appreciated them for their efforts.

Well, almost everybody loved and appreciated them.

Life in Aguilar was tough, and the men who worked the mines were tough. Some of them liked to drink, and they liked to enjoy the women at the hotel in town, which happened to be located directly across the street from the little storefront church. What they didn't like was the idea that the new preacher was telling people getting drunk and carousing with women wasn't the way the Bible said they should behave.

One evening, the church was holding a revival meeting, with a visiting evangelist speaking "on the devil and his works". Harold had opened the service and then invited the guest to address the congregation, which had now grown to include several men and a lot more women, as well as a number of children.

The church had its main entrance in the front of the building, facing the street. Inside, benches were arranged on either side of a center aisle, which led from the entrance to a speaker's platform at the rear of the room. On the platform were a couple of wooden chairs and a small pulpit from which the speaker could address the audience.

Sitting on the platform behind the speaker, Harold could look out across the congregation and through the open door at the church entrance to the hotel building across the street. As he sat listening, he noticed a light go on in the window of one of the second-story hotel rooms. Then, to his horror, he saw a man leaning out of the window with a rifle pointed directly at Harold's head.

When they had become Christians, both Harold and Ella had decided they wanted to live their lives in a manner that would both honor and serve the Lord. Once they were married, honoring and serving God hadn't really been a subject of discussion; doing so had just become an underlying assumption of their lives together. For them, part of honoring God was to trust Him in all things and in all circumstances. It was a very simple trust, which encompassed everything they did. They lived each day in total and complete trust and faith, knowing whatever happened to them, God was always in charge—always there to love, protect, provide, and care for them.

That didn't mean they always knew what God was doing. Nor did it mean what was happening at any given moment in their lives was what they wanted or was particularly pleasant. They just believed their job was to trust God. God's job was to take care of the results.

As he looked toward the rifle pointed at him, Harold wasn't fearful. Years later, he said he had never known fear during his entire life. He knew God was in charge, and whatever happened to him and to his family was up to God. But if he wasn't afraid, he didn't want to get shot either.

Keeping his eyes on the scene across the street, Harold leaned forward in his chair and reached out to pull gently on the bottom edge of the back of the visiting preacher's suit coat to get his attention. The preacher was beginning to get into his sermon. As he did so, his voice grew louder, and he got more animated. He ignored Harold's tug.

Still looking at the rifle, Harold reached forward again and tugged a little harder. The preacher went on as though nothing had happened. Finally, Harold gave a sharp yank that almost pulled the preacher off his feet. At that, the preacher looked around, angry at being interrupted and, with substantially less than Christian charity in his voice, exclaimed, "What are you doing?"

Harold said nothing but looked and nodded in the direction of the man in the window across the street. The preacher followed his gaze. As he realized what was going on, his knees went weak, and he almost fell on Harold. Then Harold said, "I think we should pray."

Pray they did. They knelt right then, right there. The guest preacher would have to admit later those prayers were among the most fervent of his entire life.

By then many in the congregation were craning their necks to follow the gazes looking out the door. When they saw the rifle, panic set in. Several dashed for a small door at the side of the speakers' platform which led to the outside. Some grabbed their children by the hand, jumped up and ran, dragging the children out the front door, even though that brought them more fully into the line of fire for the rifleman. Many, however, saw what Harold and the preacher were doing and they, too, simply knelt to pray.

Chester Carmichael was a down-on-his-luck, unemployed miner, who fancied himself a ladies' man. Because he didn't have a regular job, he spent most of his time in the mountains above Aguilar panning for gold. Every time he'd gathered enough gold to buy a few supplies and pay for a night with the girls, Chester would head back into town to tie one on.

That night, Chester was in the bar on the first floor of the hotel carrying on a very loud, very animated conversation with several other patrons about the new young preacher in town and how he was spoiling things for the rest of them by preaching against drinking and womanizing. "I tell you, we gotta put a stop to him, or we won't be able to have any fun in this town at all," he yelled across the smoke-filled room at no one in particular.

Part of Chester's drunken bluster was intended to impress Rose Garcia, the shapely woman behind the bar who was the hotel's proprietor, the bartender, and the madam for the girls upstairs.

Rose hadn't minded the new pastor and his wife. They were always courteous to her when they met on the street, and she knew it was his duty to preach against drinking and her kind of girls. However, she had to admit it was beginning to cut into her business. And that made things altogether different!

"Rosie," Chester roared, "I'm going to get that guy out of your hair for good." With that, he stormed through the bar and up the stairs at the back to his second-floor room. In the room, he turned on the light, picked up his rifle, loaded it, and looked out the window to the building across the street. Anger filled his thoughts. *There he is. Just sittin' there lookin' so high and mighty. If I lean out this window, I can get a good shot at him.*

Like most men in the community, Chester knew guns and rifles and was a good shot, even though his drinking made him a little unsteady. It wasn't an easy shot, but it was certainly one he could make. Then he'd just slip out the back way and head up into the mountains again. By the time he came back to town, nobody would care even if they knew what he'd done.

As he leaned out the window, Chester brought the rifle up and saw he had a clear shot through the open front door of the church right to where Harold sat. He pulled the stock back against his shoulder, steadied himself, and gently pulled the trigger.

While he knelt praying, Harold fully expected to hear the crack of the rifle and to feel the pain as the bullet entered his body. Time seemed to stand still. He was hardly breathing. He just kept praying and waiting.

Across the street Chester was dumbfounded. He had pulled the trigger, and nothing had happened. Quickly, he ejected the first cartridge and inserted another. Again, he leaned out the window, took aim, and pulled the trigger.

About this time, Sam Harris arrived for church. He was late. It seemed like he'd been late all day. By dinnertime, he hadn't finished all the chores on the farm, so he'd told his wife, Mary, to go on to church without him, and he'd be along as soon as he finished feeding the cows.

As he walked up the stairs to the porch in front of the storefront church building, people came rushing out the door, almost knocking him down as they fled past. *What in the world is going on here?* Sam thought in confusion.

He grabbed one man by the arm and held him long enough to ask, "What's wrong? Why is everyone running?"

The man broke away and kept running but yelled back over his shoulder, "Across the street. There's a man with a gun!"

Sam Harris was a farmer and a man of gentle nature. He was also a man of action who was unafraid to get involved. As he turned around, he could see Chester hanging out the window aiming his rifle at the front of the building. Without hesitation Sam darted across the street, bursting through the front door of the hotel bar. Inside, it appeared no one knew what was going on upstairs, but they were all startled by his noisy entrance. He ran for the staircase at the back of the room.

By this time, Rose had guessed what Chester was up to and was sure she would somehow be blamed for what Chester was trying to do. She panicked. As Sam reached the bottom of the stairs, Rose picked up a large kitchen knife and decided she would stop him from going up to Chester's room. She lunged at him, but Sam had seen her coming. With one swift move, he grabbed her arm, spun her around, and pushed her out of the way. Then he raced up the stairs.

In his room, Chester couldn't believe it. He was furious. The second cartridge had failed to fire, same as the first one. Once, again, he ejected the shell and jammed still another into the breach of the rifle. As he did so there was a thunderous crash as Sam broke through the door. Chester didn't have time to react as Sam dove over the bed and tackled him on the fly. Chester's surprise and intoxicated state made it easy for Sam to overpower him and, with one swift punch, to render him unconscious.

Breathing quickly, Sam stood looking down at Chester lying in a heap on the floor below the open window. Beside Chester were two rifle cartridges. Both had failed to fire.

Sam picked up the unfired cartridges, took Chester's rifle, and walked out of the room and down the stairs. There, Rose sat cowering and ashamed in the corner. "Rosie, I hope you're satisfied. You could have stopped Chester if you'd wanted to. You had to know he was going to do something irresponsible. Instead, you just went along with all his wild talk. It's just a good thing he didn't kill that new preacher."

Sam walked across the street and into the church building. Up on the speakers' platform, Harold and the visiting evangelist were still praying, as were others scattered around the room. "It's OK, folks. Nobody's going to hurt you now," Sam said calmly.

Then he walked up to the platform. "Well, Harold, I guess that added a little excitement to your evening! Are you alright?" He handed Harold the cartridges adding, "These were meant for you."

Harold stood up and responded, "Yes, Sam. I think we're all fine. What happened over there?"

Sam told him what he'd seen and done, and then Harold turned to the rest of the people, all of whom were getting to their feet, "Folks, I think we should probably consider tonight's meeting over. But be here early tomorrow night 'cause we have some real praising the Lord to do. He saved our lives tonight!"

Harold thanked Sam, locked up the building, and walked Ella up the stairs to their apartment.

The next evening every bench in the little building was full. People were standing against the walls along the sides. Aguilar was a small town, and everyone had heard about the attempt on the young pastor's life the night before. They considered it a miracle Chester hadn't succeeded. They wanted to see Harold and to hear what he had to say.

What he had to say as he stood before them was very simple. "Last night we found out who was ready to meet their Maker," he said. "Some of us were. Some of us weren't." He paused to let his words sink in. "Now's the time for all of us to settle that once and for all."

From there, he went on to relate the age-old Christian message that anyone can become right with God simply by accepting Jesus as God's Son and inviting Him to forgive them for their sins.

The attempt on Harold's life became the springboard for their ministry in Aguilar. It was as though people suddenly realized God is real and is directly involved in our daily lives. From then on, people knew who Harold and Ella were. The little storefront church was full or nearly full for every service after that.

Harold and Ella began a ministry to the inmates in the jail. Then they started holding regular meetings up at the Broadhill coal mining town. They were busy all the time and enjoyed knowing their ministry was growing and effective.

In early 1934, Ella told Harold she was carrying their first child. He was elated, but as was usually the case with Harold, he didn't say a lot or show much emotion about it. Throughout their lives together, that would be a struggle for Ella. Harold just didn't communicate his feelings well, but she knew he deeply loved her and, as they came, each of their children as well. She could live with that. She did know how he felt about having this first baby, though, because he proudly announced it to everyone they saw from then on.

As her pregnancy developed, Ella struggled with morning sickness and weight gain. Because they were so busy with their ministry, she ended up being exhausted most of the time, but she didn't complain. She was just happy she was going to have a baby.

The heat of July and early August, along with the dust and dirt (the Great Dust Bowl had begun by then) made Aguilar a difficult place to be heavy with child. Heavy was the right term. Ella had gained fifty pounds during her pregnancy. She was just looking forward to it being over so she could get her figure back and walk normally. Finally, it was time. Late one afternoon, Ella's contractions began, and they sent for the doctor.

By the time the doctor got there, Ella was in hard labor, but nothing was happening. After quickly examining her, the doctor knew they were in trouble and said to Harold, "We've got to get her to the hospital right now. Help me get her into my car."

They carried her to the car and headed for the hospital in Trinidad, a miserable twenty-five-mile drive over a winding, bumpy road. Ella thought she'd never make it. They stopped along the way where the doctor knew there was a telephone so he could call ahead to warn the hospital to be prepared for them when they arrived.

The struggle continued once they reached the hospital, but at least they were equipped to handle the emergency. It lasted all night and into the next day. Ella suffered terribly, and her body was punished almost beyond repair.

All Harold could do was pace back and forth in the waiting area outside the delivery room, fearing he might lose both his wife and the baby. The doctor came in and out of the delivery room several times during the night and early morning. Each time Harold asked what was happening and how Ella and the baby were. The doctor's response was always the same, "We're doing the best we can," as he rushed off down the hall. Harold just kept pacing and praying.

Then, mercifully, God answered their prayers. Their son, Paul Birdseye Landrus was born, August 21, 1934.

Paul had suffered almost as much as Ella had. His condition was so critical the doctor called Harold into the delivery room and began a direct blood transfusion from Harold to Paul in an effort to save baby Paul's life.

The doctor told Harold for a time he thought he would have to take the baby out in pieces in order to save Ella's life. Now, here was Paul, barely hanging on, but at least alive and in one piece.

Slowly, ever so slowly, little Paul began to respond to the transfusion, the doctor's treatment, and Harold's constant prayers. Days later, when the doctor told him both Ella and Paul would make it, all Harold could do was grin and say, "Can you beat that, man, can you beat that!" to everyone in sight.

Ella's recovery was slow and painful. When they returned to Aguilar, her mother came by train from California to help take care of her and Paul. The fact there was no indoor plumbing in their apartment didn't add to Ella's comfort.

Each trip to the outhouse was a long, painful walk for her, but as the months went by her stitches healed and her strength began to return. Each time she looked at Paul, she knew it was worth the ordeal she had been through to have him.

———

In the spring before Paul's birth, Harold and Ella had written again to the Assemblies of God Foreign Missions Department in Springfield to ask they be appointed as missionaries now that they had served for nearly two years in Aguilar. As they waited for the response, they struggled with the question, if they were appointed, where did they want to go? They knew they wanted to go to Africa, but where in Africa?

When they had attended Southern California Bible College, both Harold and Ella had become acquainted with Daisy Bullard and John Torta, two of their classmates. The four of them had developed a close friendship and enjoyed spending time together. It was clear to Harold and Ella that John was more than a little smitten by Daisy.

Much to John's dismay, when Daisy completed her schooling, she told him she would be leaving almost immediately to work as a missionary in Liberia, West Africa. This was a real blow to John. He wanted to talk her out of going, but knew she felt God was calling her to go. It wouldn't do any good to try to change her mind. When they said good-bye, John thought his heart would break.

A few months later, John sat talking with Harold and said, "I've decided to go to Liberia to be a missionary."

Harold looked at him and smiled. "You wouldn't be going out there to pick a Daisy would you?"

John smiled, too. "Well, I am taking a ring with me."

John did go to Liberia, and he and Daisy were married there. They loved their lives together, serving God and enjoying each other. Later, their joy was increased with the birth of their daughter, whom they named Esther. As far as anyone knew, Esther was the first white child ever born in Liberia. Their time together, however, was to be all too short.

In Liberia, warm, moisture-laden air blows in off the eastern Atlantic Ocean and drops as much as two hundred inches of rain each year. The rains support thick jungle growth throughout the country. From Liberia, the jungle stretches eastward in a band more than two thousand miles long all the way to the Congo in Central Africa and beyond. As the rains fall, they not only water the jungles, but their runoff also creates hundreds of streams and rivers. Some of the rain, however, does not flow away in the streams and rivers. Instead, it gathers in stagnant puddles, pools, swamps, and ponds, establishing the perfect environment for malaria-bearing mosquitoes to breed.

Avoiding mosquitoes in tropical Africa is simply not possible. Like all the missionaries in Liberia, Daisy and John faithfully took their daily quinine tablets to help fight off the effects of malaria. Unfortunately, their supply of quinine was running low. They hadn't been able to purchase a large enough supply when they were in Monrovia, the capital. More was on order, but they had acquired all that was available at the time. John decided he would stop taking his so there would be enough for Daisy and little Esther until the new supply they had ordered arrived. Daisy didn't like the idea at all.

"John, we still have some quinine left. Let's just all keep taking it and trust the Lord to supply more when we need it," she urged.

John wouldn't hear it. He knew they only had a few days' worth left, and not taking his would stretch the supply for Daisy and Esther.

As it turned out, John had been right. Their supply of quinine was just enough for Daisy and Esther. They were down to their last few tablets when their new shipment arrived. As soon as it did, John resumed his daily regimen, but it was too late. The mosquitoes had already delivered their deadly cargo.

Daisy suspected John had malaria when she noticed his listlessness. "Are you alright, John?" she asked.

"I don't think so. I'm exhausted and I ache all over," he responded.

"Let me take your temperature," said Daisy as she went to their medical supplies. "And let's double your quinine right away."

Sure enough, John had a fever. Then the chills came. John would shiver with cold. No matter how many blankets Daisy put on him, John could not get warm. The chills came in waves, usually interrupted with periods when John was so hot he couldn't stand to have even a sheet over him. Daisy tried everything she could think of. Nothing helped.

After it had gone on for three or four days, John was so weak he could hardly move. Then he noticed his urine was black from blood. The malaria had progressed. It had become black-water fever. John and Daisy knew he was dying.

God can't be doing this to us, thought Daisy. *What can I do?*

But there was nothing she could do, and she knew it. John was resting for the moment. She walked into the other room and buried her face in her hands and cried.

A few days later, John was no longer strong enough to even speak to her. She was by his side when he slipped into a coma. He died a short time later.

Daisy sat quietly at John's bedside. Then, as is so often the case when people face tragedy, her inner strength came to the surface. She rose and walked out the door to begin making preparations to have her husband buried. The heat and humidity in Liberia dictated that burial be carried out within twenty-four hours, or the body would begin to deteriorate. Daisy's only hope and joy at the moment was John had died knowing they had a beautiful baby daughter.

After burying John, Daisy returned to the United States. She thought she might go back to Africa later. But she wanted to be home with family and friends to mourn John's death and to let Esther get to know her grandma and grandpa.

When she got to America, one of the things she did was visit Harold and Ella. It was wonderful for them to be together. They all missed John, but Daisy could share her experiences with Harold and Ella, which helped them all deal with John's absence.

Daisy's visit had a major impact on Harold and Ella's deliberations as to where they wanted to serve as missionaries. Initially, they had thought about going to the small West African country known as the Ivory Coast, now called Cote d'Ivoire. However, John's death and Daisy's descriptions of the work and need in Liberia settled it for Harold. As far as he was concerned, more male missionaries were needed in Liberia. There were a lot of single lady missionaries on the field, and they were doing a great job, but they needed more men. He could make a difference there. That was where he wanted to go.

He and Ella prayed about it and felt God wanted them to go to Liberia. They asked Springfield to be assigned there. A few weeks later, they received the word they had been praying and working and waiting for. They had been appointed as Assemblies of God missionaries to Liberia, West Africa.

They were to immediately begin what was called "deputation"— the raising of their financial and prayer support for their first "term" as missionaries. They had to raise enough money to pay for their fares to Liberia and for the supplies and equipment they would need to take with them. Additionally, they had to raise enough cash or pledges of future financial support to cover their living and other expenses for the initial three years they were to be in Africa. After their first term, they would return to the United States on "furlough" for a year to rest and to raise support for another term on the field. This pattern would be followed for as long as they felt the Lord wanted them to be missionaries.

They needed to raise $600 for their fares and "outfit." They needed an additional $250 per month for three years. Harold and Ella had no idea where they could possibly raise what, for them, was an enormous amount of money. After all, they had been living on $50 a year in Aguilar. Nonetheless, they were glad to be getting started at last.

The missions department suggested, since Harold and Ella were pastors in Aguilar, and, therefore, part of the Colorado "Rocky Mountain" District, they begin raising their prayer and financial support there, in Colorado.

Typically, missionaries trying to raise support would contact churches in their district and ask if they could speak at a church service to tell the congregation what they would be doing as missionaries and to ask for the congregation's prayer support and financial assistance.

Sometimes, support would come from individuals in the various churches. Sometimes, it would come directly from the churches themselves. Whether or not a particular church decided to support a missionary, if it allowed the missionary to share his or her ministry in a service, the church usually took an offering to go towards the missionary's needs. If a church or an individual elected to support a specific missionary on a regular monthly basis, they would be asked to fill out a "pledge card," indicating how much they intended to give each month, so the missionary could count on that income while they were on the foreign field.

Until they had all the cash for their initial outgoing expenses and cash or pledges to cover their monthly needs in Liberia, the missions department would not let Harold and Ella leave. By the same token, once they had been appointed as missionaries, Springfield wanted them to get to the field as quickly as possible. From then on, a constant tension existed as to where Harold and Ella stood with their fundraising and how soon they could depart for Africa.

As summer 1935 approached, the annual Rocky Mountain District Camp Meeting was about to be held. Harold and Ella decided they would attend. They thought it would be a perfect opportunity to address the assembled church leaders to ask for their support. Springfield was already pressing them to agree to leave for Liberia by mid-October. So far, they had no support at all, but felt sure the response at the camp meeting would be sufficient to meet their needs.

At about the same time, they sent out more than two hundred letters to their friends and acquaintances asking for their prayer and financial support as well. Their expectations were high. They could hardly wait to see how God would provide for them so they could go serve Him in Africa.

Your
MISSIONARIES to AFRICA

Harold and Ella Landrus and Paul

"Go ye into all the world and preach the gospel."

These are the words of our Master. Will You help us?

HOME ADDRESS:	FOREIGN ADDRESS:
406 North Garfield Avenue	Assemblies of God Mission
Alhambra, California	Cape Palamas, Liberia
U. S. A.	West Africa

Please remember us in your daily prayer.

The first prayer card Harold and Ella gave to supporters.
Baby Paul was a one-year-old.

Both Harold and Ella liked attending camp meetings. They were an opportunity to spend time with old friends. And there were always lots of missionaries home on furlough who were only too willing to tell of their experiences and adventures serving God in some far-off place in the world.

Camp meeting was a time of relaxation and fun, as well as lots of singing and preaching. Harold particularly liked the singing, and he joined in with considerable gusto. He also liked the many solos that were sung. In addition to vocalists, there were instrumentalists. There was usually a host of trumpet and trombone players, pianists, guitarists, and even violinists. Harold liked them all. He'd even learned to play the violin, and Ella had begun learning to play the saxophone. They thought it would help them draw bigger crowds when they were missionaries in Africa.

After they arrived and settled into their tent, Harold immediately set out to find one of the district officials to ask for permission to address the meeting. Walking through the campground that beautiful afternoon in the warm Colorado sun, Harold was about as happy and contented as he had ever been. He had a wonderful wife. They had a fine young son. Soon, he was sure, they would be on their way to Africa as missionaries.

He walked along the lakefront, thinking how nice it would be to go fishing. He had loved to fish ever since his oldest brother, Leonard, had taught him when he was a boy. Then he spotted an official who worked for the district. As he approached, Harold greeted him with a smile and a handshake.

"How are things in Aguilar, Harold?" the man asked. "And how are Ella and that son of yours doing? I understand they had a difficult time of it."

"Yes, yes, they did," Harold replied. "But the Lord brought them through. I'm sure you'll see them both while we're here." He paused for a moment and then went on. "Things in Aguilar are going really well. The Lord has blessed our work there, and people are receiving salvation, but I want to talk with you folks about that. As you know, we came to Colorado wanting to be missionaries. Now, because we've served out two years in Aguilar, Springfield has said we can begin our deputation work to raise our support to go to Africa."

"Well, I'm delighted for you. I'm sure you're excited as can be. We'll be praying God will supply your needs quickly."

Harold looked him in the eye and said, "I'm glad you mentioned that. You see, Ella and I would like your permission to talk with the pastors and church people attending camp meeting to ask for their support. What do you say? Can we do that?"

The man's brow creased slightly as he hesitated a moment. Then he said, "Harold, you know we'd like to help you any way we can, but I just don't believe we can do what you're asking. You see, we're going to be taking an offering to buy one of our district officers a new suit as a way of thanking him for all he's done for the district over the years. It just wouldn't work to have you asking for financial support at the same time. I'm sure you understand." He gave Harold a pat on the shoulder and walked briskly away.

Watching the man go, Harold was dumbfounded. *No, Harold* thought, *I don't understand. Buying somebody a suit is more important than helping a missionary get to the field? I don't think so!* He was taken totally by surprise by the response to his request. He was hurt, disappointed, and angry. He didn't know what to do.

Slowly, he walked back to the tent. There, Ella could immediately sense something was wrong. "What's the matter? Are you alright?" she asked. Harold told her what had happened. She was as taken aback as he had been. They sat quietly on the cot in their tent for a few minutes. Finally, she sighed and said, "Well, the Lord called us to be missionaries. I'm sure He knows we can't go without support, so we'll just have to trust Him to provide. Let's go home."

The camp meeting was not their only disappointment. In response to the letters and prayer cards they'd sent out asking for financial support, they received only one reply. A lady had pledged to contribute two dollars each month to their support. That was all. Nothing else came in.

They went back to Aguilar where they decided they would leave Colorado and return to Southern California. Maybe their friends there would be more supportive, and perhaps Dr. Britton and Bethany Church would be able to help.

Chapter 3
The Adventure Begins

When they arrived in Alhambra, Harold and Ella were delighted to be back among their friends, particularly those at Bethany. Ella was especially happy to be back with her parents whom they stayed with.

However, they were anxious to get on their way to Africa, to be about the work they believed God had called them to do. The missions department from Springfield was continually asking for reports as to how their fundraising efforts were going and urging them to commit to leaving for Liberia in October.

What can we possibly tell them? Harold thought. *We can't tell them we have no support.* So, he didn't tell Springfield anything. He simply ignored their requests for a status report.

As quickly as they could, they met with Dr. Britton to ask for his help and to tell him they felt they needed to be getting on their way. His response was he, too, believed they were called to be missionaries, and they needed to get to Africa as soon as possible.

With a warm smile, Dr. Britton looked at them both and said, "We'll do all we can to help you go. There's a youth meeting this Friday evening. Take the whole service. You can speak, Harold. Tell them what you want to do and ask them for their help. Let's see what happens."

Harold and Ella were thrilled. Now, at last, maybe they would have a start on their support.

The youth meeting was called B.G.M., which stood for Bethany Gospel Messengers. As Friday evening approached, Harold and Ella were excited but nervous. What if they didn't raise anything?

The meeting began with singing and a time of prayer. Then the leader turned the service over to Harold and Ella. They shared their call to be missionaries and their desire to go to Liberia. Harold preached a brief sermon. As he concluded, he passed out pledge cards, and they took an offering. When the service was over, both Harold and Ella rushed to the church office to see what the results had been.

Dr. Britton was as anxious as they were and helped tally the money and the pledge cards. It had been a generous offering. The Lord had prompted those attending to give more than a hundred dollars, which, in the mid-1930s, was extraordinary. There were also pledges of nearly that amount in monthly support. Harold and Ella could hardly contain their joy. They didn't have all they needed, but at least they had a significant start.

Then Dr. Britton said, "I really do believe it's time for you to go to Africa. And this response from the youth group proves to me Bethany should send you. You take the regular evening service next Sunday, and we'll see what the Lord provides."

Now, they were even more excited. In preparation for the service, Harold and Ella drew up a list of the supplies and equipment they needed to take with them to Africa. They also made additional pledge cards.

During the week, they received another inquiry from the foreign missions department as to their status and their ability to leave for Africa in October. Once again, Harold decided it was better not to respond to Springfield than to tell them they had less than half their support with very little time left. If the missions department knew Harold and Ella still had so much to raise, they would probably cancel their assignment to minister in Liberia, and require them to go to another field later when they had their full financial support.

The Sunday evening service was always well attended at Bethany, and a good crowd was on hand when Harold and Ella began to share what was on their hearts about being missionaries in Liberia. At the close of the service, Dr. Britton walked to the podium and gazed out at the congregation. These were his people. He was their pastor. He was responsible to lead and guide and equip this group of believers to walk as followers of Christ. He loved them dearly. Now he needed to help stretch their faith—to help them believe God could and would provide. He wanted them to understand God called them to give so others around the world might hear the saving message of the Gospel.

He said to them, "You've heard Harold and Ella express their desire to follow God's call to become missionaries in Africa." He paused and then went on, "Now is their time. They are willing to go. They need to go but can't go unless we send them. We're going to pray now and ask God to supply all their remaining needs, and then we're going to take an offering for them. They have brought a list of the supplies and equipment they need to take with them. We would like you to select items on the list and sign your name beside them indicating you will buy those items and bring them to the church for Harold and Ella to take when they go to Africa. Beyond that, they need money in the offering to pay their fares to Liberia. They also need your pledge cards as your promise to help meet their financial needs each month while they are on the field.

"Finally," he added, "we want to establish a prayer circle tonight made up of people who will commit to regularly pray for Harold and Ella all the time they are in Liberia. We're going to call it the H & E Circle. So, if you want to be part of the prayer group, please sign up tonight. As we pray the Lord will provide for Harold and Ella, I want each of you to be asking the Lord what your part should be."

Dr. Britton prayed, the pledge cards were distributed, and then the offering was taken. As the service closed, many in the congregation converged on the sign-up sheets to purchase various items for the young couple and to join the H & E Circle. Others surrounded Harold and Ella to offer their encouragement and best wishes and to tell them what a good job they had done in the service. It took considerable effort for the two of them to be courteous and to pay attention to what was being said. All they really wanted to do was find out the results of the evening's sign-up sheets and offering.

As the last of the congregation left and they headed for the church office, Dr. Britton met them at the door. He tried to keep a straight, slightly serious expression but couldn't. He looked at them with a sparkle in his eye and a wide grin. "God must believe you're supposed to go to Africa now, too," he said. "The offering was more than enough to pay for your fares and all the items on your list of supplies and equipment have been signed-off. Best of all, it looks like there will be more than twenty people praying for you every day while you're gone. Oh, and the pledge cards collected bring your monthly total to more than the budget Springfield set for you."

Harold and Ella just stood there looking at him. It was as if they hadn't heard him correctly. They simply couldn't believe it. Tears began to fill their eyes. Harold put his arm around Ella's shoulder and then said, "Dr. Britton, we don't know what to say or how to thank you. You were the only one who really had faith in us and believed God wanted us to do this."

"You don't need to thank me, Harold," Dr. Britton responded. "Thank God. He's the One who called you, and He's the One who is providing for you."

Then Harold thought of something. "Dr. Britton, can I use your phone? I need to send a Telegram to Springfield to let them know we're going, and we can make that October boat to Liberia." His smile was as big as Ella had ever seen it.

Those were happy days for Harold and Ella as their equipment and supplies began arriving at the church, brought in by members of the congregation who had gone out and purchased them. Soon, they had everything from Coleman lanterns to flashlights, to beds and bedding, to jungle clothing. Everyone seemed caught up in the excitement of Harold and Ella's preparations.

As the supplies and equipment came in, they had to be packed for the long drive to New York and for the even longer sea voyage to the western coast of Africa. It was a busy time and a time of hard work for Harold and Ella, but it was also a time full of joy and anticipation, because they knew they were finally really going to go. They had gone to Bible school. They had served their apprenticeship in Aguilar. The Lord had provided their support. Now they were, indeed, at long last, going to Africa.

They made a hasty trip to the Bay area in Northern California to say goodbye to Harold's mother and his family and then headed back to Alhambra to finish packing.

Wilbur Bullard, Daisy Torta's brother, was to drive them to New York. They were to pick up Daisy on the way because she was going with them, on the same ship, back to Liberia. She was carrying a tombstone to place on her beloved John's grave.

Finally, the day for their departure arrived. They needed to be in New York by October 15th. They decided to leave about a week early to give them sufficient driving time. They loaded their gear into a small trailer behind Wilbur's big Buick and said goodbye to Ella's folks and a large gathering of their friends from Bethany who stood around the front yard of Ella's parents' house. Dr. Britton was there, and so was Helen Bridges, Bethany's first missions secretary.

Helen would be Harold and Ella's faithful friend and contact point at Bethany all the time they were on the field. In the years to come, she would organize countless support efforts on Harold and Ella's behalf, gathering clothing, food, medical supplies, and general supplies and equipment at the church and then packing it all into fifty-five-gallon steel drums for shipment to Liberia. She wasn't a missionary on a foreign field, but Helen had a missionary's heart. She was a person they always knew they could count on as a source of help, encouragement, and wisdom. Between them, Helen and Dr. Britton were determined Bethany should be the focal point for meeting as many of Harold and Ella's needs as possible. They never failed to do so during the nearly thirty-five years Harold and Ella were on the field.

Just before they got into the car, Dr. Britton called Harold and Ella into the circle of their friends and family and led them in prayer. He prayed God would guide and protect them and He would bless their ministry in Africa.

As they drove off, Ella couldn't help shedding a few tears. They had dreamed and worked and prayed for this day for many years. Nonetheless, leaving everyone and everything behind and venturing into the total unknown was not an easy thing to do.

What lay before them only God knew. She worried about their safety, particularly little Paul's. He was now fourteen months old and beginning to walk. Africa could be a very dangerous place for him. Many of their friends had questioned whether it was wise for them to even consider taking him with them.

However, Ella had done what would become a pattern for the rest of her life when faced with important decisions and critical times. She would say she had "prayed through" and had "gotten the victory". This meant she had prayed about the matter enough that God had given her a deep inner peace of heart and mind about it. She had taken the matter to the Lord and had committed it to Him. She was doing what He had called her to do. She had given her life to Him. She would trust Him to do whatever He, in His perfect wisdom and ultimate power, determined was best. It was not always easy to live that kind of faith. Man can't always see or understand what God is doing, but both she and Harold knew that kind of faith was the only thing that gave worth and meaning to life.

As they began their journey heading east on Route 66, they went with a confidence that, no matter what lay before them, all of it was in God's secure and loving hands. That was more than sufficient.

They were going first to South Bend, Indiana, to pick up Daisy and her daughter, Esther. They'd go on to New York from there. It was a long drive, but Wilbur's Buick was reasonably comfortable. The weather across the deserts of eastern California, Arizona, and New Mexico was mercifully mild, for which they were most grateful, because the Buick didn't have air-conditioning.

They enjoyed the wonderful red, orange, and yellow fall colors of the trees as they reached Kansas and Missouri. Then they took a ferry across the Mississippi and went on into Illinois and Indiana. Ella loved the farms with their gently rolling fields, their tidy homes, and their well-maintained barns and silos. However, most of her time was devoted to keeping Paul occupied. So much time in an automobile was considerably more than Paul was interested in spending, but he handled it pretty well.

Early one afternoon, they were driving through Indiana, looking forward to getting to Daisy's by early evening. Wilbur was driving, quietly humming a tune as he contemplated a good home-cooked meal at Daisy's. Harold was in the front seat with him. Ella and Paul were in the back seat. Suddenly, the trailer hitch snapped, and the trailer they were towing broke loose.

Wilbur looked quickly into the rearview mirror as he responded to the noise and to the surge forward the car made as it escaped the load it had been pulling. He saw what was happening as though it was in slow motion. For a brief moment, the trailer continued to follow along behind the car, the tongue scraping on the pavement in a shower of sparks. Then the tongue slid to one side. The trailer was launched upward and forward, turning upside down and spilling its contents in midair.

Harold and Ella's supplies and equipment flew in every direction as the trailer crashed back to the ground and rolled over sideways once while still sliding down the road towards the back of Wilbur's Buick. It came to a stop, right side up, sitting in the middle of the road.

Wilbur stopped the car and pulled to the side of the road. Harold and Ella were craning their necks looking out the back to see what had happened. As the dust settled, they got out and walked back to survey the damage.

"Well, thank the Lord the car is OK, and nobody was hurt," Ella said as they got to the trailer. She was carrying Paul, whose eyes were as wide as could be as the three adults stood shaking their heads.

Miraculously, the trailer seemed to be in reasonably good condition. It had some dents and scrapes but looked like it was still functional. They dragged it off the road and Harold and Ella began gathering their possessions. Most seemed to have survived, at least to the extent they could be repaired and used, although some items, like the lanterns, were obviously broken beyond repair and would have to be replaced.

In the meantime, Wilbur went back to the car to check the trailer hitch. It was torn and twisted too badly to use. They would have to get it repaired before they could even attempt to tow the trailer. He returned to help gather the supplies and equipment strewn across the road and told Harold they'd have to get the hitch repaired before they could continue.

Paul was beginning to fuss by then because he was hungry. They hadn't had lunch yet and were planning on stopping to eat at the next town. Harold said, "Ella, we'll finish picking this stuff up. Then I think I should go with Wilbur into the next town so we can get the hitch fixed. We'll get back here as quick as we can, but I don't think we should leave all of this here without someone staying to keep an eye on it. What do you think?"

She didn't like the idea of being stranded out there, but recognized it was probably the best thing for them to do. "I can stay and watch our stuff, but you should take Paul with you so you can get him something to eat. He can't wait 'til you get back."

They gathered things together and put them back in the trailer. Then Harold, Wilbur, and Paul drove off to get the hitch repaired, leaving Ella sitting on her suitcase beside the trailer at the side of the road all alone. As she watched them drive off into the distance, she couldn't help thinking. *We've just gotten started, and already this has happened. I'm afraid to even think what the rest of this trip will be like!* She smiled at herself and decided this just gave her a good opportunity to be alone on a beautiful afternoon, in a beautiful place, to talk with the Lord a little.

The fellows made good time and returned shortly, with the hitch repaired, Paul fed, and a sandwich and soda for Ella. They remounted the hitch, hooked the trailer up, and were on their way again.

In spite of the delays, they made it to Daisy's early enough for Wilbur to get his home-cooked dinner. It was wonderful for them to all be together. They talked late into the evening but were up at dawn the next morning. Daisy and her daughter, Esther, were now traveling with them, making it significantly more crowded. If they could, they wanted to drive all the way to New York that day.

It proved to be a very long day. They arrived in New York City at 3:00 a.m. the following morning after driving for more than twenty hours. Once there, they realized their limited exposure to the "big" cities of Los Angeles and San Francisco hadn't come close to preparing them for New York City. It was huge, and they were lost.

They knew they were to go to the mission house on Summit Street. The mission house had been established to provide hotel-style accommodations for missionaries waiting for their ship to leave or for those just returning to the United States from service overseas. The facility provided clean, comfortable rooms and good meals at a minimal cost. Those running the facility endeavored to help the missionaries in any way they could with last-minute needs before their departures. The problem was Harold, Ella, Wilbur, and Daisy had no idea how to get there.

Even though some might say New York City never sleeps, at three in the morning, it probably comes as close as it ever gets. The streets were basically deserted, with only an occasional car or a truck rumbling through. They saw no shops or stores with lights on signifying they were open. They continued to drive, looking for someone they might get directions from, not sure what else to do. They came to a stoplight, and a taxi pulled up beside them on Harold's side of the car. Harold thought, *if anybody knows how to get around in this town, he sure does.*

Quickly, he rolled the window down and waved to the driver next to him. The cabbie rolled his window down in time to hear Harold call out, "Can you tell us how to get to Summit Street?"

The cabbie thought for a moment and then, in a strong Brooklyn accent, called back, "Summit Street is only a block long. Dat's da problem. I don't think you'll ever find it, even if I gives you perfect directions."

"Well, we're missionaries goin' to Africa, and we have to stay there for a few days. So, we need you to tell us, and we'll just do the best we can," Harold answered.

"OK, OK." Pausing, the cabbie said, "Tell ya what. You's jus' folla me. I'll take ya there." Then off he went.

Wilbur quickly pulled in behind the taxi, shaking his head that anyone, let alone a cab driver, at this time of night, would go out of their way in New York City to show them where to go.

It took some time for them to get to Summit Street, making it clearer and clearer that, without the cabbie's generous willingness to show them, they probably would have never found the mission house.

As they pulled up to the driveway, the cabbie waved and drove off. *Dat's the least I could do, them bein' missionaries and all,* he thought to himself.

After they banged on the front door for a few moments, Mrs. Shaw, the lady who ran the mission house, greeted them. She didn't seem the least upset at having been awakened in the middle of the night. "Well, you folks must be awfully tired—especially those darling children. Let's get you right to your rooms," she said.

"We apologize for waking you," Ella offered.

"Oh, don't give it another thought. I'm glad you made it here safely and were able to find us. That's a real problem for most people," Mrs. Shaw responded.

Harold grinned. "Well, there was this angel looking very much like a taxi driver who showed us the way. Isn't it amazing how God takes care of things?"

They collapsed into their beds and slept until noon, then went downstairs for lunch. They were famished.

"We need to contact the American-West African Line to find out exactly when our ship is leaving," said Harold as they finished lunch. "I'll give them a call."

He returned to explain they would be sailing on a ship named the *West Humhaw*, but the ship's departure had been delayed. It wouldn't sail until October 30th. They had two weeks to wait, but at least would have time to shop for gear to replace the things destroyed in the trailer mishap. The *West Humhaw* was a 12,225-ton freighter built in 1918 as part of the World War I ship construction program carried out by the United States. (Years after Harold and Ella and their group sailed on her, the *West Humhaw* would be torpedoed and sunk by a German submarine off the African coast in the Gulf of Guinea on November 8, 1943.)

Daisy, Esther, and Wilbur went to stay with Daisy and Wilbur's mother, who lived in New York. Little Esther would be staying with her grandma when Daisy left. Daisy didn't think she could handle Africa and a toddler on her own. Wilbur decided to stay to see Daisy and the Landruses off on the ship.

On October 28th, it began raining. The morning of October 30th, they received word the rain had delayed loading grain on the *West Humhaw*. They would have to wait until they were notified when to come board the ship, but should remain ready because it could be at any time.

The call came early on November 1, 1935. They were to be at the dock at ten o'clock that morning. They arrived at 9:00 a.m. and were shown to their quarters. They were served their first meal on board at lunchtime, and the ship sailed at one o'clock that afternoon. They stood at the rail waving to Wilbur and his mother and to little Esther, clutched tightly in her grandma's arms.

Ella didn't understand how Daisy could leave her baby behind. She couldn't imagine leaving Paul and knew the heartache Daisy must be feeling. She put her arm around Daisy's waist and just stood silently beside her as the ship pulled farther and farther away.

On the dock, Esther and her grandma and her Uncle Wilbur grew smaller and smaller until they finally disappeared from sight, but not from Daisy's heart.

They sailed past Ellis Island and the Statue of Liberty and then headed east, out into the vast, cold Atlantic Ocean. The storm that had brought the rain and delayed the loading in the harbor was a big one, and it was playing havoc across much of the North Atlantic. As soon as they hit the open sea, the *West Humhaw* began to rock and pitch as it fought through huge swells and twenty-foot waves. The bow would ride high on the crest of one wave and then crash downward, plowing into the base of the next one. As it did so, the entire ship shuddered under the strain. At times, it seemed the ship wouldn't right itself and would just continue down and sink, but each time the bow eventually came up, spraying water the length of the ship.

In addition to rocking up and down from bow to stern, the *West Humhaw* rolled back-and-forth precariously from port to starboard. Harold and Ella could alternately see nothing but water out of their porthole and then nothing but dark clouds above them, deluging the ship with rain. The rain, whipped by gale-force winds, slammed against the ship with a deafening roar. It was like nothing Harold and Ella had ever experienced. They didn't see how the ship could hold together under the punishment it was taking.

Ella became seasick almost immediately. For the next six days, she wasn't sure whether she'd survive or not. Little Paul didn't seem bothered by the storm and the violent motions of the ship at all—although it did make his attempts at walking much more challenging, not to mention hilarious to watch. For his part, Harold did well, except on those occasions when he had to help clean up after Ella and then change Paul's diaper, too.

Adding to Ella's discomfort, while the *West Humhaw* was primarily carrying grain from New York to Africa, when it had taken its previous voyage from Africa to New York, it had carried palm oil. Now the entire ship smelled of rancid oil. Remembering the enormous amounts of cod liver oil her mother had forced down her throat as a sick child, Ella might well have been sick even if the sea had been as calm as a backyard pond.

Six or seven days out, the storm finally subsided, the sea calmed, and they began to enjoy themselves. The *West Humhaw* was a freighter but was equipped with a number of comfortable passenger cabins, many of which were occupied by other missionaries bound not only for Liberia but also for Senegal, Sierra Leone, Guinea, and the Ivory Coast.

In addition to Paul, there were three other children on board. The missionaries held Bible studies together each day and the crew seemed to enjoy hearing them sing choruses. Their meals were excellent, and they were frequently joined by the captain when his duties permitted.

The ship was quite modern for its day. Its long black hull rode well in the water once they were clear of the storm. There were large cargo holds occupying most of the front half of the ship, and then the white superstructure, with the bridge, crew quarters, passenger cabins, galley, and so on and then additional, smaller cargo holds behind. Towering above the holds, both fore and aft, were giant cargo booms, cranes for loading and off-loading the ship.

After fourteen days of seeing nothing except ocean, they saw their first land. It was the beautiful, green Portuguese island of Madeira. The *West Humhaw* had cargo to be off-loaded at the port of Funchal, the capital, so they pulled into the harbor, and the passengers were allowed to disembark for the few hours they would be in port.

Solid, dry land—Ella was sure she had never enjoyed anything so much in her life. They walked the narrow cobblestone streets, dodging carts pulled by oxen, and snooped in the small shops in the city. Ella was particularly impressed with the embroidery for sale in many of the shops and even from street vendors. It was a cottage industry here. Hundreds of women on the island made some of the finest embroidery in the world in their homes in their spare time to supplement their families' incomes.

From a low, flat area along the coast, the island rose to magnificent, green-covered mountains. White houses and buildings with red tile roofs made it picturesque and inviting. They walked, soaking in the sights and smells and the warm sunshine, with little Paul walking between them holding one of their hands on either side. Having learned to walk on the rocking ship, Paul needed a little help navigating dry land that didn't move beneath him.

Ella smiled at Harold and said, "Let's just be missionaries here. I've had about all the boat ride I'll ever want."

They laughed together and then headed back to the dock. It was time to board the *West Humhaw* once again.

Four days sailing brought them in a large swing around the Canary Islands and then to their first view of the coast of West Africa as they steamed toward the city of Dakar, Senegal. They saw haze and dust in the sky before they saw the low, flat land itself. At the western edge of the Sahara Desert, Dakar is hot, dry, and dusty. Sand and dust blow everywhere. The Sahara is so vast brownish-red dust can often be seen in the northern sky as far south as Sierra Leone and Liberia. They call this phenomenon the "harmattan". As the ship pulled closer, they could make out the flat-roofed, whitewashed buildings.

Dakar had a deepwater port, like Madeira, and the *West Humhaw* was able to pull into the harbor and up to a pier for off-loading. The city itself, however, was across the bay from the port, so the ship's crew lowered the gangplank on the side opposite the pier and the passengers were loaded into a small boat they hired to take them to the town.

It took about twenty minutes for the little motorboat to cross the bay and bring them to a wharf at the edge of town. As they stepped off the boat, Harold and Ella glanced at each other. They had just set foot on African soil for the first time. It wasn't Liberia. Senegal wasn't at all like Liberia would be. It certainly wasn't where they would live and work. But, at long last, it was Africa!

"The Lord has indeed done exceedingly abundantly in our behalf," said Harold, quoting the Bible. "Praise His name. We're in Africa."

Tears filled Ella's eyes. Holding Harold's arm, all she could do was whisper, "My, my, my!"

They had no more than gotten off the motorboat when they were surrounded by a friendly, but decidedly intense crowd of white-robed, fez-hatted Africans, all insisting they buy the hand-made leather goods and other trinkets they held up towards them.

Only one member of the small group from the ship, Mr. George Stadsklev, spoke French, the official language of Senegal. George and his wife and their three children were bound for the Ivory Coast to serve as missionaries there. The rest of the missionaries couldn't speak any French, nor any of the native dialects. So, smiling and nodding at the eager salesmen and women around them, the little band of missionaries worked their way through the crowd and walked to the native market area.

There, the sights and sounds and smells simply amazed them. Fruits and vegetables and, meat and fish were spread on mats or cloth on the ground. French bread was cut into small pieces for sale. There were flies and bugs everywhere. Dirty hands touched and felt everything. Noticing that, the missionaries quickly lost any appetite they might have had, but it was all fascinating to experience.

They walked further into town and browsed in some of the shops owned by Lebanese merchants and found some pith helmets to wear to protect them from the tropical sun. Paul didn't seem to mind wearing his hat, which made them most grateful, because they knew he needed to wear it from then on or run the risk of sun-stroke.

Soon, it was time to take the motorboat back across the bay and to board the *West Humhaw* again. From Dakar, the ship began hopping down the west coast of the African continent, stopping every few hours to drop off cargo at the next major town along the way—"major town" being a very relative term. The next stop was Conakry, capital city of Guinea.

At Conakry, there was no deepwater port. The ship had to anchor off the coast, and the passengers went ashore on small open boats paddled by eight to ten oarsmen. The sea was calm, so the ship could lower the gangplank to just above water level, and the passengers could walk relatively easily down to the waiting boats for ferrying to shore.

The pattern was the same at the next stop, Freetown, Sierra Leone. At both Conakry and Freetown, Harold and some of the other missionaries went ashore, while Ella stayed on board with Paul. She thought it was just too hot and humid for him until he could better get used to it.

Freetown got its name because it became one of the places where slaves were returned to Africa and set free after the abolition of slavery in Europe and America. Daisy went ashore at Freetown to visit some friends who were missionaries there.

From Freetown, they went to Monrovia, Liberia, and had their first view of the country that would be their home for at least the next three years. Here, again, they had to anchor offshore and take a small boat to get to the city. They did the same at the town of Marshall, just a few miles to the south.

Finally, the *West Humhaw* reached Cape Palmas, along the southern coast of Liberia. She had to drop anchor about two miles out because the coast was rocky, and there were both a coral reef and a sandbar hindering access to the shore. The sea was much rougher here than it had been at any of their previous stops. The badly rusted hulks of two ships lay in the shallows near the shore, testimony that the coast and currents here could be deadly.

It was November 25, 1935. It had taken twenty-five days for the *West Humhaw* to get them there from New York, but they had made it.

Their new home lay off to the east. They could see the green of the jungle lying low near the water and a few of the buildings in the town. After their dry, dusty days in Colorado, Ella loved the lush, green vegetation. Even anchored this far out, they could smell the jungle. They couldn't begin to imagine the adventures that lay ahead. But, for now, they were just grateful to God they were here. He had called them here. He had brought them here. All they needed now was to get ashore.

Chapter 4
Liberia at Last

G oing ashore proved to be a major adventure all in itself. They were anchored well off the coast to avoid the reef and sandbar, but that far out, the sea was rough and the *West Humhaw* rode up and down considerably on the swells and surface waves.

Surfboats, each paddled by six to eight oarsmen, came out from the beach at Cape Palmas. Not only did the passengers need to be brought ashore, several tons of cargo, including the Landruses' and Daisy's supplies and equipment, along with John's tombstone, had to be ferried to the beach as well.

The boats were about twenty feet long and completely open above their wooden sides. They bobbed and pitched as they pulled up to the side of the *West Humhaw*. With both the ship and the surfboats moving as much as they were, it was impossible to simply lower the gangplank and allow the passengers to walk down to the boats. They wouldn't have made it. The only solution was to lower the passengers from the deck of the ship directly into the surfboats using what was called a "mammy chair."

The mammy chair was a cubicle-shaped metal framework, open on the top and most of the way down the sides and ends. It had a floor and two wooden benches facing each other with a small space between them. Passengers climbed into the mammy chair and were then hoisted by the ship's cargo booms up and over the side of the ship and lowered thirty or forty feet down to the bouncing surfboat waiting below. It made for a thrill ride that could rival the offerings at any amusement park.

A mammy chair ride from the ship to a waiting surfboat below.

Ella was sure she didn't want to take that wild ride but knew there wasn't any choice. Her real concern was Paul, but she needn't have worried. He loved every minute of it.

Three or four at a time, the passengers were lowered to the bouncing surfboats. Each boat would take on six to eight passengers, and then the oarsmen paddled off towards the shore to be followed by the next boat. The boats then returned for more passengers until all were off-loaded. Then came the task of taking the cargo to shore. For this, the *West Humhaw*'s cranes were rigged with huge cargo nets instead of the mammy chairs, but the process was very much the same.

It was a long, rough, wet ride from the side of the ship to shore. As they headed toward the coast, Harold and Ella, with little Paul sitting between them, strained to catch glimpses of their new home as the bow of the surfboat alternately rose and dipped through the waves. The closer they got to shore, the rougher the water became, a result of the waves breaking against the reef and the sandbar.

The oarsmen strained to control the wildly bucking boat as they attempted to align it to pass over one of the narrow safe passages through the submerged reef. Ella wondered how these men could possibly know where the safe places were, but they didn't seem to be at all worried. She whispered a quick prayer for their safety and held on to Paul's hand a little tighter. The roar of the crashing waves was overpowering. Then they were caught in the rush of the surf toward the shore. It was thrusting them forward toward the reef with frightening speed.

The little boat seemed to be flying across the water. Ella was sure they were going to be slammed into the reef. If they were, they would all surely die. They wouldn't have a chance of surviving the pounding water. Suddenly, the boat surged upward, riding the crest of a wave. They braced themselves for the inevitable crash into the reef. Then the boat shot forward and dropped down. The water around them became calm and smooth. They had cleared the reef. The thundering roar of the waves against the reef was receding behind them. They were in a peaceful lagoon.

Harold looked at Ella. "That was about as wild a boat ride as I want for a while," he said, smiling at her. Ella let out a sigh of relief and loosened her grip on Paul's hand. They could relax now and enjoy the remaining ride past the lighthouse and up the mouth of the river to a small wharf at the end of the street leading first to the Customs House and then to the small town beyond it called Cape Palmas. The oarsmen grinned at each other, knowing what was routine for them had been a terrifying experience for these first timers.

When the surfboat pulled up to the wharf, Harold and Ella could hardly believe they were there. It had taken so long. Until now, it had almost seemed it might never happen. Something would go wrong, and they wouldn't make it.

Now they were about to step onto Liberian soil and to begin their ministry in Africa.

Harold nearly jumped out of the boat. Then Ella handed Paul to him, and she stepped out. Once again, tears filled their eyes. "Thank you, Lord," whispered Ella. "Thank you for being so faithful in bringing us here, after calling us so many years ago."

They were greeted by a throng of curious nationals and three white missionaries—Miss Emily DeGroat; Ed Simmons; and Ed's wife, Louise. Miss DeGroat had been a missionary in Liberia years before but had returned to America. She had not been in Liberia for some time. Now, she was back. This was Ed and Louise's first term as missionaries. The three of them, along with veteran missionary Florence Brisbin and newcomer Florence Steidel had arrived in Cape Palmas together by ship just a few weeks earlier.

As they introduced themselves, Harold noticed the missionaries had no vehicle with them, and he began wondering how they were going to get all their supplies and equipment, along with Daisy's, off the wharf and up to the mission house in town. When he mentioned it, Miss DeGroat explained the mission had no vehicle at Cape Palmas nor anywhere in southern Liberia. Everything had to be carried by native porters unless a local merchant was willing to assist them with one of his trucks. Even then, the trucks could only haul for short distances. The roads were dirt, and they existed only in Cape Palmas and for about twenty-five miles east, out to the town of Pleebo. From Pleebo, there was one very rough road north to Tchien and on west to Monrovia. There were no roads into the interior to any of the mission stations, only footpaths.

About then, a man drove up in a beat-up, old pickup truck and walked up to the group. "Oh, Emil, I'm glad you're here," said Emily. "Let me introduce you to our new friends." She then introduced Harold, Ella, and Daisy to Emil Frey. Emil was a French merchant in town, and Emily had convinced him to come along to meet the Landruses and Daisy and to volunteer his truck to haul their gear.

Now, here was Emil, at the wharf, doing his good deed. "You folks go along to the customs house to get signed in, I'll see to your things and bring them up in the truck."

"We appreciate that, Mister," replied Harold. "I'd sure hate to have to carry all that stuff. Thanks."

Cape Palmas wasn't much of a town, just an odd collection of several hundred buildings scattered about. A few of the more substantial ones were made of stone or concrete block, some with thatched roofs, most with corrugated roofs of rusting galvanized steel. For the most part, these were rather loosely located along what years of use had worn into a central roadway. There was no pavement, just bare dirt, which turned to sticky mud with the almost daily rains and to dust almost immediately when the sun was shining.

The less substantial buildings had mud walls and thatched roofs. These were spread out in all directions on side paths off the main road, or down along the shore, where an occasional dugout canoe had been pulled up on the sand once the day's fishing had been completed. Everything had an air of decay and deterioration about it, except for the President's vacation house, which sat in considerable splendor, at least in comparison to everything else, off by the lighthouse out on the point.

Despite its generally run-down condition and its haphazard assortment of nondescript buildings, Cape Palmas was the largest town in southern Liberia and, as such, was considered astonishingly modern and progressive by the natives in the interior. Years later, when Harold and Ella would send one of the mission boys to Cape to deliver a message, he would return in absolute awe. "Ma," he would say to Ella, "such fine, fine houses. Do you think they will have such fine houses in heaven?"

As the small band of missionaries walked up the road, naked black children scampered everywhere. They ran back and forth chasing each other, stopping occasionally to gather in small groups to discuss the strange child walking up the street with his parents. His skin was so white, and his hair was so light and fine textured. Most had never seen a white child before. For that matter, neither had many of their parents. Paul became an instant celebrity and, over the years, a favorite among the natives.

Emily led them up the street to the customs house, where they presented their passports to the customs official on duty.

Dressed in a khaki, military-style shirt at least three sizes too large, with one epaulet torn and hanging to the side, wearing khaki shorts, and barefoot, the customs officer, nonetheless, acted as though he was outfitted in the finest, most flawless uniform of the highest-ranking official in the land.

Standing as tall as his five-foot-three-inch frame would stretch, he examined their credentials in minute detail, stamping them with dignified care and then signing them with a flourish.

"Let us now examine your possessions," he said with an almost British accent as Mr. Frey pulled up outside in his truck.

Harold and Ella looked briefly at each other. This was the part they were worried about. They had been told duty on their belongings could be very high, and on their limited budget, that could present a real problem. Poorly paid and usually with large families to support, it was not uncommon for officials to use their positions to coax a little "dash," or bribe, from unsuspecting foreigners. They wondered what this man would require of them.

For what seemed like an eternity, as Harold and Ella agonized over the anticipated results, the little customs officer climbed through their cartons of goods and luggage, looking closely at everything they owned. As he opened each new box or suitcase, he would let out a studied "hmmm" and scribble notes on a small pad with his pencil. Because he used the pencil so often and had sharpened it so many times with his knife, he was operating with only the last inch and a half or so. However, this pencil stub was obviously a prized possession, and after each use, he carefully tucked it behind his ear.

Finally, he stood up straight and began tabulating the notes he had made, glancing occasionally at the stacks of belongings, double-checking he had covered it all. Then, with his most practiced, and what he assumed was an appropriately authoritative voice, he announced to them, "Duty on your possessions will be five dollars and seventy cents."

Harold and Ella and the other missionaries could hardly believe their ears. Duty that small was unheard of. They glanced at each other, and then Emily nudged Harold, who stepped forward and took out some American currency. (At the time, Liberia did not print its own paper currency. It minted its own coinage, but American cash was the standard medium of exchange.) Harold handed the money to the customs official and reached out to shake his hand.

Taking Harold's hand, the man flashed them all a broad smile and said enthusiastically, "Welcome to Liberia!"

Liberia is a small country, with a coastline stretching about 350 miles along the western coast of the African continent. It is bordered by Sierra Leone on the north and Guinea and Cote d'Ivoire on the east and south. The country extends inland from the ocean for varying distances ranging from about 75 to 190 miles. It is hot and humid. Much of the country is covered with thick tropical jungle, rising and falling above almost continuous ridges and hills that are usually only several hundred feet in elevation.

The name Liberia means "free." The nation was founded as a home for freed slaves from America and Europe. The first group of eighty-eight freed slaves arrived April 22, 1822, sent by the American Colonization Societies. These societies had been established a few years earlier by abolitionists intent not only on ending slavery in America but also on returning the freed slaves to their native Africa.

As good as the idea may have sounded to its supporters, it was not without its problems, both immediate and long-term.

In the short run, being freed from slavery in America did not equip those freed with the skills, knowledge, and experience necessary to survive on an uncivilized and decidedly hostile shore. Twenty-nine of the first contingent died within a few months.

However, with little but their courage and grit, the remainder hung on, building shelters and learning how to live off the land and sea. As more and more arrived, swelling their numbers to the thousands, settlements grew. Eventually, a government patterned after that of the United States was formed, with its capital named Monrovia in honor of President James Monroe of America.

Over the years, a particularly close relationship has always existed between the United States and Liberia. American aid has been substantial. Two American companies, Firestone and Goodrich, have for decades been the backbone of the Liberian economy, with large rubber plantations employing thousands of Liberian workers.

Beyond the difficulties of day-to-day survival, when the freed slaves arrived, they were seen as invaders by the indigenous tribes in the area. Slaves had been taken from all over Africa. Few, if any, of them ever returned to any part of the continent. Freed slaves sent to Liberia in the 1800s were the children and grandchildren and even the great-grandchildren of those who had been originally sold into slavery. They had no direct ties to Liberia or to any other African country for that matter. They were not considered fellow tribesmen or brother Africans by the native tribes. They were foreigners, and the indigenous tribes did all they could to force them out. There were frequent bloody confrontations. But in the end, the newcomers prevailed, and the tribal people retreated into the interior.

To this day, a division exists between those who are descendants of the freed slaves, at one time called Americo-Liberians, and those who trace their history to the native tribes of the land. The descendants of the freed slaves did not come to Africa with any sense of being truly African. They just happened to share the same dark skin as the native Africans. Instead, they brought culture and traditions that were uniquely their own, a blend of many divergent African traditions from the distant past, forced together because of slavery, mixed with bits and pieces of what America and Europe had to offer, and bound together through generations of suffering and struggle. They didn't have anything linking them culturally, socially, or linguistically to the existing native tribes of Liberia.

What they eventually did have, however, was greater strength and power than the local tribes people. As a result, they controlled political life in Liberia. The indigenous tribes had, to a large degree, been left without a voice in how the country was governed. Symbolic of that fact, English was the "official" language of the country because it was what the freed slaves and their descendants spoke. In the country's interior, dozens of tribal languages are spoken, with very few able to speak English at all, other than those educated at mission schools. The missionaries had to have interpreters with them wherever they went in the interior. The bloody civil wars in Liberia during the 1990s can be traced to the clash of cultures that had begun nearly two hundred years earlier.

From the customs house, the small group followed Mr. Frey's truck up the dirt road to the Cape Palmas mission house, again surrounded by a growing crowd of children and adults. As they arrived, Harold and Ella looked carefully at what Emily DeGroat said would be their home for the next three years or longer.

Once they had been appointed as missionaries by the Assemblies of God Foreign Missions Department in Springfield, Harold and Ella had, at their request, been assigned to serve in Liberia. However, their specific duties once they reached Liberia were to be determined by the field council, made up of all the Assemblies of God missionaries then serving in the country. The council appointed a superintendent to oversee the activities of the missionaries, to serve as spokesperson for the entire missionary contingent, and to act on the council's behalf for matters arising between council meetings.

Normally, the council met once each year at an annual convention, which was a time when all the missionaries tried to get together for fellowship and mutual support, as well as to deal with business issues relating to their individual and collective ministries. Because travel was so difficult, meeting more frequently was impractical. However, the superintendent could call an emergency meeting at any time he or she deemed it necessary.

Out of the newly arrived missionaries, the council had decided Daisy would be sent to minister with Ed and Louise Simmons at Feroka, a station in the interior that was a three-day trek through the jungle from Cape Palmas. Florence Steidel would work with the Palipo tribe, three or four days away. Florence Brisbin, who had arrived with the Simmonses and Miss Steidel, was returning to her work at Pleebo, at the end of the road and only an hour or so from Cape Palmas if they had a vehicle, but a full day's walk without one.

Map of Liberia with the tribal areas, mission stations, and key towns during the time of Harold and Ella's ministry.

Harold and Ella would be replacing Lois Shelton, who had taken John and Daisy Torta's place when John died. Lois would be going interior, and the Landruses would be stationed at Cape Palmas to serve as the business agents for the field.

Their duties would include handling finances between the various missionaries and Springfield, ordering supplies for the dozen or so missionaries in country at the time, and arranging for delivery of those supplies to the mission stations scattered throughout the interior of the country. They would also provide lodging and a rest stop for missionaries traveling into and out of the country. Additionally, they would preach, teach, and hold evangelistic meetings in Cape Palmas and the surrounding area in support of three or four existing native Assemblies of God churches.

Harold wasn't thrilled with the thought of all the paperwork and accounting associated with their assignment. This didn't strike him as real missionary work, even though he recognized someone had to do it. John Torta had been business agent before his death, so Harold agreed to try to fill John's shoes as best he could.

The missionaries spent a few days together at the mission house, resting from the long voyage, getting acquainted, and Lois giving Harold and Ella a quick lesson on the duties they faced.

Many of the local native pastors and their families as well as influential members of their congregations came to welcome the new missionaries to Liberia.

One afternoon sitting on the porch with Lois Shelton, Ella remarked, "I'm surprised so many of the nationals have American names. I thought they'd have African ones."

Lois chuckled and explained, "Many of the people here in town are descendants of freed slaves from America and Europe, so their names are derived from their American and European ancestors. Some of the people interior will have American-sounding names, too, because once they become Christians, they want either a name from the Bible or an American name to symbolize that their old lives are over, and now they are new creatures because Christ has taken away their sins. It's an important thing for them, and it certainly makes it easier for us to pronounce their names!"

Ella nodded her understanding and looked around the room, still marveling about really being in Africa.

Lois added, "You'll also find, even though English is supposed to be the official language here, almost no one in the interior speaks it. Most speak their tribal language. Some do speak pidgin English though, so if you listen carefully, you can probably make out some of what they are saying. It will take time for you to get used to it. I think it traces back to the English the freed slaves spoke. The natives picked up bits and pieces, and the pidgin is what it's become."

"One other thing you'll find is the natives will call you 'Ma' and 'Pa' once they get to know you. These are very much terms of respect and appreciation. They refer to us as being their spiritual mothers and fathers because we are sharing Jesus with them," Lois explained.

After spending a few days with Harold and Ella, the other missionaries left to go to their various stations. It was time for all of them to get to work. The Landruses were anxious to get started as well, but a little concerned whether they could handle it all on their own.

Theirs was a complicated, time-consuming, patience-trying job and one, after Lois left, they were pretty much on their own to figure out how to do. It was also a job upon which all the other missionaries were absolutely dependent. Without their finances and supplies, the missionaries couldn't carry out their ministries. Harold and Ella would be the link holding it all together, making it all possible. Everything every missionary needed, from food to toilet paper, fuel to furniture, rice to refrigerators (kerosene-powered), would have to be found, purchased, received, packed, transported, and accounted for. The Landruses had to do or arrange for all of it.

If a needed item could not be found in Cape Palmas, Harold and Ella would have to find it elsewhere in Africa or overseas. This was most often the case because the stores in town had very little to offer. At Daisy's urging, Harold and Ella had brought drums of flour and powdered milk for Paul with them from America in anticipation they would not be able to purchase them in Liberia. Sure enough, that proved to be the case.

Once a needed item was located and purchased, it would have to be paid and accounted for with the appropriate missionary's funds. When the goods were received at Cape Palmas, they had to be checked and any problems handled. Then the goods had to be packed to protect them from breakage and the rain. Finally, porters had to be hired to carry the goods from Cape Palmas to the correct mission station, a difficult journey of one to four or even five days, depending on the station. As an added duty, Harold and Ella served as the recipients for incoming mail for all the missionaries, forwarding it to them with their shipments of supplies and equipment.

＊

Harold and Ella liked their new home. The mission house was situated along the main street and was constructed of rock and concrete walls, with wooden roof trusses and a corrugated metal roof. It had neither indoor plumbing nor electricity. A well and the outhouse were located in the backyard. There was a nice grass lawn on one side of the house. This became a recreation area for them when they found a long-forgotten croquet set left by a previous missionary in one of the storerooms.

The house had three floors and an attic. The first, or ground floor, had two large rooms. One was for receiving and storing goods waiting to be sent out to missionaries in the field. The other they used as a meeting place for Bible studies and prayer meetings. On the second floor was a kitchen, dining room, living room, and two bedrooms. The third floor had three more bedrooms for the many guests they had passing through. When they had a large number of visitors, it was crowded, but they all made do.

Ella loved sitting on the covered second-floor porch, just off the living room, enjoying the spectacular view of the bay and the sea. Occasionally, they were treated to a gentle breeze off the Atlantic, which helped to stir the hot, humid air surrounding them like a thick, stifling cocoon.

Harold and Ella tackled their assignment with enthusiasm. They began immediately to meet with Mr. Frey and the other local merchants to determine what supplies and equipment were available in Cape Palmas. To their disappointment, not much. They had to order almost everything to be brought in from Monrovia, the capital, or from out of the country, which was an expensive and time-consuming process. When goods did arrive, hauling them to the mission house and preparing them for the long trek interior was an equally daunting responsibility.

They hadn't been there a week when Harold, exhausted from helping a team of men carry huge loads of supplies up from the wharf, said, "Ella, we have to get a vehicle to carry this stuff around. I never thought about transportation being such a big problem here."

"Well, why don't you write home and ask people to donate money for one?" Ella responded.

That afternoon, he sat down and wrote his first letter home since arriving in Africa. It included a request for financial help in purchasing a badly needed vehicle. Nine months later, he was able to write home again, "We praise the Lord for this big blessing Chevrolet service car, for which the missionaries on this field have been praying."

The vehicle could carry eight passengers, or the seats could be removed to carry three passengers and a truckload of cargo. It meant supplies could be driven from Cape Palmas to Pleebo before having to be carried inland, saving a day on the trail. It also meant tired, weary missionaries returning to the coast from the interior could be picked up at Pleebo, saving them an additional day's walk.

On one trip back to Cape Palmas after driving a missionary out to Pleebo, Harold and Ella saw a man walking along the side of the road going in their direction. They stopped to ask if he'd like a ride and then recognized he was one of the regular porters they hired to carry loads to missionaries in the interior. He had been walking for several days and was going to Cape to pick up another load.

"Matthew, you look beat, man, like you could use a lift. Would you like to ride into town with us?" Harold asked.

Matthew wore his load carrier on his back. Called a "cane jar," it was made of small branches and jungle vine the people called "tie-tie." It was used to help carry his load if he carried it on his back, rather than on his head, which was more customary. Tired from his long walk and unwilling to admit he had never ridden in a vehicle before, Matthew said, "OK, Pa," and climbed in.

As soon as Harold let the clutch out and the car began moving, Matthew buried his face in his hands in fear. "Oh, Pa," he wailed.

Then, since the seats were out of the back, he lay down with his face hidden all the way to Cape Palmas. Harold and Ella couldn't help feeling a little sorry for him, but it did give them a good chuckle, and it would give Matthew a story he would not stop telling his friends. He had actually ridden in a fine motor vehicle. None of his friends had ever dreamed of being so fortunate.

Beyond hauling people and supplies between Cape Palmas and Pleebo, the vehicle enabled Harold and Ella to expand the area of their ministry. They could now reach several more villages in the area, as well as the jail, which was some distance out of town on the Pleebo road. They immediately began a ministry among the inmates.

However, long before they had the vehicle, only a few weeks after their arrival, both Harold and Ella had taken trips to visit some of the interior mission stations. These and later trips gave them a better idea what life was like in the "bush" and what was going on throughout the region.

Less than a month after the *West Humhaw* had dropped them off, Harold agreed to stay at home with Paul, who was suffering terribly from heat rash, and continue their work at Cape Palmas, while Ella, Daisy Torta, Lois Shelton, and Florence Steidel took a trip north along the coast.

This first trip introduced Ella to travel through the jungle. It was more challenging, more time-consuming, and more exhausting than anything she could have imagined. It was only a two-day trip, but it represented the way they would have to travel during their first several terms as missionaries in Africa.

To take care of the four missionary ladies and carry the supplies required for the trip, a total of twenty-four native porters were needed. Several of them were native boys who attended Bible school at one of the mission stations and regularly volunteered to help the missionaries when they were traveling. It provided a way for the boys to earn a little money. Porters were each paid seventy-five cents a day, plus their ration of rice and, if they were lucky, some meat, usually monkey meat, shot along the way.

Sixteen of the porters were to be hammock men, four for each missionary. The others were to carry drinking water, camp cots, clothes, lanterns, Ella's saxophone, and the other essentials they needed, along with sufficient food and rice to support the porters and the missionary ladies on the journey. All these items were wrapped in canvas to protect them from the rain and then carried balanced on the natives' heads or, occasionally, on their backs on a "cane jar" like the one Matthew had carried.

The hammock men arranged themselves side-by-side, two in front and two in the rear of a hammock swung between two long poles, which ran from front to back, one on either side. Balancing the poles on their heads, the men stood up, lifting the hammock, which then hung suspended between them. The missionary was to sit in the hammock to be carried down the trail. (If anything, it was even more cumbersome and awkward than it is to describe!)

In retrospect, Ella realized her first attempt at climbing into the hammock and riding in it probably had to look comical. But at the time, she was totally preoccupied with simply trying to stay in the thing.

She had watched Daisy get into her hammock and tried to imitate what Daisy had done. She carefully sat down and then swung one leg over, so she was basically straddling the hammock. At that moment, believing she was situated, the porters started off down the path, with Ella hanging on for dear life.

On the trail, the men didn't stay in step, it was impossible for them to do so, but the result was the passenger was bounced in all directions simultaneously. Beyond adjusting to the bumpy ride, Ella was convinced she was too big for the space in the hammock.

There was a lightweight cloth netting draped over a makeshift framework over the hammock. This was obviously intended to help protect the missionaries from mosquitoes, but Ella couldn't sit up in the hammock without hitting her head on the top, and when she tried to lean back it would knock her helmet off. Having been told repeatedly she shouldn't go anywhere without her pith helmet to protect her from the tropical sun, Ella was not sure how to solve the problem. Finally, she noticed Daisy was riding with her feet up in the hammock, not draped over the sides. She tried it, and to her delight, she fit a whole lot better. Nevertheless, the next several hours of bouncing and jostling left her convinced she'd have been better off walking.

Ella in a later, somewhat "improved" hammock.

Along the way, when they came to a particularly steep or difficult section on the trail, the hammock men would stop and say, "You come down, Ma. You too heavy now."

As requested, the ladies were only too happy to get out and walk for a while.

Rivers and fast-moving streams were frightening for Ella. Often the hammock men would not stop at the bank, but just wade right in, not knowing how deep the water might be. As the water got deeper and deeper, the men would lift the hammock off their heads and hold it up with their hands stretched as far in the air as they could. With the mosquito net around her, Ella worried, if the current was too strong or one of the men slipped and lost his balance, she would be dumped in the river with the hammock on top of her.

There were times when all the ladies got their feet wet, but none fell in.

On this first trip, they crossed one stream more than ten times. Ella wasn't sure which was winding the most, the stream or the jungle path.

Adding to the adventure was the fact that, much of the time, the teams of hammock men would try to race each other. If one team slowed briefly, the next in line would scurry past them laughing, oblivious to the thrashing their running and jostling was inflicting on their passengers.

Along the way, the men were constantly talking back and forth and frequently sang songs the missionaries had taught them, making for both a bumpy and a noisy ride.

Harold and Ella did not want to ride in hammocks. They did not like riding in hammocks. They would much rather walk—not just because the hammocks were difficult to ride in, but also because they didn't like the idea of being treated in anyway special. They were there to serve the natives, not be carried by them through the jungle. However, the natives insisted the missionaries be carried. Recognizing it was an argument they weren't going to win, Harold and Ella rode some of the time to appease their hammock men. They also realized, by hiring hammock men, they were providing much-needed employment for the men. On the trail, Harold and Ella had no objection to the children riding. They were considerably safer that way.

Ella was constantly amazed by the jungle itself. It was thick and alive, encroaching across the pathway in places so the lead porters had to carry long machete-type knives they called "cutlasses" to cut the growth back, allowing them to pass. Above them, the trees and vines reached across the path, making the trail a dense, green tunnel.

When they finally reached the first village, Ella's team was some distance in the lead. It was a strange feeling for her to enter her first native village with no other missionaries and no interpreter at her side. Immediately, she was surrounded by curious children. As she climbed out of the hammock, she began to remove the dark glasses she had been wearing. Instantly, the children scattered in fear. Each time she made a move, the children would run and then slowly move back toward her as their wonder at this strange white woman overcame their momentary fear.

I wish I could tell them about Jesus, thought Ella. But she knew she couldn't until the others arrived. She had no way to communicate with these people. She just waited, wondering at the lives of these curious children, their bare-breasted mothers, and their loincloth-clad fathers.

They didn't stay long in the village and left shortly after the others caught up with them. An hour or so later, they reached another village, which surprisingly had a name. They called it Middletown. As they entered, Ella saw what the missionaries called "jujus" hanging in front of the huts. These were strange fetishes the natives had obtained from the local witch doctor to ward off evil spirits. These fetishes might be some dried chicken bones tied together or just a few small stones in a little pouch. The fetishes contained nothing of value, but they carried powerful medicine as far as the people were concerned. They often placed them at the entrances to their huts, or on sticks on their farms, or wore them to ward off danger and sickness.

Ella once met a man who said he was a warrior. When he wore his juju, he believed nothing could harm him. His enemies could not kill him.

The witch doctors had a good thing going and they knew it. To place an evil curse on someone, or to remove one, a witch doctor might charge as much as several chickens, a goat, or even a cow.

Ella was already learning the people in Liberia were animists. They believed everything, from rocks and trees to rivers and mountains, had a spirit. They also believed everything was controlled by the spirits, particularly evil spirits, and they lived in constant fear and superstition. If a person got sick, they believed it was because someone, an enemy, had "witched" them, meaning they had asked the witch doctor to place an evil spell on them.

They built their huts in a circular shape, not square, because they feared evil spirits could hide in the corners.

Coming from a Christian background and a predominantly Christian culture, it was difficult for Ella to comprehend how controlled these people were by their fears and the powers of the witch doctors. It was even more of a challenge to think about how the missionaries could effectively communicate God's love, compassion, and forgiveness to these people.

It was getting late in the day, and the ladies decided they needed to spend the night in the village, before heading back to Cape Palmas in the morning. This turned out to be like nothing Ella had experienced or could have ever imagined.

They went to the village chief and asked permission to spend the night. He was happy to have them, as it added to his stature to be able to offer help to white people. He invited them to "talk God talk" in the morning, meaning they could share about Jesus with the villagers. The chief offered them an empty hut at the edge of the village in which they could sleep.

As it applied to the hut they were directed to use, "empty" was a relative term. It was, indeed, empty of human occupants. It was not, however, empty of every creepy-crawly thing Ella and the others could have dreamed of, not to mention the large rats and mice that seemed to be a little annoyed at having to share their domain.

The hut was, of course, round. Its walls were made of sticks covered with thick mud. The roof was thatched palm fronds. The floor was pounded dirt with a thin cow dung slurry applied for good measure. There was a fire in the middle of the floor, and they sat on the ground to try to avoid the thick, eye-watering smoke. The only opening was a small doorway that seemed to allow every bug in the vicinity free access but didn't lessen the smoke one bit. Toward the peak of the roof was a framed, attic-like structure, where the villagers stored rice to keep it dry and smoked meat to preserve it, if they were fortunate enough to have any meat.

A boy named James and boys from one of the mission stations helped set up cots and mosquito nets for the ladies and began preparing rice for supper. The other porters and hammock men fixed rice for themselves. Each ate a tin can's worth of rice twice a day. As often as it was available, they covered the rice with palm butter, a thick gravy-like sauce made from nuts off the local palm trees. Meat or fish were a special treat for them. If there was any, it was added to the palm butter. Later, the porters liked trips when Harold was along because he would go off hunting with a few of the men and bring back deer, monkey, or some other game to add to the palm butter pot.

The Africans ate with their fingers. When the missionaries were ready to eat, it seemed everyone in the village gathered to watch them because they ate with spoons and forks. It would take a long time before Ella got used to being such a curiosity. She and her family were constantly watched and studied everywhere they went.

As darkness surrounded them, they climbed into their cots and under their mosquito nets. Tired as they were, Ella was sure they would sleep soundly through the night, but that was not the case. The hut was hot, rats kept scampering around, and the bugs and night creatures in the jungle made more racket than Ella believed was possible. As morning came, they were greeted by the gentle, joyful singing of the men around their fires.

They held an early Sunday morning service there in the middle of the village. Ella brought out her saxophone much to the delight of the natives. Too soon, it seemed to be over, and it was time to load up and begin the long trek back to Cape Palmas.

When she arrived home, Ella was anxious to tell Harold about all she had experienced but decided it could wait until after she'd had a good hot bath (with water warmed over the kitchen stove).

Shortly after, Harold took his first trip. It was longer than Ella's and took him to many of the mission stations they were responsible for supporting. Like the others, he tried the hammock, but folding his lanky frame into it made him cramped and uncomfortable. Most of the time, he chose to walk.

He returned to Cape Palmas almost two weeks later, delighted to be home but burning with the desire to minister in the bush.

"Ella, we've got to get interior. That's where the real missionary work is," he said his first night home. "I know they need someone here, but we need to be where the people are—where they haven't heard about Jesus. There are four churches here in Cape. The local native pastors are doing a fine job. They don't really need us. They need us back in the jungle." His eyes sparkled with his enthusiasm.

"Well," Ella responded, "you know I'd be willing to go, but the field council will never let us leave here without someone to replace us. I just don't see how it's possible."

"I know you're right," Harold sighed. "But let's start prayin' about it. The Lord has to let us go. He just has to." He paused and then added, "I'll tell you, though, we have to find a better, faster way to travel in this country, or none of the missionaries are ever going to get much work done."

In addition to traveling interior, the Landruses had also begun preaching and ministering in Cape Palmas. Harold was asked to speak at the local native Assembly of God churches. He would play his violin, and Ella her saxophone, which never failed to help draw a crowd. Unfortunately, before much time had passed, the hot, wet climate rendered both of their instruments virtually unusable.

Ella started a weekly children's ministry as well, sharing Bible stories with the children and illustrating them using flannel graphs.

As for their primary duty, the ordering and shipping of supplies and equipment was unending. By the end of their first year, there were more than two dozen Assemblies of God missionaries in Liberia, twice as many as when they had started. Harold and Ella were responsible for supporting all but three or four of them, who were stationed at Tchien and in Monrovia in the northern part of the country. The remainder were their responsibility.

It seemed there were always missionaries staying with them, either arriving or heading off to the United States for furlough. Ella always went out of her way to be a good hostess for however long her guests stayed, which was frequently several weeks.

Samuel, a young native boy from the Barrobo tribe, helped in the kitchen. Preparing their meals was a full-time task because the facilities were very limited, and everything had to be prepared from scratch. Food had to be purchased from local vendors. Water had to be drawn from the well in the backyard and then boiled for twenty minutes to make it safe for drinking and cooking. Bread and rolls had to be baked in a wood-burning stove, after the wood had been gathered and cut. Without Samuel, Ella simply wouldn't have had time to do anything else. He became like one of the family, trusted and relied upon to keep them safe from diseases brought about by contaminated food.

Their lives settled into a routine, acquiring needed supplies and equipment, shipping them interior to the mission stations, ministering in the local churches and the surrounding villages, and growing more comfortable with and accustomed to their circumstances.

Ella did most of the bookkeeping and handled a lot of the paperwork. Harold did the purchasing and arranging for the porters carrying goods back to the missionaries. Paul just kept growing and, as he approached two, kept finding more and more things to get into.

Their routine was punctuated with trips to the interior. Each new trek served only to convince Harold even more that the place they needed to be was at one of the remote mission stations located in the deep jungles of the interior.

The periodic arrival of a freighter off the coast also helped break their routine. A ship always generated a great deal of excitement because everyone knew that needed supplies and equipment would be coming ashore. For the missionaries, it also meant much anticipated mail from home might be on board as well. What a blessing when it was. What a disappointment when it was not.

There were often gifts, too. Boxes or fifty-five-gallon drums for Harold, Ella, and Paul from the family or from their faithful friends and supporters at Bethany were always welcome.

Dr. Britton, Helen Bridges, and others had begun what they called "Christmas in August" at the church. In August, they collected gifts and presents for the Landruses and other missionaries the church supported and then packed them for shipment, hoping they would arrive on the field in time for real Christmas.

As their second Easter in Africa neared, Harold and Ella were busy getting supplies out and looking forward to Good Friday and Easter morning services when they heard a large commotion outside. Walking to the balcony and looking down on the street below, they saw a large crowd of mostly men and boys yelling and shouting, running through the town, and dragging a stuffed dummy. As they did so, many of them would beat the dummy with sticks or throw stones at it. With each blow that was landed, the crowd roared its approval.

"What in the world are they doing?" Ella asked.

"I have no idea," Harold answered.

At that moment Samuel joined them. "They are beating Judas for what he did to Jesus," he explained and then added, "They aren't really Christian people. But it has become a tradition they follow. Each year they do this. It has become something of a celebration for them, even though it has no real meaning."

This was just one of the many strange, unexpected things Harold and Ella were coming to expect in Liberia.

Another had become their frequent encounters with Liberia's bugs and insects. It seemed every month or so, beyond the ever-present mosquitoes, they also had to do battle with some other pesky critter. One of these they simply called a "jigger". They all had them at one time or another. These tiny bugs hopped like fleas and most often attached themselves to their feet and legs. There they burrowed under the skin and laid their eggs. At first, they did not hurt but, instead, itched. When the eggs hatched, the larvae spread throughout their victim and began devouring the human flesh. Many of the people had parts of their toes and feet eaten away by jiggers.

Ella was constantly on the alert for the initial itching, particularly with Paul. When they thought a jigger might be present, they looked closely for a break in the skin indicating an entry point. Then they would have to dig the jigger out with a knife, being careful to get all of it and any eggs it might have laid. It was bad enough for the adults, for two-year-old Paul it was a traumatic ordeal. Because jiggers were contracted mainly off the ground, one of the Landruses' rules was everyone had to always wear shoes or at least sandals, even in the house. That was their primary defense against these nasty pests.

Teaching Paul to wear his hat, a pith helmet, to avoid heat stroke when he was out in the blazing tropical sun was another challenge. However, after a few stern scoldings just to make the point abundantly clear to him, he finally got the message. Eventually, they couldn't get him to take it off even in the house.

With each new difficulty they faced, Harold and Ella knew their best defense was to pray, to do what they could, and to trust God would protect and help them. Having done that, they left it in God's hands and simply refused to worry about it.

As Christmas 1936 approached, Harold and Ella began making plans to attend the annual convention. All of the Assemblies of God missionaries in Liberia looked forward to these yearly gatherings. They provided a much-needed time for fellowship and prayer as well as for dealing with business matters relating to the ministry throughout the country. This year the convention was being held in a place called Hooyah, a village in the Barrobo tribal territory. The mission station there was run by Pastor Samson, one of the most respected and effective of the native pastors. The field council had decided to hold the convention there as a means of honoring and showing their support for Pastor Samson.

The Landruses intended to participate in the convention and then to visit the Elseas, missionaries in the town of Koweka in the Bwebo tribe. Afterward, they would go through Neweka to see the girls' school on their way back to Cape Palmas.

They hadn't given up hope they could be stationed in the interior. But as convention time neared, they were convinced no assignment changes would be made. Maybe next year, they thought.

In the meantime, their ministry at Cape Palmas was steadily growing. Ella was having as many as eighty or ninety attendees at her children's Sunday school sessions. Their efforts with the inmates at the jail along the Pleebo road were showing promising results. Their work in the villages surrounding Cape Palmas was rewarded with new converts almost every week.

They were also busy serving as host and hostess for many of the missionaries passing through. They enjoyed this because it gave them an opportunity to learn what was going on in the interior.

In November and December 1936, one of their houseguests was Louise Simmons, who was expecting her first child. Because she was a trained nurse, Florence Steidel came out from Neweka to assist with the birth.

For his part, Paul was just a growing boy, playing with his native friends and learning to speak the local dialects as quickly as he learned English. Because the government wanted to make it the official national language, the missionaries taught and preached in English.

When they were in the interior, the missionaries normally needed interpreters to communicate with the nationals. At times, two or even three interpreters were necessary because the members of the audience might speak two or three completely different dialects. By the time Paul reached the age of eleven or twelve, he could speak nearly a dozen of the native dialects fluently and understand perhaps a dozen more, enabling him to serve as Harold and Ella's interpreter much of the time. The natives called interpreting "passing word".

Because there would be so many missionaries and native pastors at the convention in Hooyah, Ella decided to take Samuel and three other young workers with them to help with the cooking and other support tasks for the gathering. It was especially exciting for Samuel, as it would afford him the opportunity to visit his friends and family among the Barrobo tribe.

Both Harold and Ella were looking forward to the convention. They would get to see their missionary friends and would have a great time of spiritual renewal and inspiration.

It was an exhausting four-day trip to Hooyah and required nearly fifty porters, but it would prove to be worth their effort.

At the convention, to Harold and Ella's complete astonishment, the Elseas who had been ministering to the Bwebo tribe, deep in the interior, requested they be allowed to take over as business agents in Cape Palmas and that Harold and Ella switch with them and be assigned to their station at Bwebo.

The station was in the town of Koweka, in the Bwebo tribal area. However, the missionaries usually referred to locations simply by the name of the tribe, such as Bwebo, Palipo, and Gedapo. There was no need to identify the location any more specifically. There would only be one mission station in the entire tribal area.

Harold and Ella were overjoyed. "I can't believe this is happening," said Ella. "We had prayed and prayed about this but had no idea the Lord would really work it out for us! We thought He wanted us to wait until sometime later. God is so good to us."

Harold wrote home, "We are happy about it. Ella is as glad as I am. I feel we can do some real missionary work this coming year. Pray for us as we start this new work."

In one of her letters, Ella wrote, "Now we can do real missionary work. Praise God. Pray that God will use us in the saving of many souls."

Harold and Ella felt they could at last be about the work God had really called them to do. They couldn't wait to get started.

Rather than return to Cape Palmas after the convention, it was decided Harold and Ella would go with the Elseas directly to Bwebo. They would check out the station and then Harold would go back to Cape to arrange for their goods and equipment to be transported interior. The Elseas would go with him to Cape to take up the business agent duties. Because she had served as business agent previously, Daisy Torta agreed to meet the Elseas there to train them and to help get them started. Doing this would get Harold and Ella to Bwebo on a permanent basis as quickly as possible.

Chapter 5
Bwebo and a Baby

The Bwebo tribe sent porters to help carry the gear the Landruses had taken to Hooyah for the convention to the Bwebo mission station. They sent nearly two dozen men, women, and children anxious to meet the new missionaries coming to work among their people. Harold and Ella could hardly contain their excitement.

Once again, they faced a long hard trek through the jungle. Once again, they needed to have all their food, bedding, cots, drinking water, and the rest of what they needed for the journey packed and carried by the porters. This time however, it didn't seem so bad. This time, they were going interior, to Bwebo, to stay.

Harold walked ahead of the caravan most of the time, hunting for monkeys and other game to feed them all. The pathway was wet and slippery and completely overgrown in many places, slowing their progress considerably. Passing through each new village along the way, the entire population would turn out to say, "How do," to these strange white people. The natives, young and old, would walk up close to them to see them better and reach out to touch their white skin and their soft hair. They were particularly fascinated by the white child being carried on the back of one of the porters.

As they approached Koweka and the Bwebo mission station, they were greeted by a throng of people, all crowding about them to welcome them and thank them for coming. Chief William, chief of the local tribal group, and King Tom, the paramount, or head chief of the entire tribe, were both there to welcome them. Harold and Ella couldn't believe how glad these people were to have missionaries among them. They truly wanted them there and were grateful someone was going to be filling the Elseas' place.

The natives carried them to the church, near the center of town. It was a relatively large building with mud walls and a thatched roof, but it was quickly filled to overflowing as the people began to sing. The songs had been taught to them by missionaries, but they had been changed to reflect their own uniquely African rhythms and infectious joy and enthusiasm. Accompanied by drums and "shake-shakes", rattles woven of "tie-tie" vine with seeds inside, the noise was thunderous, but joyous and happy.

When he felt they had sung enough, Chief William motioned for silence and gave a brief speech welcoming the Landrus family. Then the native pastor offered a prayer, and everyone began lining up to personally shake hands with each of them.

Following their welcome, still singing and shouting their happiness, everyone escorted the Landruses to the mission house, their new home for the next two and a half years.

The house had a thatched roof. Its walls were mud and the floor pounded dirt. It had four rooms—two bedrooms, a living room, and a kitchen with a wood-burning stove. There was no plumbing or electricity. Interior lighting was provided by two kerosene lamps. Water was carried from the stream down the hill and then boiled for drinking and cooking. There was an outhouse in the backyard.

The family's home at the Bwebo mission station.

The best part, as far as Ella was concerned, was it had a covered porch in front and along both sides. A coat of local clay made the dried mud walls appear to be whitewashed, giving the house a far more substantial look than it deserved.

While many might consider a mud house with pounded dirt floors and thatched roof a hardship, Harold and Ella were ecstatic. Just days after their arrival, Ella wrote to her sister, "Yes, Lillian, I think of what you said once, that 'I was born with a silver spoon in my mouth'. God has blessed us, and we feel so unworthy of it all. We do praise Him for it."

In addition to the house, they had acquired a bit of a farm as well. They had purchased the Elseas' three goats and several chickens, four Plymouth Rock hens and a rooster the Elseas had brought from the United States, plus twenty-eight "country" chickens acquired in Liberia. These would provide the Landruses with milk, eggs, and meat.

At the time, a shortage of rice was creating severe hardship throughout the country, and Harold and Ella had to send teams of local men as far as four days walk to find rice to buy for the family. The prices had been driven up by the lack of supply, and they were hard-pressed to stretch their budget to pay for it all, particularly since they had purchased the Elseas' livestock and other supplies. The Elseas had worked hard and spent considerable money to make the station livable. They even had curtains in the house! Harold and Ella were grateful for what they had and trusted the Lord would provide the finances they needed to survive and to carry out their ministry.

As hard as the rice shortage was for the Landrus family, it was even more difficult for the natives. Ella was greeted almost daily by someone at her door asking for rice to feed their hungry family.

The natives looked upon the missionaries not only as people bringing them knowledge of God's love and salvation through Jesus Christ, but also as sources of help and assistance in virtually every aspect of their lives. If an argument developed between two villagers or between a man and one of his wives, they frequently took this disagreement, or "palaver" as they called it, to the missionaries to be settled. Together they would "talk palaver", meaning they would discuss a means of resolving the dispute.

If a family member was sick or hurt, they would go to the missionaries for medical treatment. The fact that most of the missionaries had little or no medical training made no difference. The natives simply expected them to know what to do and how to do it.

Requests for medical help were a particular challenge, especially if the natives involved were Christians. The missionaries didn't want them going to the witch doctor for help, but if the missionaries didn't try to treat them, they had nowhere else to go. So, like most other missionaries at stations deep in the interior, even without medical training, Ella held clinic every day to see what she could do to alleviate some of the physical suffering so often surrounding them.

Bwebo became her first experience as "Doctor" Landrus. Shortly after they arrived, she was approached by a man calling to her for help. "Ma, Ma, my foot she is hurt," he said.

Ella turned him around to see the back of his leg and found a large, infected gash probably six or seven inches long. "How did this happen?" she asked.

The man went on to explain that three years earlier, he had cut himself with his cutlass while clearing an area in the jungle to grow rice. He had gone to the witch doctor who had placed a potion of cow dung and water on it, and even though the witch doctor had charged him an outrageous fee of three chickens, the "medicine" had not worked. The sore had crusted over, but had then kept breaking open and oozing and bleeding, month after month. He had walked for many hours, suffering terribly with each step, to ask Ella for help.

She whispered a prayer, "Lord, please heal this poor man's leg and then heal his heart with the love of Jesus." Then she began to clean the wound as best she could. Hoping to stem the infection, she poured iodine over it. The man let out a yell as the iodine stung in the open sore.

Ella knew most of the people believed the more the "medicine" hurt, the better it must be. He no doubt thought this was very powerful medicine! She gently wrapped the wound, telling him about Jesus as she did so. Finally, she sent him on his way, with instructions not to let the witch doctor touch it and to leave the bandage on until it healed properly. As was often the case, she would never know what came of her physical and spiritual ministry to this man. She had done what she could and now had to trust God would take care of the results.

Beyond resolving palavers and mending bodies, Ella often sewed dresses and trousers for the Christians. She liked to see them clothed rather than half naked.

For his part, Harold did what he could to help supplement their meat supply with frequent hunting excursions into the deep bush.

One of the native women the Landruses met at Bwebo was a lady everyone simply called "Mama Ruth". She had two sons, Peter and Lawyer. Peter and young Paul were about the same age and became fast friends. They spent hours playing together with little toy trucks and cars sent from America by Paul's Grandma and Grandpa Pratt.

A witch doctor, or "devil doctor" as Ella more often referred to them, had purchased Ruth when she was a young girl. When she was older, his intent was to make her one of his wives. In the meantime, however, her family had given her permission to go to Neweka to attend the girls' school there run by Florence Steidel and other missionaries. While there, she had accepted Christ into her life and had become a Christian.

When she reached the age of twelve, the witch doctor had come to Neweka and forcibly taken Ruth back to his village to make her his wife. Ruth's response was to promptly run away, back to the mission station. Several days later, the witch doctor returned to collect Ruth once again. The missionaries tried everything they could to talk him out of taking her, but to no avail. He dragged her off screaming and crying, but she escaped once more and ran back to the missionaries, pleading for them to protect her.

When the witch doctor arrived again to collect his "bride," one of the missionaries tried to talk him into leaving her alone.

"I have paid a cow and a goat for her," the witch doctor protested. "She belongs to me."

After thinking for a moment, the missionary responded, "You bought Ruth when she was a young girl. What will you take for her now?"

The witch doctor was surprised by the question but blurted out, "Thirty-five dollars."

"Done," responded the missionary, pulling the money from his billfold.

From that point on, as far as the natives were concerned, Ruth belonged to the missionary, who immediately granted her freedom. Now, years later, Mama Ruth and her husband, Ernest, were helpers at the Bwebo mission station. Ernest helped around the compound and did some preaching. Mama Ruth served as the Landruses' interpreter. Their help and friendship were a constant blessing to the Landrus family throughout much of the next three decades.

Settling into life among the Bwebo tribe was a challenge. Perhaps the most difficult thing for Harold and Ella was trying to understand how the people, even many who said they were Christians, were so completely controlled by fear, superstition, and the devil doctors.

A month or two after the Landruses arrived, people in the village began to die.

Five died in one week, with more the following. As the weeks went by and the dying continued, the people were convinced the deaths were being caused by some sort of evil spell or curse. They began sacrificing chickens and goats and even a wild pig to try to appease the evil spirits. They called upon the witch doctors to make medicine to end the dying. They revived the "devil laws," which they had discarded when the Elseas had come to minister among them a few years earlier.

These devil laws were simply strange rules the witch doctors prescribed, saying the people had to follow in order to be safe from the evil spirits.

Harold and Ella were astonished at the requirements of some of these devil laws. No one could carry a monkey through the town with its head on. No one could carry a wet fish basket through town. No one could pick palm nuts while it was raining. No one could kill a bush goat and bring it to town the same day. The first pig killed had to be offered to a tree. The "laws" made no sense and, when they had no effect, only served to draw the people into further fear and confusion.

While all this went on, a total of twenty-four, mostly men and boys from one extended family, died.

They would have a headache for a day or two and then call for one of the three witch doctors in town, two men and one woman, to come treat them. The next day, they would be dead.

The people suspected the witch doctors were involved in the deaths but were too afraid to say so.

One day, a villager saw one of the witch doctors placing something on the thatched roof of a hut belonging to the town chief's brother, Harry. Upon investigation, he found a small piece of dirty cloth with some devil medicine wrapped inside. The man told the town chief, and the chief confronted the devil doctor. "Why have you put this devil medicine on Harry's hut?" he asked.

The witch doctor answered he had been told by the paramount chief, the highest chief in the tribe, to kill Harry because the paramount chief had himself been told by a witch doctor he would have big, big power if he killed all his people.

Harold and Ella were devastated so many of the people were returning to their old ways and turning their backs on their Christian experience. As Harold later put it in a letter home, "We prayed much about what to do because we felt it would break our hearts to see them go back to devil worship instead of going on with the Lord."

The Landruses decided they had to take drastic action. It could mean the end to their ministry in Bwebo, but Harold felt it was the right thing for them to do.

They called the town chief and all the people together in front of the chief's hut. As the people gathered, Harold held up his hands asking for quiet. "We are suffering terribly here with all these deaths. But turning from the Lord and going back to the devil ways is not the answer," he said simply.

Some of the Christians who had remained faithful responded by quietly saying, "Yes, Pa. You are right, Pa." Others who had slipped back into their old ways bowed their heads and stared at the ground.

Then Harold continued, "Ella and I have been praying and have decided it is time for you to choose who you are going to follow. If you want to follow Jesus, we will stay, and we will try to help you and to teach you God's ways. If you want to go back to the devil ways, it is up to you. But if you do, we will leave."

Instantly, there was a collective gasp from the people. "No, Pa," they shouted. "You cannot go. We want you to stay."

One by one dozens stepped forward, begging the Landruses to stay and promising they would not go back to the devil ways.

Finally, the town chief said solemnly, "Ma and Pa Landrus, we have done a bad thing. We want you to stay. We want you to talk God talk. I say no more devil ways in our village." With that, he ordered the witch doctors out of the village and told them not to return.

While Harold and Ella never knew exactly what had happened, they suspected the witch doctors were poisoning the people in a last, desperate effort to maintain control over them and to prevent them from becoming Christians.

Just as the devil doctor crisis ended, a crisis of another kind confronted Harold and Ella.

As Ella was putting Paul into bed one evening, she noticed a small red spot on his ankle. She wondered, *what can that be?* She touched it gently. It didn't seem to be tender, and Paul appeared to feel fine. Thinking it was probably nothing, she tucked him in and headed into the living room to catch up with her letter writing. She didn't even mention the spot to Harold.

The next morning, the spot was much larger and spreading up Paul's leg. Ella was truly worried. *Lord, Harold and I came here prepared to face whatever dangers existed, but our baby didn't have a choice. He had to come with us. You can't let anything happen to him. You just can't!*

Harold entered the room and immediately saw the spot on Paul's leg. His heart sank but he gave no indication of worry. "Well, son, what have we got here?" he asked. He gathered Paul in his arms and then said, "Let's pray. Lord, we don't know what this is on Paul's leg, but we ask you to protect him and to take it away and make him well." Then he put Paul back in bed.

"I don't have any idea what this is or what to do, do you?" he asked Ella.

All she could do was shake her head in silence.

Over the next four days, the red spot grew and spread up Paul's leg, almost reaching his hip. Only it did not stay red, it turned black. As it spread, Paul's leg began to swell. It became so swollen he couldn't walk. With the spread came a fever.

Harold and Ella simply didn't know what to do. They prayed as hard as they'd ever prayed in their lives. They tried to keep Paul as comfortable as they could, washing his face and body with a cool cloth to combat the fever. They asked the native Christians to pray for Paul, which they all did with extra fervor. Paul was a favorite among them.

Amid their struggle, two men working for the Firestone Rubber Company came through the village looking for men to hire to work on the rubber plantation near Cape Palmas. When they called at the Landruses' house, they couldn't believe the way Paul's leg looked and how sick he was.

"You people really need to get that boy to the doctor at Firestone. I've been in Liberia a long time but have never seen anything like this before," one of the men said.

"We appreciate that, Mister," Harold responded, "But we're afraid he couldn't take three or four days on those jungle trails. We can't do much for him here, but it's more than we could do for him on the trail. We've asked the Lord to heal him, and we're just going to have to trust Him to do it."

The Firestone men looked at each other and shrugged. The second man said, "Well, for your little boy's sake, I hope God is listening to those prayers." With that the men said goodbye and headed on their way.

God was listening to those prayers. Over the course of the next few days, the Lord healed Paul. Within a week, he was back to normal as though nothing had happened.

About six months later, the same thing was to repeat itself, but afterward, it never came again.

Paul's recovery was an enormous relief to Harold and Ella. It was also another demonstration to them and to the natives of the power of prayer and of the faithfulness of God.

Despite the trials and struggles of their clash with the devil ways and with Paul's illness, Harold wrote home only a couple of weeks later, "We are happy and busy as can be here on this new station. We sure like the work here in the interior. It is what we came to do and feel that we are in the center of His will. Of course, that makes the joy bells ring in our hearts."

As the weeks and months passed, the Landruses kept expanding their ministry. They had a large church and a Bible school and held clinic every morning. At the same time, they were busy caring for their chickens and goats and tending to the vegetable garden Ella had started along the side of the house.

Harold was anxious to preach in the dozen or so villages in the surrounding area. He developed something of a circuit he followed, going to them each week. When one of the natives complained he never knew when Harold would be coming, Harold explained he came the same day every week.

"But, Pa, I don't know when that is," the man said.

Harold thought about it for a moment and then, bending down to pick up six pebbles from the ground, said, "Keep these in your pocket. Throw one away each day. When you throw away the last stone, I'll be here the next day. Each time I come, pick up six new stones." Harold had provided the man with a simple calendar so he would know when to come to the village for "God talk".

As he was laboring up and down the jungle trails to the various villages on his circuit, Harold kept thinking, *there must be a faster, easier way of doing this. We waste too much of our time getting from one place to another. It takes away time we could better use ministering to the people.*

∽

Not many months later, Ed Simmons, one of the missionaries they had met when they first arrived in Liberia, sent a runner with a message for Harold proposing the two of them undertake a preaching excursion several days to the north and east into areas where missionaries had never gone. Harold was more than willing. This was an opportunity to share the Gospel with people who had never heard it. He had also learned there might be some horses to the north or even eastward into French Guinea. He wanted to see about buying a couple to ride on his preaching circuit. He reasoned horses would make travel both faster and certainly far more comfortable.

Ella wasn't too happy with the idea of Harold being gone for such a long time. They estimated he and Ed would be gone at least four weeks and, perhaps, longer. She had twice missed her monthly cycle and suspected she might be pregnant but hadn't mentioned anything to Harold. She knew he was excited about going so said nothing to try to change his mind.

When Ed arrived at the Bwebo station with his porters, Harold was ready with his own, mostly young Christian men from the village. A quick good-bye to Ella and Paul, and off they went.

Day after day, they struggled through the thick jungle on paths that often disappeared in the tangle of vines and undergrowth. When it wasn't raining, which made the going that much more difficult, the heat and humidity were sapping every bit of their strength. However, at each new village, they shared the age-old Gospel story. And as they did so, their strength seemed to be renewed.

Interpreting was difficult. As they moved from one tribal area to another, fewer and fewer of their porters knew the local dialects, but they prayed the Lord would somehow get the message across. And, one way or another, they felt it was, indeed, getting communicated.

Past the small town of Tchien, in the central highlands, they came to a village where, to their surprise, they found horses. Harold immediately spotted a nice-looking mare and inquired about buying her.

The local clan chief told him, "She belongs to the paramount chief and a Mandingo man who are up near the district commissioner's office." Further discussion indicated they would have to go about nine hours farther up the trail to reach the district commissioner's office.

Upon arriving there, they were greeted by the paramount chief himself. "What are you doing here?" the chief asked.

"We are missionaries making God talk. We also saw a nice horse back down the trail, and I'd like to buy her if the price is right," Harold responded.

"I am the chief; you must deal with me for the horse. What will you pay?"

"It looks like a good horse to me. I'll give you forty dollars for her," said Harold.

"If you pay me that much, we have a deal," said the chief quickly.

"We'll pick her up on our way back," Harold said. Then they headed on toward Guinea, sharing the Gospel at every opportunity along the way.

In Guinea, they happened upon a young boy riding another horse. Harold examined the horse and judged him to be about three years old. He thought the horse was probably too young and small for him to ride regularly, but it would be a fine horse for Ella. He purchased it for twenty-five dollars and loaded it with some of their supplies. Then he and Ed decided it was time to begin heading back to Liberia and their wives, but not before Harold bought a little burrow he had seen in another of the villages and thought would be a perfect pack animal.

After days of travel, they returned to the village where they expected to pick up the mare Harold had purchased from the paramount chief. The local clan chief greeted them and said, "Here is your horse."

On the way in, Harold and Ed had noticed horse tracks coming into the village from another direction. Now, standing before him were two mares. The clan chief was trying to give Harold the second one, the one that had been brought in since their first visit. It was old and had only one good eye. "No, Chief, that is not my horse. I bought this one over here," he said, pointing to the younger mare he had purchased.

"No. You bought this one," said the chief stubbornly.

They went back and forth for several minutes, with the chief intent on demonstrating to the villagers he could outsmart these white missionaries. Finally, Harold reached into his gear and took out his hunting rifle. Apparently, the chief thought Harold was going to shoot him and quickly agreed the young, healthy mare was, in fact, the one Harold had purchased.

Attempting to saddle the mare became like something out of a Keystone Cops movie. At first, the horse tried to run Harold down and then to bite him. That spooked the other mare and the horse they had brought from Guinea.

Suddenly, all three horses were running wild, kicking and bolting throughout the village, scattering the inhabitants in every direction and wreaking havoc on huts, pens, gardens, and anything else in their paths. It took hours to capture the horses and to calm them. The natives, trying to be helpful, probably only served to make matters worse as they ran around screaming and waving their hands at the frightened animals, thinking they were helping to corral them.

Once the mare was securely tethered, Harold blindfolded her and saddled her. Thinking he was about to ride a bucking bronco, he swung his leg over her and removed the blindfold. To his delight, she neither bucked, nor kicked, but rode as easily as could be.

Loading their supplies once again, they began riding down the trail toward home—two white missionaries, two horses, a burrow, and a small band of porters. Their horse adventures, however, were not completely over.

At still another village along the way, they saw a large white stallion Harold knew immediately was exactly the horse for him. The horse was owned by a retired army officer, who explained, "This is a good horse, and he will drink palm wine and dance, too!" Intent on demonstrating, he saddled the horse, put on his spurs, and climbed on.

As he did so, the native boys nearby began beating on their drums. Sure enough, the horse danced. Harold bought the horse from him but refused to use spurs or the curved bit the officer used. It had a knife blade welded to it and cut the horse's mouth each time the man pulled on it. That was the punishment the man had used to train the horse to dance.

Once again, they pulled themselves together and started down the trail toward Bwebo—with three horses this time. At the first village they approached, the local boys recognized the big white stallion as the dancing horse and ran for their drums.

The moment they began beating them, the horse exploded. It was all Harold could do to keep from falling off. He couldn't stop the horse, and he couldn't get off safely either. The horse raced down a hill in panic with Harold hanging on for dear life, his hat flying in the air. At the bottom of the hill was a swamp with a small, spindly wooden footbridge extending across it. Harold was sure the bridge would never hold him and the horse but was powerless to do anything about it.

The horse hit the bridge at full gallop. The fragile bridge quaked and shuddered under the strain but held together as the horse raced along it. Then Harold realized a section of the bridge ahead had no timbers on it. He was sure they were about to rush headlong into the swamp and tried to prepare for the crash. The stallion made a giant leap across the gap and was then on firm ground on the other side racing up a steep hill.

Near the top of the hill, the horse slowed enough for Harold to slide off. Still holding the reins and digging his heels in for all he was worth, he was at last able to control the animal and bring him to a stop.

Panting to catch his breath, he decided to rest for a while before he went back to find Ed and the others. Then he saw Ed coming up the hill with the other horses, the burrow, and the porters with all their supplies.

"Well, Harold," Ed said with a grin, "I guess we don't want the people in the next village beating their drums celebrating our arrival do we? By the way, here's your hat! Do you think we can go home now?" he asked, shaking his head and laughing.

~

While Harold and Ed were having their preaching and horse adventures, Ella was having a somewhat smaller, but equally challenging adventure of her own.

After Harold had left, she began worrying—if she really was pregnant, she should probably try to get to the Firestone doctor near Cape Palmas for a checkup. Paul's delivery had been so traumatic; if anything similar were to happen with this baby, out in the bush, she knew neither of them would survive.

She organized a team of porters and set out on the three-day journey through the jungle, knowing she faced three days more when she returned. The rains had been heavy, and the streams and rivers were swollen and raging. There were no real bridges, just logs stretched across, and many of them were submerged under the water.

Every time Ella inched her way over one of those slippery, moss-covered logs, she was sure she would lose her footing and be swept away by the fast-moving current. But the Lord was with her, and she made it safely to the Firestone rubber plantation, where she went immediately to the company's infirmary.

There, the doctor confirmed, yes, she was expecting, and there appeared to be no problems with the pregnancy. The doctor told her she was probably in her third month. Ella told him of the struggle with Paul's birth.

"You really need to come here when the baby is due so we can give you proper medical care, just in case any problems develop," the doctor urged. He told her to come back in late February or early March, well ahead of her anticipated delivery date.

Happy but still a little apprehensive, Ella made the long journey back to Bwebo, arriving exhausted, but glad to be home and anxious to share her news with Harold.

Several days later, Ella heard all sorts of yelling and commotion as the villagers ran out to greet Ed and Harold and to see the remarkable beasts they were riding. Only one or two of them had ever seen or even heard of a horse before. They laughed and chattered happily as the porters called out stories of their adventure and of Pa Landrus's wild ride on his new horse.

As Ella came out to meet them, Harold called to her, "Come see the nice horse I have for you to ride, Ella."

"I'm sorry," she said. "I can't ride your horse." She paused as she saw confusion on Harold's face. "I'm going to have your baby instead!"

Harold almost fell off his horse. He jumped down and hugged her and then, with a broad grin, turned to Ed and said, "Can you beat that, man! Can you beat that! Praise the Lord!"

They settled back into the routine of their mission life. They held clinic each morning, conducted the Bible school, and held Sunday services, and Harold rode his horse off to the outlying villages to hold services. He had built a makeshift shelter that served as a barn for the horses and the burrow.

Ella thought having the horses was probably a silly idea, but she recognized Harold liked riding rather than walking. Besides, she had decided he did look rather dashing sitting so tall and straight on that big white horse.

Harold on his horse.

The natives were fascinated by the horses, and large crowds gathered whenever Harold rode into a town or village. The burrow was another story. He might be good for carrying supplies, but the village women were frightened by his braying. They thought he was a demon. Late one night, several of them snuck into the corral and poisoned him. The next morning, Harold found him dead.

Over the next few months, first one and then another and, finally, the last of the horses died as well—although their deaths seemed to be from natural rather than human causes. The heat, humidity, jungle diseases, and lack of proper feed had gradually taken their toll.

Paul, approaching four years old, was completely at home, playing with Mama Ruth's son Peter and other native boys from the village and learning their language almost as quickly as he was English.

⁓

During the time he and Ed Simmons had been on the trail together, Harold had thought not just about acquiring the horses they were looking for, but also about eventually bringing an airplane to Liberia to help support all of the missionaries there. He had shared his thoughts with Ed.

"I think that might be a really good idea, Harold," he said. "Think of all the time we could save traveling. You could fly supplies in. If one of our people was sick or injured, that would be the quickest, safest way to get them out for medical help. You ought to see what the missions department says."

Encouraged by Ed's positive response, when Harold returned to Bwebo, he wrote to the foreign missions department in Springfield, telling them of the need for a good plane with a good young pilot to assist with the ministry in Liberia.

Several months later, the normal response time for mail from West Africa to the United States and back again, he received a reply. The reply stated, if the field council of the other missionaries in Liberia thought it was a good idea as well, Springfield would agree to it. Of course, the Landruses would have to raise their own funds to purchase the plane.

After receiving Springfield's reply, Harold was anxiously looking forward to the approaching annual convention, so he could present his idea to the assembled missionaries and native Christians.

At the convention, much to his disappointment, Ella and Ed Simmons were the only members of the field council in support of Harold's plan.

One of the missionaries summed it up for all of them, when he said, "Harold, you and Ella are good missionaries. We need you here, doing what you do." Then he went on, "We have more than twenty missionaries buried in this country. We refer to it as the 'white man's graveyard'. We don't need to bury another one who killed himself flying an airplane over this miserable jungle!"

So much for Harold's dream of flying—at least for the time being.

Shortly thereafter, it was time for them to undertake the journey to Cape Palmas in anticipation of the birth of the baby Ella was carrying. Ella was glad she would soon be giving birth but wasn't looking forward to three days through the jungle to get there. She was large and heavy with her pregnancy, and it was becoming difficult for her to move around easily.

Upon reaching Cape Palmas, they settled into the mission house, now run by the Elseas. Rather than going to the doctor at Firestone, they sent for Florence Steidel, asking her to come serve as nurse and midwife.

In addition to Miss Steidel, Harold learned there was a Swiss doctor in town. When he went to see if the doctor would be available to help when the baby came, he learned the man was no longer practicing medicine but was, instead, working as an automobile mechanic. The man did, however, agree to come assist when Ella's time came.

Waiting was never something Harold did very well. Cooped up in Cape Palmas waiting for the baby day after day had him pacing the floors with nervous energy. One day he announced, "Ella, I'm going down to the river to see if I can catch us all some dinner." With that, he headed out the door, fishing pole in hand, happy to have something constructive to do.

That, of course, had to be the day when Ella went into labor. Florence was already there, and they sent for the Swiss doctor turned auto mechanic. Later in the afternoon, their second child, Ruth Ella Landrus, arrived, strong and healthy. Ella was also doing well, with no complications. It was March 21, 1938.

When he returned, fish in hand, Harold was delighted at Ruth's birth, but more than a little embarrassed at having missed the big event.

For his help with the delivery, they gave the "doctor/mechanic" a tent as compensation. He appeared to be almost as delighted with his tent as Harold and Ella were to have baby Ruth.

They remained at the Cape Palmas mission house for a few weeks to allow Ella to regain her strength and to make sure Ruth was fine. Then, they began their return through the jungle to Bwebo.

They had built a special hammock for Ruth and Paul to ride in together. Ruth rode in a small box-like structure, and behind her, Paul rode in a small seat. Both were covered with mosquito netting. The entire arrangement was carried as one hammock by the porters. When Ruth would cry, Paul tried to calm her by saying, "Don't cry, Ruthie, I'm here with you."

As their first night on the trail approached, they stopped at a native village, hoping to spend the night. Unfortunately, the village chief was not there, and he was the only one with the authority to permit them to stay in one of the village huts.

"I don't want to travel at night," said Harold. "But let's see if we can make it to the next village before it gets dark."

Off they went, entering the next village just as the sun was setting. Only the village chief was not at home there either.

Harold said reluctantly, "Well, we're not going any further tonight. We'll just have to set up our cots and sleep out here in the open."

As they were doing so, the chief and his family arrived back in the village. He offered them his hut after his wife had prepared dinner for them. Then the villagers danced and beat their drums all night as a sign of their happiness that the white missionaries with their little white children were staying with them.

Their arrival back at Bwebo was cause for great celebration for the natives. They, too, sang and danced and beat their drums all night long. Ruth became the focus of much attention, discussion, and admiration.

Harold, Ella, Paul, and baby Ruth at the Bwebo house.

They picked up their ministry again and continued for another year. Then it was time for them to leave for their first furlough back in the United States. Before Harold, Ella and the children left, the natives held a big gathering to present them with parting gifts and to thank them for their work amongst them. It was difficult to leave. They loved what they were doing. They loved the people, and the people loved them. Ella had to admit, though, she was looking forward to going back to America.

They had to wait in Cape Palmas for several days while Mr. Frey tried to book their passage to England. While there, they celebrated Ruth's first birthday. Then it was time for them to climb into the surfboats and be rowed out to their waiting freighter, the MV *Sabo*.

Ella hated the thought of trying to climb the gangplank up the side of the ship. The seas were rough, and she was afraid one of the children would fall. For some reason, they weren't using the mammy chairs this time, so they had no choice. Up they climbed—thankfully, without a hitch. They left for England April 14, 1939.

Because they were traveling by freighter, they had to make many stops along the way to off-load and to take on cargo. They stopped a number of times along the Liberian coast and then at Freetown in Sierra Leone; Dakar, Senegal; and Los Palmas in the Canary Islands. There, much to Ella's dismay, Harold insisted upon buying a canary bird to take home with them. Then they sailed on to England and up the Thames to London.

Upon docking in London, a British health official, a medical doctor, came onboard to check the passengers before they disembarked. During the voyage, Ruth had developed impetigo, a small rash on her lip. When the doctor saw her, he took her from Ella's arms and began carrying her off the boat.

"Wait. What are you doing with my baby?" Ella called.

Glancing over his shoulder but without pausing, the doctor responded, "I'm taking her to Graves End. It's a hospital. I'm placing her in quarantine."

"Hold it, Mister," said Harold following him. "You can't just take our daughter away from us. She's only one year old. There's nothing wrong with her."

"Listen, I know you don't like this, but you people have been in Africa. There's no telling what this is. I have my job to do, and I can't take any chances that what she has can be spread to others. That's it. After you clear customs, you can go out to Graves End to see what they have to say."

Harold and Ella were stunned. Ruth was screaming. She hadn't been around many white people in her short life, and now she was being taken by one from her mother. Paul was crying. The ship's captain and the crew were outraged, but it was all to no avail. The doctor disappeared quickly down the gangplank, across the wharf, and into a waiting car, his arms securely wrapped around little Ruth.

The crew helped Harold, Ella, and Paul gather their luggage and get to the customs office. It seemed like an eternity before they were finally ushered through. What was all the more remarkable was they had taken Ruth away, but had paid no attention to Harold's canary. Harold asked, "What shall we do about our baby?"

One of the customs officials knew what had happened with Ruth. She said, "Go out to the hospital at Graves End. They can tell you what is to happen with your baby. Unfortunately, there is no bus. The only way you can get there is to walk. It's quite a distance, but I'm sure you can make it." Then she gave them directions, the final portion of which was a long, long walk down the railroad tracks to the hospital.

Following her directions, they walked along the streets of London. It was cold, particularly after having been used to the heat and humidity of Liberia. They stopped briefly to buy a coat for Paul and then continued until they reached the tracks and on towards Graves End. Beyond it being cold, the fog was beginning to come in and the tracks were completely deserted. Isolated, cold, tired, and feeling pretty down, Harold and Ella were both thinking, *this place is certainly aptly named Graves End.*

After walking for a considerable distance, Paul had grown tired, so Ella carried him. Harold carried his canary, with a diaper draped over the cage to shelter it from the cold. They walked in silence until they at last reached a large rather inhospitable-looking, gray building with a sign over the entrance that read, "Graves End Hospital".

Approaching the nurses' station inside, they explained who they were and why they were there.

"Oh, I don't know why the doctor brought your daughter here. This isn't an isolation hospital," the nurse complained.

"Well, does that mean we can have her now?" asked Harold.

"No, you can't. The doctor isn't here, and no one can release her but him. I don't know when you can have her," the nurse responded curtly.

Then Ella spoke up, "This is our baby. We've brought her some clothes. Can we at least see her?"

"We can't use your clothes. We don't have any diapers but are using towels, so she's just fine. As for seeing her, we just got her to sleep. I don't want her to wake up and see you. She'll just start crying all over again!"

Ella had had about enough of this. "I want to see my baby!" she said emphatically.

Sensing these people had been pushed about as far as they could be pushed, the nurse relented and said, "All right! You can peek at her through the door, but you can't go into the room. Then you really must leave."

As they reached the room, Ella looked quickly in to see Ruth sleeping soundly. Then the nurse indicated it was time for them to go.

The walk back down the railroad tracks from the hospital seemed like the longest walk they'd ever taken. Their hearts were heavy, and their moods as dark and somber as the chilling fog that engulfed them.

When they got back into the city proper, they began looking for a place to spend the night. The rates at the first hotel were so steep Harold said they'd look elsewhere. By the time they'd reached another one, they were all so tired and cold he said, "I don't care what this hotel costs. We're staying here!"

Unable to get much sleep for worry over Ruth, they rose early the next morning and contacted some Swedish missionaries they had met on the boat. They helped them track down the doctor who had taken Ruth.

When they reached him by phone, the doctor said he wouldn't allow the baby to stay anywhere in London. He would release her to them only once they had booked passage from England to America and they could take her directly from the hospital to the ship.

It took almost a week before their passage could be arranged. Each day Harold, Ella, and Paul made the long walk out to Graves End, where they were only allowed to catch a brief glance of little Ruth before they were told to leave. They couldn't hold her, talk to her, or comfort her.

Their last walk down the railroad tracks from Graves End was decidedly happier than any before. They had gathered Ruth from the hospital and left immediately for South Hampton, where they boarded the Cunard-White Star Line's HMV *Georgic* sailing for New York on May 1, 1939. The *Georgic* was built for the White Star Line as a passenger ship. She was 712 feet long, with an 82.5-foot beam and 27,759 gross tons. A year later, she would be converted into a troop ship for service in World War II. They steamed into New York Harbor at 10:00 p.m. on May 12th.

Ella was delighted to be back in America. After four years of struggles, four years away from all that was familiar, four years of adventure, four years of ministry, four years of hardship, four years of happiness, they were no longer foreigners in a foreign land. They were, once again, Americans in America.

Chapter 6
Palipo

After their arrival, the family stayed in New York for a few days and decided to visit the World's Fair. They also needed some time to locate and purchase a car, first to take them to California, and then to serve them for the period of their furlough.

They found just what Harold wanted at an out of the way used car lot. It was a 1937 Chevrolet, in good condition, for which they paid $425. Packing all they had in the little Chevrolet was a considerable challenge, but they managed and headed west on June 1, 1939.

After visiting their friends at Bethany Church and Ella's family in Alhambra, the four of them set out for Colorado, Idaho, and Wyoming to try to raise financial support for their return to Liberia. Over the course of the next two years, they put more than fifty-two thousand miles on the Chevy. Most of those miles included towing a small trailer behind for the kids to stay in as they went from town to town, church to church, seeking support.

The Landruses were only supposed to be in the United States on furlough for one year. However, during that year, Hitler's armies were overrunning Europe. Britain was standing on its own against the German war machine. The United States was not yet directly involved. Nonetheless, there were already shortages of gas, tires, and the like, making the Landruses' travels around the country significantly more difficult.

Their big problem was they couldn't book passage on a ship back to Africa. The Atlantic was alive with wolf packs of German U-boats and Italian submarines. Hundreds of ships had already been sent to the bottom of the sea. Harold and Ella's furlough was extended to a second year, most of which was spent trying to find passage on a ship that would take them to Africa.

It was to no avail. No steamship line would take them with the children. A few were willing if the children didn't go, but not with Paul and Ruth. Leaving the children behind was never an option as far as Harold and Ella were concerned, so they just kept pressing on. They lived in the small apartment above Ella's parents' garage in Alhambra, when they weren't on the road raising funds.

After months of dashed hopes and discouragement, thinking they might have a lead on booking passage only to have it evaporate, they were in Idaho when they received a message from Dr. Britton, their dear friend and mentor from Bethany Church. He, too, had been trying to find a ship for them and had finally succeeded.

An Egyptian ship the *El Nil* was going to be sailing from New York sometime towards the end of May 1941. Built as a passenger ship for the German East Africa Line in 1916, she was christened the *Marie Woerman*. Following World War I, the ship was handed over to Great Britain as war reparations, renamed the *Tjerimi*, and placed in service between Rotterdam and Java. In 1933, the ship had been sold to an Egyptian shipping company and renamed again, this time the *El Nil*. If Harold and Ella could get approval from Springfield and could get there in time, Dr. Britton would book their passage.

Springfield cabled their "go-ahead," and the Landruses returned to Southern California to say hasty good-byes. The local newspaper, the *Post-Advocate*, which had covered their wedding in 1931, sent a reporter to interview them before they left. When asked why they were willing to depart during a time of war, Ella replied, "The thrill of being in God's will, even if that means tragedy on the seas, cannot be compared with anything else we might be offered. Our children, too, have a mission among the heathen, and we ask your prayers that the Lord will keep them safe."

They journeyed, again, to New York. There they met their friends Carl and Velma Hixenbaugh at the mission house on Summit Street where Harold, Ella, and Paul had stayed before sailing for Africa on their first trip. The Hixenbaughs were going to Liberia as well.

Harold and Ella had first met the Hixenbaughs while they were pastoring in Aguilar. They had recommended Carl and Velma to the Assemblies of God Foreign Missions Department as prospective missionaries. This would be the Hixenbaughs' first term, and they were glad to be able to link up with the Landruses who could tell them what it would be like and help them adjust to their new life in Africa.

With a few days' extra time before they sailed, Harold was able to sell the trusty Chevrolet. He got $375 for it. Returning to the missions house, Harold happily told Carl, "Two years and fifty-two thousand miles only cost us fifty bucks with that car. The Lord is really looking after us!"

Carl smiled and responded, "I certainly hope He's looking after us when we're on that ship!"

The *El Nil* departed New York Harbor on May 12, 1941, bound first for Trinidad in the Caribbean. Unlike the freighter the Landruses had sailed on before, which carried only a dozen or so passengers, the *El Nil* was designed primarily to carry passengers. Built to accommodate 248 passengers, there were nearly 300 on board, about 100 of them missionaries, as they sailed past the Statue of Liberty and out into the dangers of the open Atlantic.

Most of the missionaries were with the Seventh Day Adventist denomination. Like the Landruses and the Hixenbaughs, they had had difficulty arranging transportation and were now glad to be headed in the right direction even though, for some of them, their fields of ministry lay well beyond Liberia. For all of them, this was at least a first big step.

The trip down the East Coast of the United States and into the warm waters of the Caribbean was uneventful. From Trinidad, they were scheduled to turn eastward to brave the dangerous crossing to the west coast of Africa. Everyone on board was completely unsure what lay before them.

They docked at Trinidad and were told they would be in port for several days before sailing. The Landruses and other passengers spent the time enjoying the people and the beautiful tropical climate of the island.

One evening, the passengers had gathered for dinner on the *El Nil*. The captain, looking tired and worried, asked for their attention. He had an announcement to make. "Ladies and gentlemen," he said, "I have some disturbing news to share with you." The passengers glanced nervously at each other as the captain continued, "We have received word our sister ship, the *Zam Zam* has been sunk, apparently by an Italian submarine, just a couple of days off the African coast."

As a murmur of concern ran through the crowd, he went on, "I believe it is simply too dangerous for you to proceed any further. I urge you to consider leaving the ship and returning to the United States. It is the only way I can assure your safety."

One of the passengers called out, "But, Captain, what are you and the crew going to do?"

"We really have no choice. We are going to go on, hoping we can elude this marauder. I won't tell you exactly where we will go or when we will leave, but you will have time to get your belongings off the ship in the morning. Thank you and good night."

Harold and Ella and the children were sitting with Carl and Velma. They looked at each other, not knowing what to say. Finally, Harold said, "We need to pray about this tonight. I don't believe the Lord has brought us this far to turn back now. What do you think, Carl?"

"I'm inclined to agree with you, Harold. We'd better be sure God really wants us to go on, though, because it could cost all of us our lives."

The next morning, all but a handful of missionaries had elected to leave the ship and return to the United States. The Landruses and Hixenbaughs were among those few who went to the captain and told him they wanted to continue.

"I admire your desire to serve God in Africa," he told them. "But I must tell you, I certainly question your judgment!" Then with a shrug he added, "But if you're intent on coming along, I won't tell you no."

"We'll be sailing within the next twelve hours. We will observe strict blackout conditions. No lights are to be visible from the ship. There will be no smoking on deck." Then he smiled. "Although I guess you missionaries don't do that anyway, do you?"

They sailed just after dark. Once at sea, they zigzagged every fifteen minutes, steaming first in one direction and then changing course about ninety degrees and then back to the original course fifteen minutes later. The intent was to throw off any submarines that might have detected their presence. Once it located a target, the submarine would expect it to follow the same course. By switching back and forth, the captain hoped to escape an attack if they had been spotted.

It was a nerve-racking voyage. During the day, everyone scanned the horizon, hoping they wouldn't see the telltale wake of a periscope rising out of the water. One night, they saw distant lights and immediately held a prayer meeting, praying it wasn't the raider that had sunk the *Zam Zam*. It apparently was not. No attack came during the night.

When they left Trinidad, the captain had told them he would probably sail for South Africa. From there, they would try to work their way up Africa's west coast to Liberia, hugging the coast for some degree of safety. However, they went instead to Lagos, Nigeria, only to find the mouth of the harbor had been blocked when a barge had been torpedoed a few days earlier. Apparently, the Italian raider was still in the vicinity. Now, because they couldn't get into the harbor, they would have to lay offshore at anchor, making them a sitting target for the submarine.

The next few days brought nothing but confusion and uneasiness for Harold and Ella and the others onboard the *El Nil*. With the ship anchored off the coast, the captain went ashore to see if he could get instructions from his steamship company as to what he was to do. There was some talk they might sail for England, which caused them considerable alarm. England was in the middle of the war zone, and the danger would be much greater if they sailed there.

The passengers spent restless nights sleeping with their clothes on in case the submarine attacked and they had to abandon ship.

After the long voyage from Trinidad and several days anchored off the Nigerian coast, the *El Nil* began running short of food and water. The captain decided to sail for Takoradi, a port in Ghana westward along the African coast to see if they could replenish their supplies.

At Takoradi, the harbor was full of other ships. They couldn't accommodate the *El Nil*. They were, however, able to replenish the ship's water supply. After waiting several more days at sea worrying about being torpedoed, a berth became available, and they finally made it into the relative safety of the harbor.

Unable to acquire much food but with water and fuel replenished, the *El Nil's* captain gathered the passengers together and explained he had been instructed to sail for South Africa. The passengers could go with him or disembark in Ghana.

Not sure what to do, Harold, Carl, and a few of the other passengers went into town early the next morning to see if they could find places for them all to stay. They didn't want to leave the ship until they knew they had someplace to go. Besides, local laws dictated they couldn't enter the country unless they had accommodations and could be vouched for by a resident.

If the missionaries could stay in Ghana for a while, they would try to catch another ship to take them to Liberia or wherever else they needed to go. Before they went ashore, the captain told them the ship must sail with the noon tide. They only had a short time to look for accommodations in town.

The morning drew on, and the men hadn't returned. The captain reminded Ella, Velma, and the others who had remained onboard he had to sail with the tide at noon. "If the others aren't back by then, we're sailing for South Africa without them. I'm sorry. I don't know how they will ever catch up with you, but I have no choice. We must leave."

Ella and Velma were frantic. They couldn't sail off to South Africa without Harold and Carl. They prayed and prayed that God would send their husbands back in time. But by noon, the men hadn't returned, and the *El Nil* dropped her mooring lines and steamed out of the harbor.

Ella, Velma, and the others simply didn't know what to do. They prayed even harder, "Lord, you have to help us. We need to be with our husbands and get to Liberia so we can be about your work."

As the ship cleared the harbor and entered deeper water, they came across a small local steamer plying the coastline hauling fruit and vegetables between Takoradi, Saltpond, Accra, and Keta along the Ghanaian coast. Because he had been unable to take on much food for the voyage in Takoradi, the captain stopped the ship and hailed the little steamer to come alongside so he could purchase some of the provisions it carried. When they had done so, the *El Nil* prepared to get underway again.

Just then the captain spotted a small boat racing toward them from the harbor. Grabbing his binoculars, he saw the boat was filled with the husbands and sons of the women on board. "Well, ladies, God must have heard those prayers of yours," he said, shaking his head in disbelief. "Guess who's coming to get you."

Ella, Velma, and the others were overjoyed. The captain delayed hoisting anchor and waited for the men to reach them. When they got to the ship, the disappointed men told everyone they had been unable to find places to stay. They would have to go on with the captain and the crew to South Africa.

To their surprise, the captain said, "I have another announcement for you. We have received a radio message. The port at Lagos is now open. We will go back there before we sail for South Africa. Perhaps you will be able to arrange to stay there."

None of them could believe what they had heard. Not only had God brought them all back together again, but now, He was making it possible for them to stop in Nigeria, which would make getting to Liberia far easier than from South Africa.

Arriving in Lagos, the men went ashore once again, looking for places they could stay. They met a local Methodist missionary named Mann. They never learned his first name. He had introduced himself as Mr. Mann, and that was how he was addressed the entire time they were in Nigeria.

To their delight, he arranged accommodations for everyone with various members of the congregation in the church he pastored. Harold, Ella, and the children stayed with Mr. Mann. His wife had returned to England when the war broke out so she could care for her ailing parents. He was alone and missing her. He was grateful to have their company.

It took more than a week before they were able to book passage on the Barber Line for Cape Palmas, Liberia. In the meantime, Harold and Carl spent a number of very enjoyable days with Mr. Mann in his small sailboat gliding back and forth across the Lagos harbor, while Ella and Velma took care of Paul and Ruth playing on the beach.

At last, they were able to board the ship for Liberia. It was the SS *West Lashaway*. Unlike the *El Nil*, which was of Egyptian registry, this ship was American, owned by the American West African Line. The difference was critical to their safety at sea. Egypt was already involved in World War II. In July 1941, America was not.

Harold and Ella were delighted to learn the *West Lashaway's* captain was Captain Walters, the same man who had commanded the *West Humhaw* on their first voyage to Africa, six years earlier. He explained that, rather than traveling in blackout conditions, they would be doing the opposite. The ship would be fully lit at night. Giant American flags had been painted on both sides of the ship, and these would be spotlighted at night as well. The intent was to help make it plain to any submariners this was not a combatant but, rather, an American flag carrier not involved in the ever-growing conflict.

What they assumed would be a two-day voyage to Liberia turned out to take four times longer, as the *West Lashaway* stopped to load cocoa at Accra, Ghana.

Finally, on July 12, 1941, they dropped anchor off Cape Palmas. It had taken two months to the day for them to get there from the United States.

As they rode the surfboats once again to shore, Harold and Ella could hardly contain themselves. It had taken so long, but now they were back—back to Liberia, back to the place and people they had grown to love dearly. (In August 1942, after the United States had entered the war, the *West Lashaway* was sunk by a German submarine off the coast of South America.)

When they stepped onto the wharf at Cape Palmas, they were engulfed by an enthusiastic crowd of missionaries and natives all shouting their greetings. Several of the native men and boys hoisted Harold above their shoulders and began carrying him towards the missions house chanting "Pa Landrus is back. Pa Landrus is back."

They were surprised so many missionaries were there. When they asked why, Harold and Ella were told the American ambassador had urged all American missionaries and other workers in Liberia to leave the country for safer areas due to the rapidly spreading war in Europe and the likelihood America would soon be drawn into the conflict as well.

"You should turn around and go back as quickly as you can," one missionary told them. "We've been stuck here waiting for a ship to take us out. We're leaving on the ship you just arrived on. There's talk the Germans may try to take over the rubber plantations in order to deny them to the Allies. This will be no place for you and particularly your children!"

Harold looked at Ella and said, "Well, I think we're about traveled out. It took us two months to get here. I don't believe the Lord had us go through all that just to have us turn back. No. We'll stay. But thanks for your concern. We'd appreciate your prayers."

Carl and Velma Hixenbaugh elected to stay as well.

Harold and Ella were just glad to be back. The day they landed, Ella wrote to her parents, "You will never know how thrilled we are to be back in Africa. We trust the Lord will use us in the saving of many souls."

They stayed in Cape Palmas for several weeks, which enabled Harold and Carl to take a brief trip interior so Carl could get an idea what their lives would be like. It also gave Harold and Ella time to consider where they would minister this term.

When word of their arrival spread to the interior, several tribes sent delegations begging the Landruses to come be their missionaries. They were asked to return to Bwebo and thought a lot about doing so but couldn't come to a real peace in their hearts about it. Besides, another missionary, Lois Hackert, had already been assigned there.

A group from the Palipo tribe arrived, sent by the paramount chief to plead with them to come to Palipo.

When the Landruses arrived for their first term in Africa, they had been assigned to serve as business agents in Cape Palmas. At the same time, Florence Steidel was sent with Miss Martha Ramsey to minister to the Palipo tribe, four days interior. There, they had a fruitful ministry teaching and, because Florence was a registered nurse, also doing medical work. About halfway through her term, however, a major problem arose that ultimately forced both of them to leave Palipo and to complete their terms elsewhere.

One of the many superstitions the people held was that, when a witch doctor, or the "Que" (Kwee) as they called him, came into a town or village, the women and children were not to look at him. They were to hide in their huts until the Que had left.

When the Que arrived, there was much shouting and high-pitched wailing. The drums were beaten loudly. It was chaos. To this day, more than seventy-five years later, Ruth remembers the fear even she felt when the Que came through town.

If the women looked upon the Que, they were told their eyes would pop out. The men supported this idea because they felt, if their wives were afraid, they would be more submissive and obedient.

Florence Steidel was a devoted missionary who considered the Liberian people to be "my people." She was not about to run and hide when what she viewed as the personification of evil itself came to town, particularly if he showed up on what was supposed to be a church night. She would not be intimidated. She was not afraid. She knew the power of Christ was far superior to that of any heathen witch doctor.

When the Que came, Florence looked at him. He knew she had looked at him and was furious. It was a direct challenge to his control over the people of the village. He threatened the village and the chief. He told them great evil would befall them. In the end, the tribe's fear overcame their desire to have a missionary among them, and they insisted Florence and Miss Ramsey leave.

They were heartbroken—not just because they were being forced to leave, but also because the natives' fear was so deep and the few Christian converts among them did not have the strength to resist their fear. Florence and Martha left Palipo and went to help at the girls' school at Neweka. Little did Florence know, what she viewed as a defeat at Palipo was laying the foundation for a wonderful, productive ministry a few years later when she founded a leper colony and mission station at New Hope Town.

After Miss Steidel and Miss Ramsey had been forced to leave, the Palipo tribe had begun to change its mind. The Christians in the tribe were continuing to grow in number and in influence. The paramount chief, Chief William, had become a believer and a supporter. When he heard Ma and Pa Landrus were back in Liberia, he decided to ask them to come be missionaries to the Palipo people.

He sent a delegation to Cape Palmas with the promise, if the Landruses would come, he would send fifty porters to carry them and all their belongings free of charge. He also pledged the tribe would keep the Que out of town when church services were to be held so they would never have "palaver" about it again.

After hearing their plea and several days and nights of prayer, Harold said, "I do believe Palipo is where the Lord wants us. What do you think, Ella?"

"I believe so, too," she responded quietly.

They immediately began making preparations for the journey to Palipo. Because the Cape Palmas mission now had a vehicle, the one they had purchased when they were business agents, they could be driven to Pleebo and start the trek through the jungle from there. It would save them a full day's walk. Nevertheless, it would be followed by two, possibly three hard days on the trail, with at least one overnight stay, maybe two in a native village along the way.

Paul was seven years old and as happy as could be to be back in Africa. At just over three, Ruth was also delighted. It didn't take long for her to get used to the special treatment she and Paul received from the natives. They were favorites and were treated as such wherever they went.

With their supplies and belongings on the heads of dozens of porters, Harold and Ella were anxious to reach Palipo. As they approached, hundreds of people rushed out to greet them. Grabbing their hammocks from the hammock men, they lifted them high above their heads and ran through the town, carrying them in and out and weaving between the huts, singing and chanting.

The natives took Paul and Ruth in their arms and ran through the village with them. Neither of the children could quite understand what was happening, but at least everyone seemed happy, so they weren't frightened.

The natives carried them to the mission house where they were greeted by Chief William, and the people presented them with gifts of rice, palm nuts, chickens, and bananas. The porters took their supplies and belongings into the house.

It had been more than three years since Florence Steidel and Martha Ramsey had left, and the house was something of a mess. But the villagers had cleaned it from top to bottom for the Landruses' arrival.

For the four years of this term and four more years the following term, Palipo was to provide Harold, Ella, and the children with tests and trials, joys and triumphs, and adventures beyond their wildest imaginations.

$$\sim$$

Over the next several days, they were greeted by virtually everyone in the village, including each of Chief William's twelve wives. John Try, the native pastor, came to express his joy at their coming and his gratefulness to God for answering his prayers for a missionary to minister among them.

One afternoon, a young native named Daniel presented himself at their door, stating solemnly, "I am a cook. I cooked for Ma Steidel. I be a very good cook for you."

They decided to hire him to cook for them. For nearly thirty years, Cook Daniel faithfully served the Landruses and their family, following them wherever they were stationed in Liberia. He became a loved, trusted member of the family.

The Palipo house was very different than the one in Bwebo. In the early 1930s, an American named Charlie Jacobs had come to Liberia to build houses for missionaries. He built houses at Palipo and at Bwah and helped with several others.

Compared to what they had had at Bwebo, Ella thought it was a wonderful house. She marveled at how Mr. Jacobs could have managed to construct it in such a primitive area, with sources of supply so far away, and only natives with hand tools available to carry out the work.

The house was built on ironwood posts. (Ironwood was sufficiently hard the termites wouldn't destroy it.) The house had a wooden floor about three feet off the ground. Its walls were also made of wood.

All of the wood had been sawed by hand with what they called a "pit saw". Large trees would be cut from the forest and the logs dragged out and then suspended between two supports over a pit dug in the earth. One native would stand on top of the log with one end of a long two-handled saw. Another remained on the ground or in a pit below, to man the other end of the saw. They would cut the log lengthwise, alternately pushing and pulling the giant saw blade up and down. It was backbreaking work made more difficult by the tropical heat and humidity and by the toughness of the wood. It was aptly named "ironwood" because it seemed to be as hard as iron.

Cutting lumber with a "pit saw"

Charlie Jacobs even had corrugated metal roofing material carried over the trail from Cape Palmas, rather than settling for a thatched roof. As the natives said when they had finished helping him build it, "It is a fine, fine house!"

The house had a living room and a bedroom on one side and the kitchen and two additional bedrooms on the other. There was a small, covered porch across the front and down one side. The living room was very small, so they did most of their entertaining on the front lawn. There was no plumbing. The restroom was an outhouse in the yard behind the house.

Having lived at Bwebo without electricity and without refrigeration, Ella had persuaded Harold to purchase a small generator, or "light plant" as they called it, and a kerosene-powered refrigerator before they left the United States to return to Africa. The refrigerator and light plant had come all the way across the Atlantic on the *El Nil*. They had been transferred to the *West Lashaway*. The porters had labored mightily carrying them along the jungle trails and across rushing streams and rivers to finally get the two pieces of equipment to Palipo.

At almost every point along the journey Harold had wondered if they would be worth the effort. However, once they were set up and running, these simple appliances made an enormous difference in their daily lives.

They no longer had to operate solely by candlelight or kerosene lamps at night. Harold could turn the light plant on for a few hours in the evening, and they could read and write by an electric lamp. They had brought a shortwave radio with them as well, so they could listen to the British Broadcasting Company. Throughout World War II, being able to occasionally listen to the BBC news allowed them to know what was happening in the outside world. It helped immeasurably to combat their feeling of total isolation.

The refrigerator, which smoked considerably but seemed to work surprisingly well, enabled them to store food for several days without spoiling. It even had a small ice box. And on a very personal level, nothing tasted as good or as refreshing to Harold as a glass of water with ice in it, after a long sweltering day under the blazing African sun.

In October 1941, Ella wrote to her parents: "We are enjoying our electric lights and radio more than we can say. It makes it so much more like home. All the missionaries want us to write the news to them as we are the only ones who have these luxuries. Our native hunter shot a pigmy hippopotamus this morning and we had it for dinner tonight and have plenty more. The natives say hippo meat is the best they have. The ice box works perfectly and makes ice in such a short time. So many of the natives have never seen ice and it is fun to hand them a piece. They will drop it and yell, 'It is hot.' They are afraid to pick it up again. The other day a boy carried four buckets of water for one small piece of ice. We are so grateful for all these lovely things which make living here so much more pleasant."

~

They began settling into routine life at the Palipo station, a life typical of many remote mission outposts throughout tropical Africa.

One of Harold's first projects was to construct a classroom out in front of the house to serve as the training center for native boys and girls from the tribe. It was a difficult job for which they hired many of the local men and boys. In addition to building projects, Harold maintained the mission compound and hunted for meat to feed the family and the many natives they ministered to and who worked for them on the station.

Their ministries included morning clinic for anyone in the village with an ache or pain, a cut or bruise, or any other malady the natives were sure the missionaries could cure.

They had a boarding school for the native boys and girls, teaching them Bible lessons and beginners' level English (held in the classroom Harold had built). They conducted Bible studies for the adults and preached in outlying villages. They helped train and encourage Pastor John Try. They taught Sunday school. They distributed clothing and other items from America to the people. Ella managed to sew dozens of pairs of shorts and shirts for the boys and dresses for many of the girls.

This routine of ministry and daily living continued essentially uninterrupted for the next three and a half years, punctuated by periodic trips to Cape Palmas for supplies.

～

As it had been at Bwebo, holding clinic was a particularly challenging task for Ella. She wanted to be of help to the natives, but her lack of any formal medical training left her feeling very inadequate. Nonetheless, she carried on as best she could with limited knowledge and even more limited supplies.

One morning while she was conducting clinic on the lawn in front of the house, Chief William arrived with two of his twelve wives. His wives were a symbol of Chief William's wealth and prestige, so he liked having as many as possible. He had paid a cow, a goat, a pot, and a piece of cloth for each of them, so they represented a substantial investment. However, having that many wives did not always lead to peace and harmony at home.

As they approached, Ella could see one of the wives was holding a bloody cloth to her mouth, and the chief was reaching out with something in his hand.

On closer inspection, Ella realized what the chief was holding was his wife's two front teeth. "Big palaver," he said solemnly. "These two wives have big, big fight. Dis one, she knocked out dis other one's teeth," he said, pointing to them.

"Well, I see that, Chief, but what is it you want me to do?" asked Ella, afraid she already knew the answer.

As a good husband, Chief William would be concerned with his wife's appearance; after all, he'd paid handsomely for her.

The chief replied in a very matter of fact manner, "Ma, you fix." The idea that Ma Landrus might not be able to "fix" his wife's teeth had never occurred to the chief.

"Chief William, you know we do all we can to help you and your people, but there's nothing I can do about these teeth."

The chief insisted she do something. Shaking her head, Ella prayed quietly, "Lord, I don't know what to do about this, but I know You do. Please help me, and please demonstrate to these people just how mighty You are."

With that, she wiped out the woman's mouth and dabbed mercurochrome in the tooth sockets. After cleaning the teeth, she simply pushed them back into their sockets. "Now tell your wife not to touch her teeth or to try to eat anything solid for at least a week," she told the chief. "We have asked Jesus to heal her, and now we'll have to wait to see what happens."

"Yes, Ma. Yes, Ma," answered Chief William as he motioned for his two wives to go back to their hut.

A few days later, Ella was greeted by the chief's wife, smiling brightly, displaying that her teeth were fine once again.

"Thank you, Lord." Ella sighed. "I know that wasn't really possible in human terms, but all things are possible with You."

Years later, Chief William proudly reported to Ella his wife's teeth were indeed fine and had been as good as new since Ella had put them back in.

～

Harold's days were no less challenging.

Isaac had become a Christian during the time Florence Steidel and Martha Ramsey had been missionaries at Palipo. He had been a difficult man to get along with before then. He liked to drink palm wine, and when he was drunk, he became very mean tempered. He picked fights with others in the village. He beat his wife. He was just plain mean-spirited.

One day, he had been standing along the road with nothing particular to do when Miss Steidel started teaching a Sunday school lesson to a group of children sitting on the grass nearby. Isaac heard every word she said. It absolutely held him spellbound. It was as if he couldn't make his legs move to take him away from there. When she was finished, Isaac knew he had to talk with her, but he had no idea what to say.

As the children scampered away to play and he approached her, Ma Steidel made it easy for him. "Isaac, I think it's time we talked about Jesus," she said quietly. And they did. Right then. Right there. By the time they were finished, Isaac had asked Jesus into his life.

The transformation in him was startling. He quit drinking. He became a loving, caring husband and father. He was also determined to share with all his family and neighbors what had happened to him when he accepted Christ.

Now, years later, Ma Steidel had left, and the Landruses were the missionaries. Isaac had grown to love them just as he had Miss Steidel and he had become one of their helpers with the mission work.

Today, however, he had not been helping. Instead, he had walked several miles to visit one of his brothers in another village to tell him about Jesus. Tired and thirsty, he was on his way home, thinking he might stop by the mission house just long enough to say hello to Ma and Pa Landrus. He knew they'd want to know how it had gone with his brother, and besides, they might give him a glass of water with a piece of ice in it.

Working his way along a narrow jungle path, Isaac came to a small clearing where a farmer had cut the jungle away and burned it so he could grow some rice. There was a rather large anthill near the center of the clearing. The hill was like hundreds of others spread throughout the countryside, strange tall dirt mounds, sculptured into castle-like shapes by the tropical rains, and standing like giant sentinels keeping watch over the ever-changing jungle around them.

As he walked past the hill, through the corner of his eye, Isaac thought he caught sight of something moving. He stood motionless for a moment and looked more closely toward the anthill. Yes, there it was, again. Along the side and partway up the anthill, something was moving.

Then he recognized what the something was. It was a huge snake slowly winding its way up the hill. Isaac was amazed at how big it was. He couldn't see much of it, just a portion around his side of the hill, but it was enormous, its thick body undulating rhythmically as it moved progressively up the hill. Suddenly, the snake's head appeared from behind the hill.

It seemed for an instant Isaac and the snake looked directly into each other's eyes. The snake didn't respond at all but kept working its way up the hill. Isaac was terror stricken. He stood frozen to the spot. His heart was pounding. His mouth was dry. He wanted to run but couldn't seem to make his body work. He was even holding his breath. He just stood there unable to take his eyes off the giant snake.

Isaac was twenty-six years old and had encountered hundreds of snakes during his life. He had even killed a few. Mostly, he just avoided them, and they avoided him. They were a fact of life—something he, like everyone he knew, had grown up with. He had known of people killed by any one of the highly poisonous snakes in the country. One of his nephews had even been killed by a giant python that had dropped out of a tree, wrapped itself around him, and then slowly crushed him to death. Isaac had a healthy respect for snakes, but he had never really been much afraid of them.

What he saw now truly frightened him. He had never seen a snake even close to this big before. Finally, his brain managed to regain control of his body. He gasped, turned, and tore down the jungle path as fast as his legs would carry him, all the time yelling at the top of his voice, "Pa, Pa, come quick. Bring your gun, Pa!"

Harold had gone to the house for a drink of water after working out in the compound under the hot tropical sun since lunchtime. He was just emerging from the house, lifting his hat to wipe his brow, when he heard Isaac's yelling and saw him racing toward him. Others in the village stopped their work and watched, wondering what the matter could be as, stumbling and panting, Isaac reached the house.

"Isaac, slow down, man. What's the matter? You look like you've seen a ghost," Harold exclaimed.

As winded as he was and bending over to catch his breath, it took Isaac a few seconds before he was able to explain. "Pa, there's a snake down there." He gasped, pointing back down the path. "A big snake, Pa. Bring your gun! Bring your gun!"

"All right, settle down. I'll get my gun, and you can show me where he is," Harold said as he turned to go back into the house.

Emerging with his rifle, he checked to see a shell was in the chamber and headed down the trail with Isaac. Others, having heard the commotion, began following after them.

As they approached the clearing, Isaac was petrified. He glanced quickly from side to side sure that, defying all logic, the snake would somehow leap out of the bush and attack them. Then he stopped, his fear making him unable to go any farther. "He's up there, Pa. Around the bend, in the clearing. I saw him on the anthill. He looked like he was climbing up to the top."

"OK, Isaac. You stay here. I'll go see what I can find," Harold responded, heading toward the clearing. Once there, he immediately spotted the anthill but saw no sign of the giant snake. He walked cautiously around the anthill and then made bigger circles out to the edges of the clearing. He didn't see the snake but did find a swath of bent grass blades, indicating the slithering track the creature had left from the forest and across the clearing. At the anthill, the track disappeared in the harder dirt.

Harold looked around once again, and then up toward the top of the anthill. *Maybe Isaac is right*, he thought. *I wonder if it could be up there.*

As he briefly studied it, Harold recognized it was an old anthill— long abandoned by the ants that had built it. It even had a couple of small trees growing out of the steep sides up near the top. Once the anthill had had hard dirt sides, but the dirt was now crumbly, making it extremely difficult to climb. Holding his rifle in one hand and clawing at the dirt with the other, Harold began to climb to the top of the hill. As his head neared the crest, he could see the hill had a deep bowl-like crater in the top. It was three or four feet wide. Carefully, he peered over the edge. There, in the bottom of the bowl, perhaps three feet below his face, was the curled form of the giant snake.

It was completely still, its long body coiled around and around and piled layer upon layer. Harold couldn't really tell how big it was, but it was clearly a monster. The snake had apparently chosen the crater-shaped hole in the top of the anthill as its nest.

Harold inched back from the edge and tried to decide what to do next. *How in the world am I going to kill this thing? I don't have any idea where to begin to shoot it. Shooting its body won't do any good, and I can't see its head.* Then he thought of an idea.

"Isaac, can you hear me?" he called.

"Yes, Pa," came Isaac's timid reply from back down the path.

"Come on, man," Harold called to him. "I need your help. He's up here in the top of this anthill, but I have to find his head if I'm going to kill him."

Reluctantly and with painfully hesitant steps, Isaac came around the bend and into the clearing. "Pa, I'm scared! He's too big, Pa. He'll get us both!"

"No, he won't, Isaac. Not if you'll help me," Harold assured him. "I want you to run back to the mission station and get a shovel to dig into the hill, up here about three feet down from the top. Then you can poke the snake in the side, and maybe it'll stick its head up so I can kill it."

Isaac's eyes opened wide, "Oh, Pa! Are you sure? I don't think he will like me poking him."

Harold smiled. "That's exactly what I'm hoping, Isaac. That's exactly what I'm hoping!"

Grateful for the opportunity to leave the area of the snake, Isaac took off running. Upon reaching the mission compound, he found a shovel and headed back to the anthill, praying all the way, over and over again, "Please, Jesus, help us!"

When Isaac returned, Harold was still on the anthill waiting somewhat impatiently. "OK, man. Now I want you to dig a hole in the side of the hill."

The look on Isaac's face was one of stark terror, but Harold coaxed him to do it anyway. *The poor guy may never live this down,* Harold thought, with a grin.

For all his reluctance, Isaac tackled the hill with gusto, using the shovel to bore a hole through the side of the hill at about the level of the snake. As he got closer to where he figured the inside wall of the crater was, his pace slackened considerably. He simply couldn't bring himself to arouse what he knew was a slumbering giant. He didn't want to poke through by accident. He wanted to go through the last little bit of dirt very slowly and very gently. Isaac wanted to know exactly when the shovel would break through and hit that snake because he wanted to be ready to run.

Finally, the shovel did poke through the dirt and struck the soft muscular flesh of the snake, but it hadn't happened as gently as Isaac had wanted, and when he realized what he'd hit, he was so shocked he almost dropped the shovel. But strangely, nothing happened. The snake didn't move.

Isaac looked at Harold. "Pa, I'm sure I poked him, but nothing is happening."

Harold looked over the top and into the snake's nest. Isaac was right. Nothing was happening.

Suddenly, with amazing speed, the giant creature began to uncoil. It was as if the entire snake was exploding in size. Where the top of its body had been three feet below the edge of the rim, now it was boiling upward, being thrust up from below and soon would overflow out of the top. Harold knew he had to stop the snake from uncoiling.

Without thinking, he reacted almost instantly. He jumped into the nest on top of the writhing snake, hoping his weight would help hold the creature down. It didn't. The snake continued to unwind itself, parts of its body nearing the rim. Harold still had his rifle in one hand but couldn't do anything with it. He tried to keep his feet firmly planted on the snake's back, holding it down but couldn't do so.

Even in the midst of the struggle, it struck him as odd the snake's skin would be so slippery and slimy. As the snake continued uncoiling, Harold knew he would be thrown off balance. If the snake ever got a coil wrapped around him, it would be all over. He wouldn't stand a chance. Desperately, he reached out to grab one of the small trees growing out of the side of the hill to steady himself and perhaps give him some leverage to help hold the snake down.

It did help steady him but didn't help control the snake. Frantically, he tried slipping his arm through the sling on his rifle, to free his second hand. As he did so, he lost his grip on the rifle. It fell and, seemingly in slow motion, bounced down the side and came to rest at the bottom of the hill, out of reach and useless to him.

Meanwhile, his wild ride atop the snake continued. Reaching as far as he could, he seized hold of the other small tree.

Stretched across the hole at the top of the hill, clutching a tree in either hand, struggling with all his might against the snake erupting beneath him, Harold thought he could maybe hold him back for a short while. But he knew time was on the snake's side.

Harold was fighting a losing battle, and he knew it. His strength was beginning to ebb. This couldn't go on very much longer.

Suddenly, the snake's head shot through the hole Isaac had dug in the side of the hill, almost hitting Isaac, who flipped over backward as he ducked out of the way. And as Harold would describe it later, "When he hit the ground, he was running."

From the top of the hill, bouncing wildly as the snake was beginning to uncoil again once it had found an avenue of escape, Harold spotted the snake's head flailing back and forth sticking out of the hole in the side of the hill. He yelled at Isaac, who was just disappearing around the bend in the path. "Isaac, don't you leave me!"

Isaac slowed. "But, Pa, he's going to kill us," he shrieked.

"No, he's not. If you'll listen to me." Harold fought to calm his voice as much as he could, knowing Isaac needed all the reassurance he could get. "Come over here and trade places with me."

"No, Pa. No! He'll kill me," Isaac replied with a sob before Harold could finish what he was saying.

"Isaac, I won't let this snake kill you. But if you don't come up here right now, I might!" Harold shouted back sternly, knowing they only had moments left before things really got out of hand and trying anything to break through Isaac's fear.

Isaac hesitated briefly but then scrambled up the hill. At the top, he grabbed the two trees and stepped in on top of the snake as Harold jumped out and slid quickly down the hill. On the ground, Harold immediately retrieved his rifle and aimed at the snake.

The snake's head was waving back and forth so quickly and so violently Harold couldn't get a clear shot at it. Without hesitating, Harold let out a long loud, ear-piercing whistle. For the briefest of moments, the snake's head stopped its wild swinging and hung motionless in the air.

It was just enough time for Harold to squeeze off one round. It hit its mark, splitting the snake's skull, and killing it instantly.

In death, the snake's huge body seemed to deflate now that its muscles were no longer flexing and gyrating. Isaac was looking incredulously at the snake beneath his feet. Harold was exhausted.

"Isaac, are you alright?" Harold called out.

"I think so, Pa. I think so," Isaac responded somewhat in a daze. "But, Pa, why did you do such a thing as that? And, Pa, why did you whistle at the snake and why did it stand up like so?"

Harold shook his head. "I don't know the answers to any of those questions, Isaac, and I'm not sure I ever will."

"And Pa, would you really have killed me?" asked Isaac, his head down.

"No, Isaac. You know I would never hurt you," answered Harold softly, as he climbed the hill and put a reassuring hand on his shoulder. "I was just trying to get you to help me. You were very brave to do that."

Isaac smiled broadly and stood a little straighter atop the snake.

The crowd, which had followed them from the mission station, had reached the clearing in time to witness most of the titanic struggle and now began shouting and cheering. Harold called to them to come up the anthill. "Let's see if we can drag this thing out of here and see how big it really is."

Eager to be a part of such a legendary event, a story they themselves would tell their children and their grandchildren, everyone clambered up the hill and helped pull the snake out and onto the ground below.

As they stretched it out to its full length, there were gasps of complete astonishment. It was the biggest snake any of them had ever seen. They had heard stories of snakes so large but had never really been sure they should be believed. Now they would believe, for they had seen it with their own eyes. When they measured it, the snake was more than twenty feet long.

The giant snake and the snake eggs.

For his part, Harold was interested in inspecting the slimy, gooey stuff he kept slipping on while he tried to stand on the snake. He climbed up the anthill once again. Looking into the hole on top of the hill, he discovered the slimy stuff was clusters of snake eggs—still in a slippery pouch. There were about twenty eggs, and when the natives cut them open, they found each one contained a baby snake.

The natives skinned and then cooked and ate the snake. There was enough for everyone. Then they danced and sang through the night, celebrating Harold and Isaac's victory in such a gigantic battle.

Chapter 7

Death's Door and Elephants

One day, after they had been at Palipo for some time, Harold came into the house from working out in the compound. It was unlike him to return until closer to time for their midday meal. Ella was working in the kitchen with Cook Daniel and called over her shoulder, "My, you're back early. Lunch won't be ready for a while."

When Harold didn't respond, she took off her apron and went into the living room to see if he was alright. She knew immediately he was not. He had a terrible red rash over his face and hands, and as he took off his shirt, she could see the rash covered much of his body.

"Harold what on earth is the matter?" she asked.

"I don't know. I just feel awful," Harold mumbled as he collapsed into a chair.

"Let me check your temperature," Ella said, heading for their box of meager medical supplies.

Harold had a high fever. She got him into bed and then tried to keep him as comfortable as possible. Over the next couple of days, his fever increased, and the rash turned even brighter red.

Ella didn't know what to do. She remembered Daisy Torta's description of John's death from blackwater fever and was certain that was what Harold was suffering from. She prayed and prayed, but Harold's condition did not improve.

Little Ruth, unused to seeing her daddy in the house and in bed during the day, kept asking what was wrong. To this, Ella could only reply, "Daddy is very, very sick."

"Don't worry, Mother. Jesus will make him better," Ruth responded with the absolute confidence of a four-year-old.

However, after more than a week, Ella knew without question Harold was dying.

She decided to send a runner to the medical doctor at the Firestone rubber plantation. It would take two days in each direction, but she hoped the doctor would come, and that he could do something to save Harold's life.

With Harold so desperately ill and Paul and Ruth too young to fully understand, Ella felt more alone than at any time in her life.

Four days later, with Harold more dead than alive, the runner returned from the Firestone plantation. To Ella's disappointment, she didn't see the doctor with him. As the runner approached the house, she called out, "Where is the doctor? Why hasn't he come? Didn't you tell him Pa Landrus is dying?"

Gasping for breath, the runner responded, "I told him, Ma. But he is not coming. He say he not a 'mail-order doctor.' I'm sorry, Ma. I don't want Pa to die."

Ella was devastated. She buried her face in her hands and wept. She loved this man. How could she lose him?

Harold was delirious as the fever ravaged his body, draining him of strength and the will to survive. He was dying. Then, amid his struggle, Harold later told Ella he felt himself moving upward out of his body and heard God speaking to him—not audibly but just as real as if it had been. God asked him if he wanted to go to heaven or if he wanted to remain on earth. Harold could see Ella, Paul, and Ruth as though they were standing on a beach looking up at him as he floated above them toward heaven.

"No, Lord," Harold responded. "I don't want to go to heaven. My wife and children are here, Lord. I need to take care of them. And there is so much more work you have for me to do here. Please, let me go back."

From almost that moment, Harold's fever broke, and ever so slowly, he began to improve. But he was so weak days passed and he still couldn't get out of bed.

At that time, Miss Ruth LePers, a young single missionary woman, happened to come through. She was on her way to Cape Palmas for supplies. She had come from a mission station about a two-day walk north of Palipo, near Tchien in the central highlands. She was working there among the Konobo tribe along with Annie Cressman and a group of other Canadian missionaries working out of Tchien.

As Harold slowly recovered, Miss LePers stayed for a number of days to help Ella care for him. Between them, they managed to get Harold out of bed and into an old wooden rocking chair a previous missionary had left.

Being up and sitting in the rocker seemed to be just what Harold needed. From then on, he began to steadily improve. Miss LePers extended her stay for several days longer and then continued on her way to Cape Palmas.

Ella wrote home, "If the Firestone doctor was no 'mail-order doctor' Jesus was. He healed Harold. Praise His name."

Paul was five years old when the family had left Bwebo to go to America for their first furlough. When they arrived back in Africa at Palipo, he had been seven—old enough, Harold thought, for Paul to learn to hunt. Over the course of their next four years at Palipo, Paul went almost everywhere with his father, first learning to shoot with his BB gun and then graduating to a .22. By the time they left Palipo at the end of their term, Paul was eleven years old. He had become an excellent marksman with his daddy's higher-caliber rifles and an accomplished hunter.

Paul loved hunting. He loved being with his father. It was all he wanted to do. Harold loved being with Paul and teaching him to hunt, just as much.

Ella didn't mind Harold and Paul hunting so much of the time, and they all enjoyed the fresh meat they were able to put on the table. She worried, however, about the time it was taking away from Paul's education.

In Bwebo, on their first term, Ella had taught Paul through the help of correspondence courses from America. Now as he progressed through fourth, fifth, and into sixth grade, Ella was concerned she wasn't well enough qualified to continue teaching him.

While he was using his BB gun, Ella adopted an incentive plan for Paul to do his studies. She would give him a BB for every sentence he wrote and for every new word he learned to spell. It worked reasonably well at first. It didn't last though.

The truth was, Paul was a little like his daddy. He hated studying. All he wanted to do was hunt. He and his friends, a group of native boys headed by Peter, Mama Ruth's son, and another boy also named Peter, Peter Jahr, would go off into the jungle to hunt at every opportunity. Most of the boys only had slingshots or crude bows and arrows, but Paul had his trusty .22. He would shoot birds and monkeys. The boys would tie the monkeys' tails together to form a strap and sling them around their necks to take them back to the village as meat for supper. Any birds they killed would go into their soup.

When Ruth LePers came back through from Cape Palmas on her way to Tchien, Ella shared her concern about Paul's education. Miss LePers was a trained schoolteacher and volunteered to take Paul with her to Konabo and be his teacher.

Being separated would be difficult for the entire family, but Harold and Ella felt it was best for Paul. So, off he went with Miss LePers. He remained with her until near the end of their school term, returning only occasionally to visit them at Palipo.

Ruth was too young for school and remained with them at Palipo. She kept Ella busy teaching her the ABC's and the other basics every four-year-old must learn.

Though she was busy with her ministries, Ella struggled with their isolation. Paul was away for schooling with Miss LePers. Harold frequently went hunting, and even little Ruth was often on her own under the watchful care of a faithful native girl named Louise. There were times when more than a year would go by without Ella seeing another white person other than Harold, Paul, and Ruth. Though she deeply loved and enjoyed being with the natives, being completely removed from her culture, her friends, and her family was not easy for her.

Palipo was unbelievably remote and isolated. It was surrounded by thick jungle, which was teeming with an incredible variety of wildlife—monkeys, deer, snakes, and leopards. There were even elephants during certain times of the year.

Leopards were a particular menace. They seemed to have no fear of the humans in the village and the mission compound. On the contrary, the chickens, goats, and occasional cows these humans kept provided inviting targets for the stealthy cats. They had even been known to attack and kill children in the villages.

As they beat their rice each morning, the native women would regularly see leopards on the prowl, circling the village at the fringes of the jungle, looking for easy prey.

Being missionaries was far more dangerous than Ella had imagined it would be. She prayed continuously for the children's safety, trusting the Lord to provide the protection they needed.

Their first encounter with a leopard occurred one Sunday while they were holding church services. When they returned to the house, they discovered the pet chimpanzee they had on the back porch had been taken and killed by a leopard.

"I can't believe a leopard would be that bold," Ella said, shaking her head. "That poor little chimp. Harold, I'm worried about Ruth and the children in the village."

"Well, a few of the natives have traps and I'll set some myself to see what we can do," Harold replied.

The problem for the natives was that the traps were very expensive. Often an entire extended family would have to go in together to afford just one. Then, when a leopard did happen to step into their trap, it was often powerful enough to escape back into the jungle, dragging the trap with it. In such a case, the leopard would eventually die, but the costly trap would be gone forever.

As leopard sightings and attacks occurred more and more frequently, the natives would come to Harold and plead with him. "Pa, the leopard, it took my trap. Go get him, Pa. Go get him." Then off Harold would go with three or four natives, into the dense, dark, jungle to try, only sometimes successfully, to retrieve the trap, knowing other missionaries had been severely injured, and one even killed, attempting to do the same thing.

One evening when Harold was out on a hunting trip and Paul was at school with Miss LePers, Ella and Ruth were alone in the house. Suddenly, there was a heart-stopping scream from near the chicken coop. A leopard, bent on snatching a chicken for dinner, had stepped into one of Harold's traps. As the steel jaws of the trap closed more and more tightly around the big animal's leg, it strained all the harder to pull free. Finally, it managed to break the rope anchoring the trap to a nearby tree and, with the trap still clamped to one of its hind legs, limped across the compound toward the schoolhouse. There, it stepped on another huge steel trap. Sensing its doom, the leopard fought the new trap all the harder, screaming at the pain and growling with rage.

The leopard's growls pierced the night, awakening the villagers who all came running, frightened beyond imagination, yet irresistibly drawn to the spectacle in the dark.

Ella had grabbed her big flashlight and trained it on the leopard. As she did so, she could see its eyes, like spots of fire, but she could also see the leopard was about to break this trap loose as it had the first one. The natives were yelling, "Ma, Ma, get a gun. Shoot it. Shoot it!"

She retrieved one of Harold's extra hunting rifles just as John Try, the native pastor came up. "Here, John. You'll have to shoot him. I can't," she said much more calmly than she felt, as she handed him the rifle.

The little pastor took careful aim at the thrashing cat spotlighted in Ella's flashlight and gently squeezed the trigger. The shot was deafening, and then it was over. The giant cat lay dead at the corner of the schoolhouse.

The ensuing silence was as intense as the raging chaos had been only moments before. Then one of the natives let out a cheer. And then another. And then another, until the entire village was cheering the little pastor. He had killed what for them was a mortal enemy. He was a hero.

Ella assumed the natives would skin the leopard and, because meat was always in short supply, distribute the meat to be eaten by the villagers. However, to her surprise, the next morning, she learned the people might kill a leopard, but they would not eat leopard meat.

Pastor Try patiently explained, "The story of why our people will not eat leopard meat has been handed down from generation to generation."

He went on with the story, "Many years ago, our Palipo tribe was at war with another tribe. The other tribe was winning the battle, and the Palipo people were forced to retreat. As they were being chased by the other tribe, they came to a river, but there was no bridge, and they couldn't cross. The enemy tribe was behind them, pursuing them with clubs and spears.

"Sensing their defeat, one of the Palipo warriors desperately looked upriver. There he saw a leopard crossing the river, seemingly walking on the water. It was walking on a submerged log hidden just below the surface of the rushing water, forming a bridge to the other side. The tribe quickly followed the leopard across the river on the log bridge. Once on the other side, they cut the log free, and it washed down the river. The enemy could not get across the river to pursue them. The Palipo tribe was safe."

Looking directly into Ella's eyes as if to impress upon her the solemnity and significance of the event he had related, Pastor Try continued. "Ma, it is out of respect for the leopard, for what it has done for us, we will not eat its meat." Then, with a grin and a twinkle in his eye, he added, "But we do not respect them so much we will not kill them if we have to."

In addition to their ministry at the mission compound, Harold and Ella frequently walked to other villages, some of them considerable distances away, to preach the Gospel to still unreached tribespeople. When Paul was home from school with Miss LePers, Harold usually took Paul with him, leaving Ella and Ruth at home, often for a week, sometimes even two. Then Ella would take Ruth and leave Harold and Paul behind. These were difficult journeys, with whoever had gone usually returning home exhausted and sick, but the trips were worthwhile in their eyes because so many came to accept Christ as their Savior.

In December 1943, Ella began preparing for the family to attend another annual convention. The missionaries, along with as many of the national Christians as could make it, would be gathering between

Christmas and New Year at Neweka. Everyone looked forward to these yearly times of fellowship and worship.

Because so many people attended, it was a major challenge to provide food and lodging for them all. Most everyone would bring as much of their own food, bedding, and so forth as they could. However, a great deal of extra food was always needed. Harold was usually the one who volunteered to answer the need for meat, by hunting for large amounts of wild game. He had accepted the challenge again this year.

He had hunted off and on for several weeks and had distributed a significant amount of meat to the Christians in town for them to dry and then take with them to the convention. But he had also obtained a permit from the Liberian government to hunt for his first elephant.

The jungle elephants found in West Africa are somewhat smaller than the plains elephants of East Africa, but are, nonetheless, huge animals. They do not live permanently in Liberia but migrate in from Guinea in search of a particularly favorite fruit, which is at its tender, juicy best in November and December.

Because a single elephant devours as much as two to three hundred pounds of vegetation each day, a migrating herd can severely damage the jungle forests through which they travel. However, the forests can replenish themselves in a surprisingly short time because of the moist, rich soils and abundant rains. Far more important from the natives' standpoint, the herds regularly devastated their rice crops. These could not be so easily replaced, and their absence spelled famine and death for native families.

In the 1940s in West Africa, elephants were not an endangered species. They were simply a potential danger to the natives' lives and livelihood, and a source of much-needed meat. When the elephants passed through, small bands of only the bravest hunters would try to kill at least one of the huge beasts for meat. It would feed an entire village for weeks.

Once the hunting party had located an elephant, they would attempt to kill it utilizing a handmade spear and a shotgun. The spear had a long wooden handle with a steel point tied to one end. The shotgun was a single shot and would have been purchased in Cape Palmas or given to one of the hunters by a missionary. The spear would be jammed down the barrel of the shotgun. When the gun was fired, the spear was propelled forward with remarkable force.

As a weapon, the combination spear-shotgun left a great deal to be desired both in terms of range and accuracy. It was also extremely dangerous to use. All manner of mishaps could occur. The spear shaft could splinter on firing, sending lethal fragments in all directions. If the spear handle lodged too tightly in the barrel, the gun itself might explode. It was, however, typical of the natives' ingenuity and their ability to make do with what they had.

The real problem was, even when it worked perfectly, their primitive weapon could, at best, only wound an elephant. Once hit, the giant beast might attack the hunters or simply run into the forest, where it could take several days for the poison the natives dipped the spear tip into to take effect and the animal to finally die. During those days the elephant was charging through the forests, the hunting party would have the dangerous task of following it to ultimately claim their prize.

Once the elephant died, the hunters would cut off the bristly tail. Then, they would return to their village with the tail as quickly as possible. Upon seeing this proof of their conquest and bravery, the entire village would erupt in singing and dancing. The celebration might go on for two or three days. Only then, would the hunters return to their kill to cut up the rotting, putrefied carcass and carry huge slabs of meat and entrails home, to be eaten at still another celebration. What meat was not consumed in the celebration would be dried and then hung in the round peaks of their hut roofs, smoked above their fires, safely stored for future use.

Given the danger and difficulty of hunting on their own, the natives were delighted when they learned Pa Landrus was carefully cleaning and checking his .405 hunting rifle, and he would be setting out with a select team of trackers and hunters in search of Africa's greatest game.

After several days of trudging through the thick foliage, hacking their way with cutlasses where no trails existed, one of the natives leading the team signaled he had seen something. They all stopped immediately, and Harold crept forward to see if they had found their elusive prey.

There, not more than a hundred feet across a small clearing was a group of four elephants. There were three fully grown females and one young calf. The adults were delicately picking fruit off the overhanging trees with their trunks and then stuffing the delicious treat down their throats. They were unhurried, unafraid. The calf trotted about in childhood awkwardness, stopping occasionally to suckle from its mother.

Harold and the hunting party sat motionless, mesmerized by the peaceful, natural scene, taken in by the wonder of God's creation.

After some moments, Harold signaled to the others he wanted to move to the right to get closer and to get a better shot. He had been a hunter all his life. Now, Harold was hunting the biggest game in the world.

Killing such a magnificent animal did not bother him. It was the nature of things. If his aim was true, if the bullet found the small hole in the skull behind the elephant's ear or the one directly between the elephant's eyes, it would penetrate the skull to the brain, and the elephant would die immediately. If he missed, the animal would probably only be wounded. And whether the wound was slight or mortal, the hunters could be in grave danger. Beyond that, as a hunter, Harold wanted to kill the elephant quickly and cleanly. He didn't want to cause it undue pain or prolonged suffering.

His father had died when Harold was only a child. As he grew up on their small family farm in eastern Colorado, his oldest brother, Leonard, had taught Harold how to shoot and hunt. There were lots of rattlesnakes in the area, and Harold would shoot them whenever he had the chance. By the time he was eight, he had a string of rattles all the way around the headband of the beat-up cowboy hat he never went without.

When Harold was in high school, his mother and the children moved to central California. There, he and his middle brother, Ray, went to work for a farmer who owned hundreds of acres of cherry trees. As the cherries ripened, birds would flock to the orchard and cause heavy losses to the farmer's crop. He hired Harold and Ray to shoot the birds to protect his cherries.

Rather than supplying the boys with shotguns as would have been normal for shooting birds, the farmer gave them single-shot .22 rifles.

Every morning, he would give each of the boys two boxes of shells, fifty shells per box. It took some practice, but before long, Harold and Ray became expert shots. Every day, they could each bag ninety-six to ninety-eight birds out of their hundred rounds of ammunition.

The Lord had provided skills and experience for Harold, as a boy, that he would need years later, as a man, to protect and provide for his family in Africa. Now, his skills as a marksman were going to be tested like never before.

He maneuvered his way behind a large mahogany tree, where he had an unobstructed shot from only about sixty feet from the closest of the females. She was not the mother of the young calf, and Harold decided she would be his target. Silently, he raised his heavy rifle and took careful aim. *Lord, let this shot be true.* Then gently, as if in slow motion, he pulled the trigger.

The sound of the shot was deafening, and it seemed to echo through the trees. The target elephant died almost instantly and collapsed where she had been standing. The others, bellowing in fright and anger, charged off thrashing into the jungle. Harold and the native hunting party stayed motionless for several minutes, listening as the sound of the elephants, still crashing through the forest at full flight, slowly began to fade into the distance, and the normal sounds of the jungle resumed around them.

Then the impact of their triumph settled on them, and the natives began shouting and cheering. They lifted Harold above their heads and danced around the clearing while he held on for dear life. "All right! All right! You fellas put me down now," he yelled above their commotion.

"Pa, you did it! One shot, Pa! One shot!" they shouted.

As they let Harold down, they raced to the elephant and, taking out their knives, began cutting off the tail. "We go to village now, Pa," they said.

"I know that's what you usually do. But I want us to stay here and cut up this meat so we can take it back with us," Harold responded.

Their grumbles communicated their disappointment, but the little band began the enormous task of carving up such a huge creature.

After working all day and into the evening, they were ready to leave early the next morning. The natives carried thick slabs of elephant meat slung across their backs. The meat weighed as much or more than each man did. Still dripping with blood and beginning to smell horribly in the stale, humid tropical air, the meat attracted what, Harold was sure, had to be every fly in Africa. The journey home was one of continuous heat, sweat, and wicked fly bites. The joys of the kill were soon lost, and they lapsed into silence, other than an occasional grunt, as the relentless struggle continued hour after hour slogging through the merciless jungle. It was a journey none of them would soon forget.

Two days later, they reached the outskirts of the village and were soon surrounded by laughing children, all screaming and jabbering excitedly. The closer they got, the more people emerged from their huts to greet them. As the crowd and excitement grew, the loads seemed to feel lighter, and the hunters' moods improved with each step. Finally, they were home and were being greeted as heroes.

The drums began beating almost as soon as they had dropped their heavy loads. Shouted inquiries and hasty responses quickly told everyone in the village the story of what had happened, with a few embellishments just to make the tale more captivating. By the time they began carrying Harold and the other members of the hunting party around on their shoulders in celebration, the villagers were convinced not only had Harold killed the elephant with one shot, but it had also been an elephant charging at the hunters, who had bravely stood their ground, spears in hand ready to fight the animal to the death!

Displaying the massive tusks from Harold's first elephant kill (with Paul attempting to hold one tusk and Ruth standing in front of her daddy).

After two full days of dancing, singing, and eating, the celebration gradually ran out of steam, and the villagers set about the task of distributing and drying the meat.

A large portion was set aside to be carried to Neweka for the annual convention. With so much bounty, nearly all the villagers decided they would attend this year, if only to participate in the feasts they would have.

Ella gave a piece of meat to one woman in town who was so delighted, she said she would keep it until her daughter got married and bring the meat out for the wedding feast.

Harold enjoyed a few days of well-earned rest, while Ella continued getting the family ready for the journey to Neweka, which meant another three days of jungle trails.

Before they left for the convention, Paul returned from attending school with Miss LePers at Konabo so the family would be together for Christmas.

At various times during the year, packages from the United States would arrive for them at Cape Palmas. They would be held at the mission house there until Harold came to town for supplies. Then his team of porters would carry the packages, sometimes boxes, sometimes fifty-five-gallon drums, back to Palipo.

Often, these packages contained small pieces of cloth for Ella to distribute to the native women she was teaching to sew quilts. Other times, they were bedsheets, torn into strips and rolled to be used as bandages when Ella held morning clinic. Sometimes, the packages included small gifts for Harold, Ella, Paul, or Ruth.

Whatever the contents, opening a package from America was always a special treat, an event they tried to enjoy as a family.

In October 1944, a package had arrived addressed to six-year-old Ruth. Harold and Ella were delighted because they couldn't buy gifts for Paul or Ruth in Palipo, so Christmas was a time for celebrating Christ's birth, not for exchanging gifts. Now, it appeared Ruth would have a

Christmas gift after all, and they were as excited about it as Ruth was. There might even be gifts for all of them.

From the day of its arrival, Ruth begged to open her package, but Harold and Ella wouldn't let her. Even Paul got into it saying, "Just wait, Ruthie! It's for Christmas!" Nonetheless, through the balance of October, all of November and the first three weeks of December, every few days, little Ruth would drag out her package and shake it and dream about what wondrous present it must contain.

The smell of the package was almost present enough. It was the only thing in the house that didn't yet smell of the musty mildew of the tropics.

Christmas morning, Ruth could hardly contain herself. "Hurry, Mother. Sit here with me," she said as she plopped herself on the floor. "Daddy, can I open it now?" she asked.

"Well, I guess so. Let's see what you got, Dollie," Harold responded, using the nickname he frequently used for Ruth.

Ruth tore into her package, tossing the brown paper wrapping at Paul, who sat expectantly on the other side of the package in front of her.

As she opened the box, Ruth's expression changed from anticipation to despair. There were bandages—rolls and rolls of bandages.

"Maybe there's something underneath," Paul encouraged her. She kept digging into the box, throwing bandages aside as she did so.

She pulled the last bandage out and, with tears in her eyes, turned the box upside down. Nothing!

Ruth's disappointment was exceeded only by that felt by Harold and Ella, and even Paul. They sat quietly for several moments.

Then Harold said with a small catch in his voice, "OK, children, let's get ready for Christmas services. These people need us to tell them that Christmas is about God's gift of Jesus, not our gifts to each other."

Later that evening as they lay in bed together, Ella said softly, "If there had even been a single piece of gum in there for her, it would have been OK."

As usual, the annual convention was a major highlight of the year for the Landrus family. Harold and Ella got a chance to fellowship with their missionary friends and to catch up on the latest news. Because the Landruses would be leaving for the United States on furlough the following spring or summer, this was also the last time they would see many of their friends until, if all went well, they returned in about eighteen months. Convention gave them an opportunity to say good-bye.

Convention also meant Paul and Ruth got to be with other missionary children.

Time for missionary children to play and interact with one another was particularly important as far as their parents were concerned. Because their children normally had only native friends to play with, missionary parents feared they would grow up "native," meaning they would think more like natives and approach things from a native perspective. To a large extent, this could not be avoided. However, the missionaries did what they could; after all, they didn't expect their children to remain in Africa once they were grown and wanted their children to be able to assimilate into American society when they were older.

At ten years of age and one of the few boys on the field at the time, Paul was already the center of attention for several of the young missionary girls at the convention. He was tall and slender. He was already a good hunter. He was at home with the natives and could speak their languages perfectly. And as they timidly admitted with squeals and giggles to one another, he was just so cute!

Ella had been asked to preach the second evening of the convention. (Much of the time, she did more preaching than Harold did.) She selected a portion of Scripture from the Old Testament dealing with the life of David as her text. Traditionally, at the close of a service, the preacher gave what they referred to as an "altar call," meaning they would invite any in the audience who wanted to repent of their sins and accept Christ into their lives as their Savior, to come forward, signifying their desire to do so, and have someone pray with them.

Much to Ella's surprise and joy, when she asked if there were those in the audience who wanted to accept Christ, Paul first raised his hand and then walked to the front of the room for prayer.

Harold and Ella had, of course, raised their children in a Christian environment, but they recognized just being raised as a Christian and living by Christian values was not enough. When it came down to it, each individual had to make the personal choice as to what he or she was going to do with the person of Jesus Christ. All had the option to accept Him as Savior and Lord of their life or reject Him and live as they chose. Harold and Ella had prayed daily the Lord would draw Paul and Ruth to accept Him. Now, kneeling on the floor in the Neweka chapel, Paul became a Christian. It was a great and glorious day for them all.

Time passed quickly as they returned to Palipo following the convention and began preparing to leave on furlough. However, Harold had one last big project he wanted to complete before they left.

At the convention, he had spent considerable time talking with fellow missionary Brother E. L. Mason. No one ever called him by his first name. They all called him "E. L." or just "Mason". Mason was a pilot and had brought an airplane to Monrovia to assist with the mission work in the north. "In fact," he said, "I'd have flown the plane to Neweka for the convention, but there was no place to land."

That had settled it in Harold's mind. He would bring a plane with him next term.

At Palipo, he marked out a broad area of jungle and set a group of the male Bible school students to work each morning cutting down the maze of trees and vines.

After several weeks' work, they had cut and hacked a section about sixty feet wide and several hundred feet long. The felled trees, brush, and vines lay where they had fallen, but they were now dry and brittle.

Once he figured they were dry enough to burn, Harold lit the entire cut area on fire. It burned intensely for two days and then burned itself out. Whenever the flames approached the uncut jungle at the edges, the still growing vegetation was so moist the fire could not burn it. What Harold ended up with was a sixty-foot-wide pathway littered with charred stumps and a number of large logs the fire had not completely consumed.

Afterward, Harold put his team to work digging the stumps and using a series of pulleys to yank them out of the ground. They hauled off the unburned logs. Then by rigging a makeshift blade, they leveled the ground as best they could.

After more than two months of sweat and toil, they were finished. Harold could leave now. He was ready. At supper, Ella remarked, "I've been too afraid to ask just what it is you've been up to out there all this time."

"That's because you already know the answer, Ella." Harold grinned. "That's my first airfield!"

Ella shook her head and smiled. "You don't have an airplane and you don't even know how to fly!"

———

They closed the Palipo mission station on March 19, 1945. There were no missionaries available to substitute for them while they were on furlough, but they hoped to return the following year. They had twenty-four hammock men and twenty-six load men for the trek to Pleebo. The trip cost them fifty-three dollars, including eight dollars for the truck ride from Pleebo to Cape Palmas.

They stayed at the mission house in Cape Palmas for several weeks arranging for their transportation to America. Ella kept busy sewing clothes for them to wear when they got there.

On April 30, Brother Mason flew down to the airfield at Cape Palmas, bringing Florence Steidel and Laura Bassett with him. It was his first flight to Cape Palmas. He was to pick the Landruses up and fly them to Monrovia. His plane was a single-engine seaplane that could land on water or on land and carried six passengers. It was much too big to attempt landing on Harold's new Palipo airstrip.

Before leaving, Harold insisted he and Mason walk back to Palipo one last time so Mason could check out the airfield and see if he thought it would be adequate. He did think so, and congratulated Harold on having carved it out of such thick and inhospitable jungle.

They flew north from Cape Palmas along the coast to Sinoe on May 19, 1945. There they spent a few days visiting the Walins, missionaries who, in addition to Miss LePers, had also provided schooling for Paul during part of the term.

On their flight out of Sinoe, en route to Monrovia, Ruth broke out with the measles. A few days after reaching Monrovia, Paul came down with them as well.

They stayed in the basement of the mission house in Monrovia so the other missionary children would not become infected.

A couple weeks later, Paul and Ruth had recovered and were ready to resume their journey. Brother Mason flew them to a place called Fisherman's Lake, northeast of Monrovia. There they could book passage on one of the fabulous new flying "Clippers" Pan American World Airways had recently introduced to commercial aviation.

The Fisherman's Lake facility had been constructed as Pan Am's part of the war effort, when every pound of cargo was desperately needed to support the Allied Forces fighting in North Africa. The seaplane Clippers, heavily laden with war materials, landed at Fisherman's Lake. Then, their cargo was off-loaded and carried overland by porters to the US Army's Benson Field where land-based aircraft waited to rush the loads to the northern battle grounds. Now, as the war was nearing its end, Fisherman's Lake was being converted into a passenger as well as cargo handling station.

As their Clipper plane landed to pick them up, Harold was amazed at its size. Paul and Ruth thought it was wonderful they were going to fly in something so large and luxurious. Ella was uncomfortable about a plane being able to fly for so many hours. None of them had ever heard of a passenger plane flying non-stop completely across the Atlantic before. They were flying to Natal, Brazil, the closest point in the Western Hemisphere from Liberia. As the Pan Am brochure handed to each passenger noted, a "mere twelve hours flight".

To Ella's relief, they landed safely on June 19, 1945, in Natal, Brazil, and spent the next three weeks at the Grande Hotel endeavoring to arrange transportation for the next leg of their journey.

Hitler's armies in Europe had been crushed and American GIs were beginning to return home from South America and other far-flung corners of the American war effort. As a result, US Navy troop ships seemed to be sailing everywhere. Never bashful, Harold presented himself to the American authorities stationed in Natal and managed to book passage for the entire family on a troop ship headed for New Orleans via Trinidad and San Juan, Puerto Rico.

As civilians, they were treated like royalty. They ate their meals with the captain and the other officers. They couldn't believe how good fresh food tasted, particularly real butter on their rice. When he wasn't eating, Paul occupied himself playing checkers with the sailors.

During the voyage, a large knot developed under the skin on Ella's back, near her right shoulder. It became infected and hurt terribly. The navy medic on board gave her penicillin, but refused to lance it for fear the infection might spread. The penicillin seemed to have little effect, and she suffered for the rest of the trip.

When at last they made it up the mouth of the Mississippi to New Orleans, to their surprise, they were met by none other than E. L. Mason. He had left Liberia shortly after they had but had managed to secure passage on a ship sailing directly for the United States. Al Trotter, a friend of Mason's, was with him. Trotter quickly maneuvered them through customs and then took Ella and Harold to find a doctor, while Mason took Paul and Ruth to his house.

The doctor said there was little he could do. The skin was broken and the sore oozing, but like the navy medic, he didn't want to cut or lance it because he was concerned the infection would spread if he did. All he could do was give her additional penicillin and dress the sore. She would just have to endure it until the infection subsided.

Even with the war ending, there were major shortages of automobiles, gasoline, and tires. Nonetheless, a few days later, Harold was able to purchase a used car, and they began the long drive from Louisiana to Alhambra, California.

"Thank the Lord," said Ella as they began their drive. "I can't wait to get to where a doctor can really take care of this."

Stopping regularly to change the dressing on her back, they made it to Ella's parents' house in Alhambra on July 31, 1945.

The doctor in Alhambra was able to do no more than the others had. He told Ella to be patient. The penicillin would eventually work, and the sore would go away.

Mercifully, he was right. Within a couple of weeks, it was gone and never returned.

They were back in America again. Time to rest and recuperate. Time to begin the long preparations to go back to Africa. Time to undergo the challenges of being missionaries on furlough.

Chapter 8

Furlough: Tears, a Baby, and Wings

This, their second furlough, was to encompass three particularly significant events for the Landrus family. The first was a very private, very painful personal battle for Ella. The second was to change the family forever. And the third was to dramatically alter their ministry in Africa.

⌒

As she settled into life in Alhambra, Ella sensed something was very wrong. She couldn't figure out what it was. She had felt so lonely and isolated in Africa, but now when she could be with her friends and others she knew, she just didn't want to be around people at all. She didn't want to go anywhere. She felt like crying all the time. She had no idea why she was feeling these things. What she did know was she had to do her very best to keep whatever she was feeling to herself.

This was 1945. Missionaries were expected to be strong, non-emotional people who trusted God for all things and never, ever shared their feelings and their struggles with anyone else. It was as if, to do so, would somehow indicate they didn't believe God could handle their troubles, or they simply didn't have sufficient faith to carry them through. If that were the case, how could they possibly be missionaries?

Every Sunday, Harold and Ella, along with Paul and Ruth, would walk the couple of blocks from Ella's parents' home, where they were staying for the furlough, to Bethany Church for the morning worship services. Everyone was so glad they were back and wanted to talk with them and to hear of their adventures in Africa. This became almost unbearable for Ella. She didn't know why.

Harold was of little help to her. He had found her in the bedroom a time or two with tears running down her cheeks. He hadn't seen her like that very often, and his assumption was there was something physically wrong with her.

"Are you alright, Ella? Are you sick?" he asked.

"No, no. I'm alright. I just must be tired I guess," she answered.

Harold loved her with everything in him, but rendering emotional support and sensitivity were definitely not among Harold's strengths. He took her reply at face value and left her quietly alone, not pressing her to learn what she was facing; perhaps subconsciously recognizing he didn't know how to help her when the battle was emotional, rather than the physical dangers or hardships they faced in Africa. Those he could understand and knew how to deal with.

One Sunday morning before the services had begun, Dr. Britton spotted Ella in the foyer of the church standing off to one side, desperately trying to avoid as many people as she could, without being too obvious about it. Immediately, he sensed she was very ill at ease.

Walking up to her he said, "Good morning, Ella." Then he took her by the elbow and carefully guided her out of the sanctuary to a quiet place in the garden outside.

"Ella, are you alright? You seemed to be pretty uncomfortable in there," he said softly.

Tears immediately welled in Ella's eyes. "Oh, Dr. Britton. I don't know what's wrong with me. I feel so helpless. I don't know what to do. I feel like I'm just going out of my mind or something." She bowed her head and began to sob.

Dr. Britton said nothing, but put his arm around her and gently guided her to sit on a wooden bench in the garden. They sat there for several minutes; the silence broken only by her sobs. Dr. Britton sat quietly, patting her hand gently.

Suddenly, Ella's head shot up. "Dr. Britton, you have to go. The church service is about to begin," she wailed with terrified urgency in her voice.

With a smile, he looked at her and said, "Ella, they can start the service without me. Or they can wait until I get there. What I'm doing right now is much more important."

"You have had a difficult time of it, Ella. You don't know the strain you've been under. You've had to care for your family in a dangerous, lonely place, and you've had to be strong for them. It's OK for you to let it all out now. This is the place for you to do it because you can't do it in Africa." Looking into her eyes, he gently coached her, "I want you to go home now. Harold and the children can stay here for the church service. You go home, where you can be alone, and I want you to just let yourself cry."

"But, but ..." she started. "Are you sure? Do you think it'll be all right?"

Once again, he patted her hand. "I'm sure of it, Ella. You go along now and let yourself have a good cry."

Chastising herself the entire way, Ella almost ran home. She kept thinking, *I don't know what's the matter with me! This is ridiculous. What will people think? Oh, I don't understand what's happening!*

She stumbled into the house and then into the bedroom, where she threw herself across the bed. Then she cried.

She cried and cried. She cried until there were no more tears.

Slowly, she lifted herself from the bed and looked in the mirror. *What a mess you are,* she thought. Then it dawned on her. She did feel better. It was as though a big weight had been lifted from her.

Ella had no idea what had happened. She just knew she felt better, and she was going to make it through whatever this was.

When she thought about it later, Ella could never identify what her problem had been. It could have been the months of isolation and loneliness in Africa. It could have been almost losing Harold to blackwater fever. It could have been, at least subconsciously, she was beginning to recognize what most missionaries eventually learn—they don't belong. She no longer belonged.

She didn't belong in Africa, and she didn't belong in America. As much at home as she felt in Africa, she was still a foreigner and always would be. She was a white person in a black culture. But she also no longer belonged in America. It had passed her by. It had changed and progressed while she was living half a world away in a primitive land virtually unchanged by time. She was beginning to understand part of the price she and Harold and their children had to pay for being missionaries.

They were loved and cared for. They had lives of meaning and ministry. But they simply did not belong—anyplace.

❧

Ella's emotional struggles might also have been made more difficult due to some dramatic hormonal changes occurring in her body. Much to her surprise—after all, it had been nearly eight years since Ruth was born—she was pregnant with their third child.

Some of Harold's buddies would tease him later; even though they were sailing on a troop ship, he must have been taking advantage of the romance of the Caribbean on their voyage from Natal, Brazil, to New Orleans.

On Easter Sunday 1946, Harold and Ella, along with Paul and Ruth, joined some of their friends, including Dr. Britton and Helen Bridges, for lunch at Bernice Van Amtworth's home.

Early the next morning, Ella knew it was time for Harold to take her to the hospital. There, at 7:00 a.m. on April 22, Esther Mae Landrus was born. A healthy, happy little girl.

Considering the difficulties she had endured with Paul's birth, and the primitive conditions surrounding Ruth's arrival, Ella was more than relieved Esther could be born in a clean American hospital with no problems or complications. As she lay recovering in her hospital bed with Esther snuggled close in her arms, Ella whispered, "Thank you, Lord. Thank you for this precious baby girl. Please protect her when we go back to Africa."

❧

Almost from the moment they arrived in Alhambra, Harold began lobbying Dr. Britton for help in purchasing an airplane to take to Africa. He spoke about it every time they saw each other.

Late one Sunday evening, Dr. Britton was in his office study located in a room on the second floor of an old house next to the church. He was something of a night owl and could be found there most nights until well into the early hours of the morning. That is, he could be unless he was riding with one of the city's policemen driving patrol on the streets. Dr.

Britton liked to ride along occasionally just to be available to minister to some wayward citizen in trouble.

Harold had walked to the church about eleven o'clock hoping to catch Dr. Britton, his friend and supporter. Seeing a light in the office, Harold climbed the stairs and knocked. Through the door, he heard Dr. Britton quickly respond, "Come in."

As he entered, Harold got right to the point. "Do you have a minute we can talk?"

"Of course, I do, Harold. Come sit down here," he said, hastily moving a stack of books from the chair in front of his desk.

As Harold sat down, Dr. Britton continued. "Before you get started, I want you to know I've been thinking and praying about this airplane you want so badly." He studied Harold for a moment and then continued, "Harold, do you really believe you need an airplane? And it will benefit your ministry in Africa?"

Without hesitating, Harold responded, "Yes, sir! I surely do! We've been able to raise a little money toward it—about $600. But that leaves us nearly $3,000 short."

Dr. Britton paused, thinking about it, and then, nodding his head slightly, said, "Well, I guess we'd better buy it for you then!"

Harold could hardly believe his ears. He just sat, not knowing what to say or do.

"When would you like the money, Harold?" Dr. Britton asked.

His senses returning, Harold said with a smile, "Well, if it's all right with you, I'll take it right now!"

Dr. Britton chuckled, reached into his desk for a small cash box, and counted out the money right then and there.

Early the next morning, Harold went to the Western Union office to send a telegram to the Piper Airplane Company to place the order for his first airplane. He was as excited as he had ever been.

The plane he ordered was a three-seat Piper Cub Super Cruiser. Harold had thought long and hard about which plane he would buy if he ever got the chance. This model was sturdy enough to withstand the rough terrain landings he would have to make. It also had good cargo space, coupled with reasonable fuel capacity, giving him ample range to fly throughout Liberia. This was a critical issue for him. Gasoline wasn't easy to come by in the jungles of Liberia.

A follow-up phone call to the factory in Pennsylvania confirmed they had received his order and also the down payment he had wired to them. Since Harold and Ella would be leaving for Africa within a couple of months, they planned to stop at the factory on their way to New York.

This would enable Harold to check out the plane and to test-fly it. The Piper people would then disassemble the plane down to its major components and pack them in one large crate for trucking to New York and then for loading on the steamship for West Africa.

Harold could hardly wait for the time to arrive for them to pack, say their good-byes, and begin the long drive to New York—this time with a very special stop in Pennsylvania along the way.

In the meantime, he went to the general aviation airfield in El Monte, California and began learning how to fly.

—◦—

When they arrived at the Piper factory, the plane was everything Harold had anticipated it would be. He had flown a similar model while they were in California, but this was a newer version. Best of all, this one was his!

That man is like a kid in a candy store, thought Ella. "I'm not sure we're ever going to get your father out of that airplane once we get to Africa," she said to the children.

Paul was already dreaming of having his own plane once he was a little older.

Harold put the plane through its paces, taking off and landing on a grass strip alongside the paved factory runway. He needed to know it could land and take off from something a whole lot rougher than a traditional runway. He liked the way it handled.

After a couple of days, he was more than satisfied with his purchase. As he climbed out of the cockpit for the final time, he walked over to the waiting factory representative and shook his hand, "I think that about does it. Mister, you build a fine airplane. I'll be proud to fly it in Africa."

"Well, Mr. Landrus, we'll be proud to have you flying it over there. You folks go on to New York now. I promise we'll have this thing broken down, crated up, and following on behind you in no more than three days. We thank you for your business."

"I thank you for your help. We'll wait for it to catch up with us in New York," said Harold, shaking his hand one last time.

~

In New York, they stayed at the mission house on Summit Street once again and waited for the crated plane to arrive. It did so, as promised, three days later.

The plane was scheduled for shipment to Liberia on the freighter SS *Biafra*, a 5,405-ton cargo ship built in 1919 and owned by the Elder Dempster Line. Harold was not ticketed. In his concern over the plane, he had forgotten to book his own passage. Ella and the children were already scheduled to fly, but Harold had wanted to accompany the plane by ship. Now, he would have to fly with the rest of the family.

Harold couldn't bring himself to do that. He went down to the dock to watch the wooden crate containing his precious airplane safely loaded and securely tied on deck. He decided he'd ask to speak with the captain.

"Captain, I'm H. H. Landrus, missionary to Liberia," he said extending his hand to the man. "That crate they just loaded on board is my airplane. I'm takin' it to Africa to use in my missionary work. It's real important to me."

"I understand, Reverend Landrus. Rest assured we'll take real good care of it for you. You don't need to worry about it at all," the captain assured him.

"Well, I appreciate that, sir. And I thank you for it. But I'd be much obliged if you could see fit to allow me and my son to sail with you, just to be sure."

The captain hesitated and then smiled and said, "I guess we could find room for you. We don't want to stand in the way of the Lord's work, now do we?"

A few days later, Harold and Paul, keeping a watchful eye on their special wooden crate, sailed out of New York Harbor bound for West Africa. Ella, eight-year-old Ruth, and baby Esther flew out a few days later on a Pan Am Clipper, headed for Liberia via Lisbon, Portugal, and Dakar, Senegal.

The Landrus family in 1946 just before returning to Africa.

Mechanical problems grounded them for several days in Lisbon, but Ella and the girls didn't mind. They knew Paul and Harold would not reach Liberia for another week, so they enjoyed sight-seeing compliments of Pan Am.

The only problem Ella encountered in Lisbon was she couldn't buy milk for Esther. In Ella's word's, "God told the Pan Am man I needed milk for my baby." And it must have been so, because the Pan Am agent did, indeed, go to the American embassy and request canned milk for Esther.

That afternoon, three men from the embassy walked through the hotel lobby, each carrying two handfuls of canned milk. Directed to Ella by the hotel staff, the men dutifully delivered the milk to Ella as if they were presenting a gift to a visiting dignitary.

They resumed their flight about a week later and arrived at Roberts Field in Liberia on Thanksgiving Day, 1946, just in time to meet many of the other missionaries who had gathered to celebrate the holiday. They all rode the sixty bouncy miles to Monrovia in the back of Mason's truck.

Ella and the girls stayed in the mission house in Monrovia and waited for Harold and Paul.

⸺◠⸺

Meanwhile, out at sea, Harold and Paul were enjoying a rather uneventful voyage. They had gotten to know the crew well enough the seamen were more than willing to play a prank or two on this unsuspecting missionary and his son.

A few days out, one of the crew came running up to Harold. "Mr. Landrus, Mr. Landrus," he shouted excitedly. "Come quick. Some cargo shifted. I think your plane's been crushed."

Poor Harold could hardly believe what he was hearing. "Oh, no!" he yelled as he began running down the deck toward the spot where the crate was stowed.

As he rounded the corner of the ship's superstructure, he was prepared to see the protective crate splintered and shattered, his beautiful plane smashed and broken. What he saw instead was the crate untouched, surrounded by nearly half the crew laughing wildly at the joke they had pulled on him.

If he hadn't been so relieved Harold might have been a little angry. But he had to admit they really had him going. All he could do was grin and shake his head.

They arrived off the Liberian coast two days later.

⸺◠⸺

Like Cape Palmas at the time, Monrovia didn't have a regular port. Ships had to anchor some distance from the coast and off-load cargo onto rafts and surfboats. These were then paddled to shore, and the cargo transferred by hand to the beach. The crate with Harold's plane was no exception.

Pacing the deck of the freighter, sure they were going to drop or damage his plane, Harold could hardly watch as the cargo booms hoisted the crate and lowered it over the side to the raft waiting below.

To Harold, the raft looked smaller and smaller as the large crate was gently placed in its center. Fortunately, the sea was calm, and the raft rode smoothly, accepting its load, settling deeper into the water as the full weight of the crate began being felt on its flat deck. Peering over from the railing of the ship above, Harold was certain the raft was simply too small. Once the full weight of the crate was transferred to the raft, he knew it would just keep going down. Water would pour over the deck, the raft would sink, and his plane would be lost forever at the bottom of the sea.

Harold needn't have worried. It didn't happen. The raft did ride painfully low in the water once the entire weight of the crate was released by the freighter's cargo boom, but it remained afloat, much to Harold's relief.

He and Paul hurried down the gangplank to join the crate on the raft for the ride to shore, which went off without a hitch.

At the beach the crate was manhandled ashore by a team of waiting workers and then taken by truck to a nearby rock quarry where it was again off-loaded.

The family stayed temporarily with other missionaries at the mission house in Monrovia, while Harold and Paul went out each day to the rock quarry to work on putting the plane back together.

Mason gave them a hand assembling the plane, and within a few days Harold tightened the last fitting. Lifting his hat to wipe his brow, he said, "Well, I guess that does it. All we have to do now is see if it'll fly!"

Before anyone could say or do anything, Mason stepped to the plane and, raising his right hand toward heaven and placing his left hand on the plane, began to pray. "Lord," he said in a bold voice, "Harold has brought this plane to Liberia to do your work. I pray right now you would bless and protect Harold and this plane and that the cause of Christ would be mightily served by what Harold can do with this plane. May all who ride in it be safe. May your work be done in and through it. In Jesus's wonderful, powerful name I pray. Amen."

Harold and Paul added their own "amens". Then, looking at the plane, Harold said softly, "I'll fly it out of here tomorrow morning."

Reassembling Harold's plane.

Early the next morning Mason drove Harold and Paul out to the quarry for Harold's first attempt at flying in Africa.

The challenge, assuming they had gotten the plane back together correctly, was the takeoff. This was a rock quarry, not a runway. All they had to work with as a runway was a rock-strewn dirt truck path, which meandered through the quarry. It wasn't even straight, which Harold knew would really make things difficult.

"We probably ought to make a few minor improvements to this high-class runway we have here." Harold grinned.

They walked from the plane down the road, removing as many of the bigger rocks as they could and kicking dirt into the worst of the holes and ruts. Then they worked their way back, continuing to make what "improvements" they could.

"Harold, this might not be a good idea," Mason worried. "Maybe we should take the plane apart again and truck it to another location."

"No. I think I can make it. I don't figure the Lord had me bring this plane all the way out here just to crash the first time I try to fly it," Harold responded.

They brought five-gallon cans of gasoline they carefully emptied into the plane's fuel tanks. They also made sure the oil level in the engine was where it should be. After one last check of all the pieces they had bolted together when they reassembled the plane, Harold patted Paul on the shoulder and climbed into the cockpit.

"I'll see you fellas at the soccer field in Monrovia," he said as he began checking the instruments and flicked the switch to crank the engine over. Monrovia had no airport of its own. Incoming international flights landed about sixty miles south of the city at Roberts Field, as Ella and the girls had done just a few days earlier. Harold planned to use the city's soccer field as his makeshift landing strip, assuming he made it out of the rock quarry, and the plane held together for the short flight to the city.

The engine caught almost instantly and settled into a steady purr as Harold throttled back to let it idle, making sure everything was operating properly. He'd only get one chance at this takeoff. He couldn't risk any loss of power or any problems with the controls.

Finally, he was ready. "All right, Lord. Let's get this thing in the air," he prayed aloud.

With a brief wave to Mason and Paul, Harold maneuvered the plane onto the truck path and lined it up for his rollout and takeoff. Revving the engine, he let off the brakes, and the plane began its run, gradually picking up speed.

It went more smoothly than Harold had expected. He followed the slight bends in the road as the plane gained speed, and then, at the right moment, he pulled back on the controls. The little Piper seemed to leap into the air, just in time to avoid a rather large pile of rocks looming all too quickly just ahead.

Harold circled back over the quarry, dipping his wings as Mason and Paul scampered to the truck for a mad dash to the city. They glanced up, waving enthusiastically.

Harold couldn't help himself. He laughed out loud. This was something he had thought and dreamed and prayed about for a long, long time. Here he was. Flying his plane. Over Africa! *God is truly good*, he thought.

⁓

Navigation wasn't a problem. Once he got the plane to sufficient elevation, Harold could see the city off in the distance to the west and slightly north.

Soon he was buzzing the soccer field and then swinging around to line up for his landing. A small group of children playing on the field scattered quickly, hiding behind the palm trees along the perimeter. Some of them were frightened because they had never seen an airplane in their lives. Others teased them, acting like sophisticated, worldly citizens because they, unlike their inferior friends, had seen an airplane before. For all of them, this bright yellow machine in the sky above them was a thing of incomparable wonder and magic.

The landing went well, and Harold taxied to the edge of the field and shut the engine down. Immediately, the plane was surrounded by curious children, soon joined by a throng of similarly interested adults, all jabbering excitedly.

As entranced as they all were by the airplane, they nonetheless kept their circle several yards distant from it. After all, this was a remarkable machine, and to be there, this close to it, was a truly extraordinary event for them. Something so incomprehensible as this machine was surely to be treated with a certain degree of respect and even fear.

Mason and Paul drove up shortly, as did Ella, along with Ruth and Esther and a number of the other missionaries. All were delighted to see Harold and the plane had arrived safely, and were excited that a new era of ministry in southern Liberia was about to begin.

The following morning, after loading their gear, Harold and Paul took off with Lois Shelton for their first flight to Cape Palmas.

Navigation was, again, no problem. All they had to do was follow the coast until they reached Cape. A good airfield awaited them there, built by the Americans as part of the war effort.

Flying back to Monrovia alone, Harold picked up Ella, Ruth, and Esther the next morning and flew them to Cape Palmas.

They would stay at Cape for about a month waiting to attend the upcoming annual convention being held at Neweka.

Chapter 9

Palipo Again

The entire family was excited about going to the convention again, all but Esther, who was only seven months old at the time. It was good to be back in Liberia. It was becoming "home" to them. They would soon be able to see not only their missionary friends but many of their African friends as well.

The natives were particularly delighted to see Esther. They rarely sounded the "r" at the end of her name, calling her "Estah baby" instead.

The family was very excited Harold had his plane now. They were going to be able to fly to Neweka for the convention. An airstrip had been carved out of the jungle there just so the Landruses and the Masons could fly in. What a wonderful change that would be. This would mean a short flight, rather than a two- or three-day ordeal through the steaming jungle.

When the appointed day arrived, they happily packed the plane and took off for Neweka. Unfortunately, this flight was toward the interior, not along the coast. Navigation became an immediate problem. Below them was a seemingly endless carpet of thick green jungle rising and falling over the hills and valleys but providing no clear features from which Harold could get an idea of their location.

He wasn't worried about their safety. If necessary, he could fly back to the coast and then return to Cape Palmas. But they didn't want to go to Cape Palmas. They wanted to go to Neweka, in the interior, for the convention.

After flying for some time crisscrossing the area Harold thought was about the right location, he finally spotted the small clearing marking the Neweka mission compound and the narrow cut in the jungle indicating their landing strip.

Later, as his time in the air as a "bush pilot" increased, Harold became expert at recognizing a dead tree here, a finger of rock there, or a tiny stream as beacons from which he could navigate. The first nearly two-hour flight to Neweka became a routine twenty to thirty minutes afterward.

~

The annual convention was all they had anticipated. Their native and missionary friends were there. The singing and preaching and relaxed fellowship made them feel they really were back at home in Africa.

Six different tribes made determined appeals for Harold and Ella to come be their missionaries. Each had what they felt was a high priority need, and each made their case to the missionary field council during the convention.

Ultimately, Chief William and the Palipo tribe prevailed. When they were told the Landruses would be returning to Palipo, they sang and danced their joy. The chief promised to send many porters to carry all the supplies and equipment the family would need to, once again, set up for another three or four years of life in the remote interior.

Harold was disappointed to learn that, while they were on furlough, the airstrip he and his crew had labored so hard to complete had been left unattended and was overgrown with brush. It would be impossible for him to land there, at least for the time being. However, Chief William assured him the Palipo tribe would clear it as quickly as possible.

~

One of the African girls attending school at the Neweka mission station was Grace Scott. Her father was a native pastor ministering to the people in a small jungle village some distance away. Pastor Scott and his family had made their way to Neweka to visit Grace and to participate in the annual convention.

During the convention, Pastor Scott approached Harold with a request. "Pa Landrus, you have a fine, fine new baby daughter. I believe my daughter, Grace, should accompany you back to Palipo so she can care for Estah baby for you and Ma Landrus."

Surprised, Harold said, "Well, Pastor, we appreciate your offer. We really do. It would be a real blessing to have someone to help Ella with her. But what about Grace's schooling here in Neweka?"

"Pa, tis awright. Grace can learn from you and Ma Landrus in Palipo at your mission school there. She truly wants to care for Estah baby. She will love her and protect her so you and Ma can be missionaries and talk God talk to the people."

"OK. I'll talk it over with Ma Landrus, and we'll let you and Grace know before the convention is over," Harold responded.

A few days later, Ella approached Grace and accepted her offer to become Esther's nanny. Grace would go with them to Palipo and, for the next four years, would be like a second mother to Esther, caring for her, nurturing her, teaching her, and protecting her. Until she could walk on her own, Esther would travel strapped to Grace Scott's back wherever they went.

Grace Scott caring for "Estah baby."

Harold, Ella, the children, Grace, and the porters fought their way through the jungles once again to Palipo—only to find that, like the airstrip, the house was overgrown with vegetation and in considerable disrepair.

Their first task was to make the house livable. The school building also needed work. Once they got the major repairs completed and were somewhat settled in, they would begin Bible studies, organizing the school, and setting up for daily clinic.

Very quickly, they had more than forty natives they were responsible for supporting. Some were there to attend school. Others were hired to help with the endless tasks of maintaining the mission buildings, clearing the airstrip, tending the garden to feed them all, and assisting Harold and Ella with their daily ministry activities. It was not unusual for Harold and Ella to preach as many as forty times in a month, in addition to holding daily clinic and teaching school.

One of Ella's "extra" tasks was grinding rice flour to supplement any wheat flour they could purchase when Harold made trips to Cape Palmas for supplies. Cook Daniel always needed plenty of flour to make his delicious bread. Ella also made soap out of palm oil for them to bathe and wash clothing with.

Harold started his regular rounds preaching in the surrounding villages, but would soon be busy flying once the airstrip was cleared and he could return to Cape Palmas to fly the plane into Palipo.

The house had an attic with two small rooms. Harold converted one of them into his shortwave radio room. Each morning at six thirty sharp, his voice would boom out as he almost yelled into the microphone, "Palipo calling Neweka. Palipo calling Neweka. Come in, Carl."

Whereupon, Carl or Velma Hixenbaugh would respond, "Neweka to Palipo. Good morning, Harold." From there they would carry on a radio conversation to make sure everyone was alright and pass on any messages or needs.

Once they signed off, Harold would call the next station and then the next, checking with each missionary on the field, relaying messages, arranging for supplies, or coordinating transportation now that they could look forward to flying. The radio became their lifeline with the world outside.

After a lot of hard work, they got the airstrip cleared sufficiently for Harold to land and he walked to Cape Palmas to bring the plane in.

<hr />

A bloodcurdling scream pierced the darkness late one night, startling the sleeping family awake. At first, no one was sure what it was. Then, as angry growls joined the screams, they knew. It could only be a leopard. The screams obviously meant it was in terrible pain, but the growls that accompanied those screams also indicated it was in a rage of anger.

Several days before, the leopard had crept out of the surrounding jungle and onto the back porch of the house. It had grabbed a chicken that had escaped from the nearby coop and hauled it off for a light snack. When Ella discovered what had happened, she was immediately worried about the children. Paul and Ruth were a little older, so they were at least aware of danger and could call out for help. Esther was just about one. Even with faithful, ever-present Grace Scott caring for her, she and Grace were both at risk with a leopard prowling the outskirts of the compound. The animal's boldness even had the students, workers, and those in the village frightened.

Ella didn't consider the leopard to be evil. It was just being a leopard, doing what it was created to do. However, it did represent a threat to her family and to the natives who were there to help.

"Harold, you have to do something about that leopard. He's not afraid of coming right up to the house. I'm worried about Esther and Grace, and the women in the village are terrified," she said.

"Well, I'll be flying out tomorrow and will be gone for a couple of days. I'll set some traps along the path he took. We might get lucky and snag him. But the children will have to stay away from the traps, or they could be badly hurt. I'll have Paul and some of the boys help me set them before I leave. Just make sure everybody knows to stay away from them."

The following morning, Harold, Paul and two of the native boys located the leopard's tracks and carefully set the heavy steel traps. Covered with leaves and foliage from the jungle floor to hide them, the traps were designed to spring shut when an animal stepped on them, grabbing the animal's leg in a death grip. They were brutal, and Harold hated to use them. He was a hunter, not a trapper, but he felt it was his only alternative since he wasn't going to be there to protect his family. The natives would do all they could to help Ella and the children, but the reality was they were in as much danger, perhaps even more, than the family.

The leopard was clearly unafraid of humans and had already demonstrated he was a serious threat. It would as quickly snatch a child from the village as one of the Landruses' chickens.

Harold knew, unlike most other predatory animals that kill only to eat or to protect their territory or their young, a leopard will kill for sport. A leopard would kill not for food, not in defense, but purely because the opportunity presented itself.

After setting the traps, early the next morning Harold walked with Ella, Paul, Ruth, and Grace, with Esther securely tied to her back, out to the airstrip. "You should be OK until I get back. Hopefully, the leopard won't return, but if he does, maybe the traps will stop him. At least we have company, so there will be some help available."

Harold had flown a young missionary couple in from Monrovia a few days before. Married only a short time, the couple was embarking on their first term on the field, and they wanted to visit some of the mission stations in the interior before they took up their work in the capital city. Right then, John and Maxine were still snuggled in each other's arms, asleep in the house.

Harold climbed into the plane, folding himself into the pilot's seat; taxied down the bumpy, grass-covered runway; and took off. Ella, Paul, and the girls watched until his plane became a tiny speck and then disappeared in the distant sky. Grace, only a few years older than Paul, and the children dashed off toward the house, leaving Ella to follow quietly behind.

Once, again, Ella was struck by how alone they were, how completely isolated, even though they had visitors for a few days. If anything, their houseguests had only accentuated Ella's feeling of isolation, because visitors were so rare. During their first term in Palipo, there had often been times when months had passed without the family seeing anyone from the outside. She wondered what this term would hold.

She looked at the children as they ran toward the house, happy and seemingly totally carefree. Paul was twelve years old, going on thirteen, tall and slender like his father, working at becoming a man, already an accomplished hunter, totally at home with the natives and with the wilds of Africa.

Ruth had just turned nine and was a little princess, with pretty clothes and beautiful, long, curly hair. She was adored by the natives and everyone else around her.

Toddling along behind, holding tightly to Grace Scott's loving hand, was Esther. Such a little tyke, Esther was small and vulnerable, doing all she could to keep up with her big brother and sister.

"Lord, you have to protect them," Ella whispered. "I can't."

Paul (13), Ruth (9), and Esther (1) at Palipo.

That night, after the children were asleep and Ella sat reading her Bible, she thought she heard the growl of a leopard out in the dark, prowling the jungle looking for a good meal. She listened for a time. There was nothing but silence. If it was a leopard, she knew it probably hadn't gone far off; in fact, she was a little surprised she had heard it at all. Normally, a leopard is absolutely silent, able to stalk within striking distance of its prey without being detected or waiting for hours in a tree, ready to drop down on an unsuspecting deer or gazelle below. She sighed, blew out the kerosene reading lamp, and headed for bed, where she quickly fell into a deep, peaceful sleep.

What she didn't know was, at about the same time, the leopard had decided to try to reach some more of those tasty chickens in the coop near the house. Wary but unwilling to pass up such an easy meal, the sleek cat followed the path it had taken just a few days earlier and approached the clearing around the house. After pausing to make sure it was safe, it took one more step toward the house.

In an instant, there was a crushing blow as the jaws of the trap smashed into one of his rear legs, slashing almost to the bone. The leopard reacted immediately by trying to yank its leg away, but it would not pull free, and the trap was securely anchored to a tree, so the big cat couldn't drag it off into the bush. The more he pulled, the more it hurt. The pain was excruciating. The more it hurt, the angrier the leopard became. Growling, screaming, clawing, thrashing, biting at the air—the trapped animal found that nothing helped. Its rage knew no bounds. All it wanted was to kill.

Awakened by the noise, back in the house, Ella and the children were out of bed, racing to look out the windows. The newlyweds awoke, terrified. "What in the world is happening?" Maxine shouted. "What is that horrible sound?"

"I don't know," John responded. "But it sounds like it's just outside."

As he started to get out of bed, she grabbed his arm. "Please don't leave me. I'm scared. We don't know what it is. Please, please just stay here," she pleaded.

"It'll be all right," he said as he climbed out of bed and pulled on his robe.

He went into the living room, where Paul had pulled out his flashlight and was heading toward their room. "The noise sounds like it's coming from outside your bedroom," Paul explained.

As they entered, Maxine was sitting in bed with the covers drawn up around her in absolute terror. Her eyes were wide and showed her fright.

Paul and John hurried around the bed toward the window, with Ella, Ruth, and Esther and Grace following close behind. As Paul shone the light out the window, they all gasped as the beam settled on the wildly flailing animal at the edge of the clearing. When the light struck, the leopard paused momentarily, looking toward its source. Its eyes glowed bright yellow, reflecting its anger and hate.

"I'll get my gun," said Paul, dashing out of the room.

"Now, John, you let Paul go out there. You stay here with me," pleaded Maxine from her bed.

John looked at Maxine and then out the window at the snarling leopard. "Well, perhaps I should, just to make sure Maxine is OK," he said, grateful for a reason not to become involved in facing the leopard.

By then, Paul was out of the house, one of Harold's hunting rifles in his hand. He took careful aim, but because the leopard was thrashing around so much, his first shot did not kill him. His second, mercifully, did.

After the screaming, growling, and the blast of the two gunshots, the quiet that followed was almost a physical force.

People from the surrounding village, awakened by the entire ruckus, had come running into the compound. Some arrived with clubs, others with spears, not sure what they would find when they got there. Then they saw Paul, gun in hand, with the dead leopard a few yards in front of him. They, too, became silent at the sight. Then they realized what had happened. Paul, their young Paul, had killed a leopard. He had made the village a safer place for all of them. They began to shout and cheer, and they began to beat their drums. It was time to celebrate.

Paul was elated at having shot his first big killer cat but wished it hadn't been that way. He would have preferred the leopard be on the loose, not already caught. Like his father, he too was a hunter, not a trapper, but there would be other leopards and other hunts. For now, he had done what he needed to do. He had protected his family and the village.

When Harold returned a few days later, he was told the story in great detail by each member of the family and many from the village. He couldn't contain his pride in Paul. He smiled as the size of the leopard, the magnitude of the confrontation, and Paul's courage seemed to grow each time one of the villagers told the tale.

When Harold flew the missionary couple back to Monrovia, John and Maxine could not disguise their delight that they would be working in the city. Their first visit to the bush had been substantially more adventurous than they had ever anticipated.

Paul with his first leopard kill.

The mission compound at Palipo was extremely large. With the school buildings, the house, the farm, and chicken coop; the clinic building and various other outbuildings; and the airstrip, there was a great deal of ground to cover. Periodically, Harold found himself wishing he had a good truck to help with the work around the compound.

On one of his trips to the coast for food and supplies, he found an old jeep for sale. The American military effort during the war had included a significant presence in Liberia. The GIs had carved a large airfield, which they named Roberts Field, out of the jungle south of Monrovia to help provide air support for convoys crossing the South Atlantic. At the close of the war, this had become Monrovia's "international airport."

The Americans had also set up a small base of operations on the outskirts of Cape Palmas and had made the airstrip there, which the missionaries now used regularly.

With the war over, a great deal of surplus military equipment was being sold off, rather than being shipped back to the United States.

Always unable to pass up a piece of useful gear, particularly at a bargain price, Harold decided he had to buy the jeep. He reasoned it would be perfect for hauling supplies and building materials around the Palipo mission compound. Besides, he could use it to help level and expand the airstrip so other, larger aircraft, like Brother Mason's, could land there. The problem of getting the jeep to Palipo was not even a consideration affecting his decision to buy.

Only after the jeep had been purchased did Harold begin to address the matter of hauling it through the jungle, without roads, across uncountable rivers and streams on what, without pushing and pulling a jeep along, was a four-day journey of considerable torture.

He decided to leave his plane at Cape Palmas and hired a team of porters to help him take the jeep back to Palipo.

The porters were simply dumbfounded when they learned what Harold had in mind.

"Pa," one of them complained, "I don't tink we can do dis ting."

Another, shaking his head, stated absolutely, "Pa, dis cannot be done!"

"Of course it can," was Harold's only reply.

They drove the road from Cape Palmas to the Firestone rubber plantation at Pleebo, where they spent the night. Early the next morning, Harold purchased four empty fifty-five-gallon drums and a dozen large, rough cut two-by-eight planks each about twelve feet long. Carrying these and armed with shovels, axes, cutlasses, a block-and-tackle, and two hundred feet of heavy rope, they attacked the jungle trail. Their plan was to widen the trail to the point where Harold could drive the jeep through. Where the going was too difficult for the four-wheel drive jeep, they would use the block-and-tackle to drag the jeep forward.

They left Pleebo on June 14, 1947, hacking their way through the thick jungle undergrowth, cutting it back from the narrow footpath with their cutlasses, so they could then push and pull the jeep along the trail. It was unbelievably difficult work. Adding to their misery, it rained heavily almost every day.

Some days the going was so tough they would only make a mile or two. At night, they were all so tired they could hardly eat their ration of rice and the meat Harold hunted for along the way.

Natives from surrounding villages came from miles away just to see the jeep. Very few had ever seen a vehicle of any kind. They stood along the trail watching with fascination as this strange machine was dragged and pulled through the jungle. When a space was opened wide enough for Harold to drive the jeep for a short distance, the natives hid in fear in the bush, but they watched nonetheless, peeking, wide-eyed, through the tangle of vines and foliage. Their amazement at what they were seeing knew no bounds.

From Harold's perspective, the crowds of curious onlookers meant two things. First, and most important, when evening came and they stopped their struggle for the day, he had a perfect opportunity to preach the "God way" of Christianity to the assembled crowd before they left to return to their villages for the night.

Second, there were always a number in the crowd who were brave enough to lend a hand when the going got particularly tough. An extra fifteen or twenty pushing and pulling made an enormous difference up a steep, slippery hill. The natives could tell their children and their grandchildren of their personal involvement in this momentous event, which would surely be passed down in the tribal lore of the area for generations.

Foot by foot, yard by yard, mile by mile, they kept at it.

When they came to a stream or gully they couldn't drive or pull the jeep across, they would place the steel drums in the bottom of the streambed and lay the planks in place to form a makeshift temporary bridge.

Harold hated trying to drive across those "bridges." The planks creaked and bent, and he was sure they would break under the weight of the jeep. He also wasn't completely confident the porters were paying sufficient attention as they gave him signals right and left to guide him along the planks. He expected to drive off the edge any moment. But the Lord provided protection, and they had no major mishaps during such crossings.

One river, however, was an entirely different story.

After nearly two weeks fighting their way through the jungle, and with several miles yet to go before they got to Palipo, they encountered their third major river. This one was by far the biggest obstacle of the entire trip. Because of the unusually heavy rains that had plagued them for most of the journey, the river was raging and had grown to perhaps sixty or seventy feet across.

The exhausted porters simply dropped the ropes they had been pulling the jeep with and sat on the bank, staring with a slightly dazed look at the rushing, turbulent waters.

They knew Pa Landrus well enough to know this river would not stop him, but they had no idea how they were going to get the jeep to the other side.

Harold had known the river was there and they would have to cross it. After all, he had walked to Palipo many times before. However, he hadn't remembered the river being quite this high nor moving this fast.

"Let's set up camp here for the night," he said. "We'll get started in the morning."

Early the next morning, the porters gathered around to see what Harold had in mind. "We'll do it just the same as we did at the first two rivers," Harold explained to them.

"We'll cut cork-wood trees and make a raft," he said. "Tie the drums underneath at the corners to help keep the load level in the water. Then I'll drive the jeep up on 'er, and we'll pull the raft across, just like last time."

"But, Pa," one of them said, his voice filled with worry. "Dis river is too, too big!"

The porters were divided into teams. One would fell the trees Harold selected and marked with his cutlass, making certain they were good and straight and of similar size in diameter. Another team would drag the trees to the riverbank, where a third team would lash the tree trunks together with "tie-tie" vines from the jungle. It took all day, but by dinnertime, the raft was complete. They would make the crossing in the morning.

"Lord," Harold prayed after a dinner of rice and monkey meat, "we'll need your help tomorrow. Just, please, don't let anyone get hurt. The river could be a killer. Good night, Lord!"

They were up at dawn, ready to go.

Harold tied a rope around each of six volunteer porters and sent them out to cross the river. They began timidly, concerned both about being swept away by the current and about attracting the attention of several large crocodiles basking on the bank only a hundred or so yards downriver. Harold had thought about taking time to shoot the crocs but was concerned the blood might only attract more of them. He did keep his rifle close at hand, just in case.

One of the porters lost his footing and disappeared into the boiling water, giving Harold and the porters remaining on shore a moment of panic. But shortly, his head bobbed above the surface as he regained his footing. They were able to wade across about two-thirds of the river, with the water only up to their chests. It was very difficult for them to maintain their balance, but they could manage if they were careful.

The remaining third of the river they would have to swim. This was the dangerous part. Once they made it to the other side, they would use the ropes to pull the raft across. If the currents washed them too far downstream as they attempted to swim the final portion, Harold hoped he and the others on shore could pull them back to safety with those same ropes.

As first one and then another of the six began to swim, Harold immediately sensed they wouldn't make it. The current was too strong. It was whipping them off course and forcing them downstream. If they didn't drown first, they would surely be swept right into the path of the crocs.

While the crocs seemed to be sleeping, Harold knew they could and would move with blinding speed if a tempting meal presented itself to them.

There was nothing Harold could do. The men were too far away for him to help them. He and the others could only hold their breaths and watch as the six struggled, flailing their arms and legs as fast as they could, straining for the opposite shore. Harold couldn't take his eyes off them, but he prayed as hard as he had ever prayed.

One of them went under, but came up again and, as incredible as it seemed to Harold, the man seemed to be higher in the water. Yes, he was higher. He was wading toward the shore. He had made it. Then he reached back and helped the next man, and the next, until all had made it and fell, panting, on the far shore.

Harold and those with him let out a loud shout and danced in glee, slapping each other on the shoulders. "Can you beat that!" shouted

Harold to no one in particular, "Can you beat that! They made it! Thank you, Lord!"

"Papa God is with us, Pa," one of the porters exclaimed.

"He surely is, man. He surely is!"

They quickly lashed the ropes to the raft they had already pushed into the shallow water. Harold instructed twenty-five men to get aboard the raft just so he could test it to verify it would hold the weight of the jeep.

Satisfied it would carry the load and using a couple of planks, they made a ramp and Harold carefully drove the jeep onto the raft. It seemed to ride well, and he told the crew to push off into the river.

The plan was for the six porters on the other side to pull the raft across while those still on the first shore splayed out ropes tied to the back of the raft to help keep it straight as it hit the stronger currents in the deeper portion of the river. Once the raft was on the other side, they would use one rope to pull the remaining porters across. Harold would ride the raft, standing alongside the jeep.

All went well until the raft was about thirty feet from the far shore. There, the current caught the raft and caused it to tip badly. Harold ran to the high side to try to balance it, yelling for the others to pull faster.

Suddenly a wave caught the raft and broke several of the ropes from both ends. The raft started to spin, while the porters on either side strained on the remaining ropes to pull it straight. The jeep was too precariously perched on the raft, which now was heaving and bucking in the current.

One side of the raft tipped, and the jeep shifted slightly, setting it off balance. In a matter of seconds, the raft rolled over completely; the jeep broke its lashings and sank slowly to the bottom coming to rest on its side in about eight feet of water. Harold was thrown into the water and began immediately swimming for the other shore.

Freed from the weight of the jeep, the raft bounced up and, as the stunned porters slackened their grips on the ropes, floated down the river past the undisturbed crocodiles.

Harold couldn't believe it! After dragging himself out of the water, he sat on the shore shaking his head. *Well, Lord, at least no one was hurt!*

He looked over at the porters. They were about as tired and discouraged as he had ever seen them. Then he motioned to the porters who had remained on the first shore to swim across to join them.

After they scrambled ashore and had rested for a few minutes, Harold asked quietly, "All right, who wants to go for another swim?"

Blank looks were the only response. "Come on. All we need is to tie a rope onto the axle and we'll pull it out of there. Which one of you is man enough to do it?"

After a painfully long pause when no one said or did anything, a reluctant volunteer shrugged his shoulders and raised his hand.

The volunteer made two dives, securing two strong ropes to the rear axle of the submerged jeep. "Now I need five more who will go down with him one more time," Harold announced.

By now they had had a few minutes to regain their optimism, and several of the porters indicated their willingness. "But, Pa. What is it we are to do?" asked one of them.

"You are going to turn the jeep over so it's sitting on its wheels," Harold responded.

The porters looked at each other and then erupted in a very animated, very heated discussion in their native dialect. For the next fifteen minutes, Harold just stood there looking from one to another as they jabbered away, wondering where this conversation was headed. Finally, one of the men stepped forward and said very quietly, "Yes, Pa. We will do it!"

Harold never knew what the palaver was all about, but he was satisfied with the outcome.

The men dove into the water and managed to tip the jeep right side up on their first attempt.

Back on shore, they tied the block and tackle to a sturdy tree and joined together in pulling the jeep, now rolling quite nicely along the river bottom, up the side bank toward them. Finally, it emerged, water flowing out both sides. They pulled it to a rest on the bank and let it sit as the water continued to drain from everywhere.

As fascinated as he was with gadgets and machines, Harold never was much of a mechanic. He did know he needed to drain the water out of the engine and the gas tank and clean the spark plugs. After taking those steps, he tried to start the engine but found the battery was dead.

The next village was about a mile ahead and much of the distance was downhill. Harold decided to take the jeep there. On the way, he put the jeep in gear whenever he could to help drive the water out of the engine.

Much as he hated to, Harold left the jeep in the village, parked alongside a native hut in a makeshift lean-to. Then they walked on to Palipo.

After resting for a few days, Harold and a couple of the boys from the mission station walked past the jeep in the village and on to Cape Palmas, where he could get the battery charged and pick up his plane to fly back to Palipo.

Two weeks later, he returned to the village to see if he could get the jeep started.

After installing the battery, putting oil in the engine, gasoline in the tank, and making a few final adjustments, it was time to give the engine a try.

Harold had done all he could do. As far as he was concerned, it was up to the Lord to make it work or not work as He saw fit, and Harold would live with the results. *Lord,* he prayed silently, *please make this thing work.*

To the complete amazement of the assembled onlookers, the jeep started up on the second try and ran without a problem.

Harold and his crew set out for Palipo immediately and managed to cover the remaining few miles in just one day. It had taken nearly six weeks for Harold and his crew to get the jeep to Palipo.

Ella, Paul, Ruth, and Esther were among the first to greet them. Ella had walked out to meet them on the trail. She was sure Harold couldn't get the jeep through the swamp at the edge of town, but with its four-wheel drive and a little run at it, the jeep plowed through the swamp and then bounced into town.

The sight of the battered old jeep as Harold drove it in was frightening for many of the villagers because most had never seen any kind of vehicle before. However, it was also obvious to them it was cause for great celebration. They began to dance and cheer. They even beat the big nine-foot drum, the oldest and largest drum in the village, in honor of the occasion.

Ma Hannah, one of the native women helping them on the mission, begged Harold to take her for a ride in the jeep. She explained, "I have only walked, never ridden since my mama stopped carrying me when I was a baby."

Harold smiled and took her for a quick ride. As they began to move, her eyes widened. She clutched the dashboard in sheer terror. When he brought the jeep to a stop, she got out as quickly as she could and then, after regaining her composure slightly, asked Ella, "Is it that frightening every time you ride?"

Ella could only look at Harold and smile.

The jeep became an indispensable piece of equipment on the compound. They used it constantly for the farm and as they expanded the airstrip. Harold even thought of making roads to some of the nearer villages, so they could save time driving there instead of having to walk when they held their regular evangelistic services.

He took good care of the jeep and even painted it yellow to match his airplane.

While Harold was away hauling supplies in the jeep or off on local preaching trips or flying his plane, the loneliness Ella faced was all the more intense. They had sent Paul and Ruth to Neweka for schooling under the careful tutelage of Carl and Velma Hixenbaugh. When Harold was gone, Esther was Ella's only non-native company. They had frequent problems with the shortwave radio, so Ella couldn't contact other missionaries if there was an emergency.

They moved Grace Scott into the house, so Ella wasn't completely alone with the baby. Grace and Esther slept upstairs in the little room next to Harold's "radio room".

In one of her letters before they had the jeep, Ella wrote, "Harold left six days ago to go for the jeep ... Esther was sick with a fever the first two days after he left and then she broke out with red spots ... but Praise the Lord they have gone now and she feels fine."

The small, day-to-day struggles with illness or food shortages or palavers in the town were all the harder for her when she had to face them alone.

⟞⟝

Harold and Ella thoroughly enjoyed Esther. When both Paul and Ruth were away at school, she became the focus of their family life. She was beginning to talk and could say several words, including "nana" when she wanted a banana, her favorite fruit.

As she approached a year and a half old, rather than words, she had developed a series of sounds she made to indicate the things she was talking about. She made separate noises for the airplane, the jeep, and a host of other things and creatures, including their pet chimpanzees named "Big Boy", "Little Boy", and "Small Boy".

Esther was unafraid of anything and willing to explore each new thing that attracted her attention. Ella was grateful for Grace Scott's faithful, ever-protective eye over her.

⟞⟝

With Harold gone so much of the time, Ella took on the burden of running the mission.

The Landruses felt responsible for providing for the students in their school, as well as natives they hired to help with work around the mission station. In all, there were more than fifty people to feed and clothe.

Because supplies were so difficult to obtain, even with Harold's plane, the farm became a major part of their daily lives. They planted 385 white pineapple plants Annie Cressman had sent them from her mission station in the central highlands near Tchien.

They planted nearly 800 sugar cane heads and countless vegetables and fruit trees, including banana, orange, and avocado. All of these needed to be tended, weeded, and harvested. They didn't need to be watered. The rains took care of that.

They also maintained a large chicken coop. Chickens provided both eggs and meat. When Harold graded the airstrip with an old plow blade he had attached to the front of the jeep, the chickens followed along behind, feasting on the bugs and worms he turned up.

Enlarging and maintaining the airstrip was another major, ongoing task. They removed more than two-hundred tree stumps as they made the strip longer and wider. Erosion from the rains and the rapid growth of the jungle foliage required constant attention. They even constructed a bamboo "hangar" for the plane.

Fortunately, Harold was home when one of the mission boys came running up to the house yelling, "Pa, Pa, come quick! A snake, Pa, a snake! In the house for chickens."

Harold needed no further prodding and took off running toward the chicken coop.

As he approached, he could see nothing on the outside, but could hear the chickens in an uproar inside.

The coop was a rather short, rectangular-shaped shed fully enclosed with wooden sides and a corrugated metal roof. There was a low door on one side that served as the entrance. The chickens were often allowed to roam free around the compound during the day and then closed into the coop at night. As evening was approaching, one of the students had shut the chickens in, and the door was closed.

Harold grabbed the handle on the door and pulled. It opened with a creak, and he was greeted by an explosion of feathers as chickens fled past him to safety outside.

Though evening was near, it was still rather bright outside, and, as he stooped and stepped through the door into the coop, it took a few moments for Harold's eyes to adjust to the relative darkness inside. Before they fully adjusted, he saw a fleeting movement out of the corner of his eye. At ground level, it was the tail of the startled snake as it darted to escape out a knothole in the bottom of one of the pieces of side planking.

Without thinking, Harold reacted instantly. He reached down and grabbed the end of the snake just before it disappeared out of the hole.

At this point, Harold realized what he'd done. He had the snake and was in no immediate danger. The hole was small enough the snake could not double back on itself to attack him, no matter how hard it tried. However, Harold didn't want to risk letting go of the snake because he had no idea where it might go. He was pretty sure it was a black mamba, one of the fastest snakes in the world—and also one of the deadliest.

As the snake pulled and flexed in Harold's hand, he began thinking about what to do next. His options seemed awfully limited. He knew he couldn't stay this way for long. He would soon lose his grip on the flailing snake.

Then an idea began to form. *If I can reach that door with my foot,* he thought, *just maybe I can do this. Let's give it a try.*

He stretched one leg as far as he could and, while maintaining his grip on the snake, kicked the door to the coop open. Then in one swift, fluid movement, as another cloud of panicked chickens flew out the door with him, he yanked the snake back through the hole and quickly jumped outside.

Before it could curl back to attack him, Harold began swinging the snake in a giant circle over his head, like a cowboy's lariat. Staggering slightly but keeping his balance while swinging the snake in an arc above him, Harold walked as quickly as he could toward a nearby palm tree and, with a sharp snapping motion, wrapped the snake around the tree, killing it instantly.

When he laid the snake out on the grass in front of the house, Harold recognized, as he had thought, it was a "black mamba".

He had killed one of the world's most poisonous snakes bare-handed. And it was a whopper. It measured almost ten feet in length.

Ella stood with Esther and several of the students watching Harold measure the snake. "Well, that's one snake we won't have to worry about," she said. "I don't mind a snake I can see. What really bothers me is finding a snakeskin in the house like I did last week, but no snake. I always wonder where he is!"

Ella with a snake killed in the Palipo school room.

Snakes posed a major threat to their chickens. A single snake had left thirteen chickens dead in one episode, and Harold had killed three cobras in just one week. Marauding leopards were a similar menace. Despite these predators, their flocks of chickens and ducks steadily grew larger. Near the end of their first year back in Palipo, Harold had to build a new chicken coop to house more than ninety chickens and a dozen ducks. They regularly collected twelve to fifteen eggs a day, which was a real blessing as they worked to feed all those for whom they felt responsible.

~

Scarcely a week would pass without a family coming to the house to beg the Landruses to take just one more child, their child, into the mission's school. All knew, if their children were able to attend, the missionaries would not only teach them but also care for them, clothe them, and feed them.

The Palipo mission boys' school had grown to more than fifty in enrollment. And, even though they hadn't really wanted to do so, Harold and Ella had begun a new girls' school as well, because the girls' school at Neweka could not accommodate any more students.

Paul and Ruth spent a portion of their time at Neweka attending school with several other missionary children. Carl and Velma Hixenbaugh were in charge there, but Miss Laura Pape was the schoolteacher.

After three or four months, Paul and Ruth would plead to go home to Palipo to be with their family for a month or two. During these periods, Ella would do her best as substitute teacher, but she knew she couldn't replace Miss Pape's professional teaching.

Paul couldn't wait for these trips home, where he could do what he most wanted to do—hunt.

While Paul and Ruth were attending school at Neweka, Paul helped provide food for the students by hunting for monkeys. Monkey meat soup was a frequent and greatly appreciated meal.

One evening, when Paul came in from hunting later than he was supposed to, Carl Hixenbaugh disciplined him by taking his gun away.

The missionary girls all loved Paul and, as might be expected of young teenagers, felt his punishment was far too severe. They cried through the night on his behalf, begging Mr. Hixenbaugh to give Paul's gun back to him. A few days later, he returned Paul's precious .22 rifle.

Paul shot his first bush goat when he and Ruth returned to Palipo. The whole family agreed, along with pygmy hippopotamus, it was the best meat they had ever eaten.

Day after day, the pattern of their lives was constant. It was a life of sweating, struggling, working, preaching, hunting, flying, farming, and caring, deep in the heart of Liberia's unrelenting jungle.

Chapter 10
Flying High

From the beginning, Harold's airplane was an enormous help to the entire missionary community. As soon as they could do so, missionaries at virtually every station began cutting airstrips for him to land on.

During this, their first term with the plane, more than a dozen airstrips were hacked out of the jungle. They were rough and, often, too short and too narrow, but Harold managed to fly into all of them regularly.

Using their radio network, Harold would contact every mission station each morning to see if there were special needs only he and his plane could fill.

He brought them supplies. He delivered their mail. He provided transportation, cutting their travel time from days through the jungle to minutes above it. This was particularly critical when a missionary was sick or injured.

The other missionaries jokingly referred to Ella as the "airplane widow". With Harold flying so much of the time, he seemed to be gone more than he was around.

In addition to flying supplies and passengers, Harold used the plane to travel to places like the Firestone rubber plantation near Pleebo, outside of Cape Palmas, where he could hold evangelistic meetings. At one such meeting he had more than four hundred in attendance.

Ella was always worried something would happen to Harold while he was flying. There were just so many things that could go wrong. Maintenance was a continuous problem, even though the plane was rugged and Harold did his best at keeping it in good flying condition. Gasoline was often contaminated, and the plane's engine would sputter and spit, but it kept running. The airstrips were nothing more than bumpy patches of weeds and rocks in the middle of the jungle. Each landing and takeoff was fraught with danger.

Ella's biggest concern was the plane would crash and Harold would be injured, unable to get out of the plane, with no hope of help. If his plane went down, he might never be found. She might never know what happened to him.

The thought of Harold crashing in the jungle was a burden of considerable weight for Ella. Trapped and injured in his airplane in the thick of the jungle, Harold would have no chance of survival. If he didn't die first of his injuries, he would be attacked and eaten by a leopard or a snake.

Worse yet, as far as she was concerned, he could be attacked by driver ants.

She had heard of it happening before and could imagine nothing more horrible. One of their chimpanzees had been tied up on the porch while they had been gone one morning. When they returned, they found the chimp had been killed and eaten by driver ants.

Hidden in the depths of the jungle, driver ants are colonies of literally millions upon millions of large stinging ants. Normally, they live off the abandoned remains of leopard kills, animals that have died of natural causes, or animals trapped and unable to escape from deep mud around a water hole or stream.

When they detect food, a driver ant colony moves as a coordinated army. They descend upon their prey in long columns from multiple directions, all attacking at once. Each column is made up of so many ants it looks like a giant moving black ribbon, which may range from a few inches to a foot or more in width. If their target is unable to move away, they overwhelm it by the sheer force of their numbers. Drivers have been known to devour an entire elephant in a matter of hours.

In Liberia, if a python kills a deer, it will make wide circles around the kill sensing with its tongue for any signs of driver ants. Only if there are none will it swallow its prey, because once it does so, it will go dormant for several days. If driver ants were to arrive when the snake was in a dormant state, they would kill and eat the snake before it could escape.

Whenever he flew, Ella prayed Harold would not crash, but prayed even more, if he did, he would not be attacked by driver ants.

～

By mid-1947, less than a year after he arrived with his plane, Harold had already logged nearly three hundred hours of flight time. He was flying to Monrovia for supplies when he noticed the plane had begun vibrating slightly. He could feel it in the controls first and then in the seat of his pants as he sat in the pilot's seat. His instruments didn't indicate anything wrong, but he knew something had to be causing this unusual tremor throughout the plane.

He still had forty-five minutes before he reached the soccer field he landed on in Monrovia. He rarely flew into Roberts Field. It was too far out. The soccer field was right in town. *I wonder if I can make it,* he thought. *Nothing but jungle down there. Seems to be flying OK. Lord, I think I need your help here!*

The Lord heard his prayer. Harold landed without incident in Monrovia. However, the vibration had increased with intensity the longer he had flown. He was sure it was from the engine, and he knew he had to get it checked out before he could fly again.

The problem was, even with the help of Ed Mason, who had his own, larger mission plane in Monrovia, Harold couldn't find anyone who could properly test the engine for him. He cabled Piper Aircraft in America to tell them what he had encountered. Their response was he needed to ship the engine back to the United States so they could check it out thoroughly at the factory and make any necessary repairs.

It took several days for the telegrams to go back and forth to Piper. Additionally, Harold had needed almost a week to remove the engine, get it crated, and make arrangements for it to be transported on the next ship to America.

He was staying at the mission house in Monrovia, which had a shortwave radio. However, he had been unable to reach Ella back in Palipo via the radio, and he knew she would be worrying about him. He decided to send a runner to give her the news about the plane and to tell her not to worry. He would ask Mason to fly him to Neweka. He'd walk home from there.

Unfortunately, the runner never made it to Palipo with his message for Ella.

Harold had told her he would be back in a couple of days, but his trips frequently took longer than he expected. Ella wasn't particularly worried when four or five days passed without Harold's return and without any word from him.

She had more than enough to keep her mind occupied, speaking at chapel, holding clinic each day, and directing work on the farm and the rest of the mission station.

After ten days, however, she did begin to worry. He might not have been able to get back by now, but he always would have sent a message, one way or another, if he was able.

Thankfully, she got the radio working and was able to reach Anna Stafshalt, the Assembly of God missionary in the Barrobo tribal area. Anna said she had heard nothing from Monrovia or any of the other mission stations about Harold, but she would ask Florence Bassett to come be with Ella in case there was bad news.

Much to Ella's relief, dear Miss Bassett arrived after a two-day, twenty-mile trek through the jungle. She had made the grueling journey just because she was Ella's friend and didn't want her to be alone in Palipo if something had happened to Harold.

They waited another two weeks—still nothing. Ella was sure Harold was either dead or seriously injured, but all she could do was continue to wait. As much as she worried, she still had a quiet peace about it. She had again "prayed through" and "gotten the victory." She knew whatever had happened to Harold, the Lord was still in charge. He would sustain and keep her, no matter what she had to face in the next days or weeks.

One afternoon, as they were concluding a Bible study with a large group of the native women, Ella heard a faint sound in the distance. "Florence," she said grabbing her arm, "I believe I hear a plane."

Ella's heart was pounding as they raced outside to try to catch a glimpse of it. By then, the sound was louder. It was a plane for certain. "There it is," Florence yelled, pointing at a small speck in the deep blue sky.

"Yes, I see it," Ella responded. "But it's not Harold's plane. It's Mason's. He can't land here though. Our field's too small for his big plane. I wonder what he's doing."

Mason piloted the plane in closer and swooped down to buzz the airstrip. As he did so, he opened his window and dropped a letter, which floated gently down, landing only a few yards from them. One of the mission boys grabbed it off the ground and quickly brought it to Ella.

Ella's hands were trembling as she took the letter. She was certain it brought grim news. Without looking, she handed the letter to Miss Bassett. "You read it. I'm afraid to." But as she did so, Ella saw the handwriting on the envelope.

It was Harold's. At least he was alive. "No. I'll read my own letter," she said with a rush of joy, reaching for the letter.

Harold's letter explained what had happened. The vibration in the plane, the delays in Monrovia, and his attempts to get word to her—it was all there. Best of all, Harold was above them in Mason's plane. They would fly on to Neweka, with its bigger airstrip, and Harold would start walking home the next day.

Ella could hardly contain her happiness. "Thank you, Lord. Thank you, Lord," she repeated over and over.

Tears of joy filled her eyes as Harold approached Palipo a couple of days later, and she ran to meet him. As she threw her arms around him, she thought she had never been so glad to see him in her entire life. Afterward, Ella was a little embarrassed she had hugged and kissed Harold in front of some of the natives. The Africans didn't hug and didn't display affection in front of other people.

***

Loss of the plane was a difficult blow, not only to Harold and Ella but also to the entire team of missionaries on the field.

It would be several months before the plane could fly again. Until then, all of the missionaries faced endless, grueling treks through the jungle. Food, supplies, and mail could only be obtained with days of toil, sweat, and danger under the hot, moist canopy of tropical trees and vines.

The most critical issue was medical attention. With the plane, they all knew if illness or injury occurred, help was a relatively short flight away. Without it, they faced substantially increased risks, with little or no possibility of either help coming to them from the outside or of them traveling to where medical assistance would be available.

It seemed to Ella they had no more than just learned the plane was going to be out of service for some time when emergencies at her morning clinic began to multiply. To make matters worse, their radio went out again as well, leaving them with no contact with the outside world except by runner through the jungle.

<hr />

Mama Ruth, who had been purchased and freed from a witch doctor, and first joined the Landruses in Bwebo, and then again on their first term at Palipo, heard they were back in Liberia and immediately sent word she would come as quickly as possible. She wanted to work with them, to be their interpreter, and to be a missionary alongside them.

The entire family was delighted when she and her husband, Ernest, and their two boys, Peter and Lawyer, finally arrived.

Peter and Paul were inseparable whenever Paul was home from school at Neweka. Having grown up together, they were almost like brothers. They had played for hours as young boys, making toys out of anything their imaginations could dream up. Now, in their early teens, their passion was hunting. They eagerly spent all day on their own in the jungles hunting monkeys or deer.

On one such hunt, several other teenage boys from the village had joined them. They were in single file with Paul in the lead, Peter immediately behind him. Following Peter was a string of eight or nine other boys, including a boy named Paul Jahr.

The going was tough. The jungle was particularly thick, and the boys were all swinging their cutlasses, hacking a trail through the dense undergrowth.

The cutlasses' long metal blades were often pounded out of the steel from a fifty-five-gallon drum. The blades were razor sharp and had wooden handles tied to one end. They were used like a machete to hack a trail through the jungle.

As Paul Jahr swung his cutlass with his right hand, his left hand extended behind him to maintain his natural balance. Just at that moment, the boy behind him reached forward slightly to swing his cutlass at a vine protruding across the trail they were making. It was a thick vine, and he put considerable force and speed into his swing. Concentrating on cutting the vine, he didn't see Paul Jahr's hand as it swung back towards him.

In an instant, the cutlass knifed through Paul Jahr's middle finger, severing it at the second knuckle. He screamed. Chaos ensued. Bright red blood seemed to be everywhere.

One of the boys pulled a tattered T-shirt over his head and thrust it at Paul Landrus, who had turned and was kneeling beside Paul Jahr trying desperately to stop the bleeding. His patient was shaking, but calm. With the shirt, they were able to at least stem the flow of blood.

"We'll get you back right away," he said trying to reassure the frightened teenager.

One of the boys grabbed the severed finger off the jungle floor, and they all began to return to the mission station as quickly as they could. Fortunately, it was not far, and it was back along the path they had already cleared. They were young and strong. They almost ran, supporting the injured boy as they went.

When they burst into the compound, they went straight to the house. Ella had heard the commotion as they raced across the grounds and met them on the porch. "What is it, Paul?" she called. "What's wrong?"

"It's Paul Jahr, Mother. He's cut off his finger."

Gently, she unwrapped the shirt from Paul's finger so she could examine it. "Oh, Paul. I'm so sorry. Does it hurt terribly?"

"Not so bad, Ma," he responded, trying to be brave.

"Well, it's going to hurt now," she said as she poured alcohol over the wound.

Paul Jahr screamed. Then they handed her the end of his finger. "Well, I don't know what I can do with this," she said. *Lord, I don't know what to do. I don't know how to help him. I'm not a doctor!* was all that went through her mind.

She washed the severed finger in alcohol and then put it back in place on the finger stump on his hand. She bandaged it tightly and spoke to Paul gently as she did so, "Paul, you've lost some blood, but I think you'll be OK. I'm not sure about this finger though. I want us to pray and then we'll send you to Cape Palmas to the Firestone doctor. He may be able to do something."

"Ma, I know de Lord, He can do anyfing. He will make it well," Paul said much more positively than he really felt.

If only we had the plane, Ella thought. *Harold could get him to the doctor in less than an hour. I have no idea what three days through the jungle will do.*

But she had done what she could. She prayed. Then she sent him on his way.

A group of mission boys accompanied the injured boy on the trek to Cape Palmas and escorted him to the Firestone doctor.

They told the doctor what had happened before he began to unwrap the finger. With a slightly skeptical look on his face, he asked, "Can you move it?"

Paul wiggled the finger just a little bit.

"Does it hurt?" the doctor asked.

"No," was the boy's only response.

The doctor paused, thinking about what he knew had to be impossible. *A severed finger can't be reattached simply by sticking it back in place and bandaging it.* Yet, here it was, directly in front of him. He shook his head. He had often said the missionaries got the worst of the medical needs because the natives would only go to them in the most severe circumstances when tribal remedies and witch doctor rituals had already been tried and proven useless.

Then, these missionaries, most of whom had no medical training, would do their best with what they had, and the results amazed him. The missionaries certainly weren't always successful, but they frequently were. They were when all the medical science he knew said they couldn't possibly be. Africa and these missionaries were full of things he would never be able to explain.

"Well, then, I guess it must be OK. There's nothing more I can do. Leave the bandage on for another week. Then you should be able to remove it."

"Praise, God!" Paul Jahr shouted with a broad, happy smile, "He has healed my finger!"

It was a boisterous, happy journey back to Palipo, with all of them anxious to share the news of another miracle of God.

~

A second medical crisis did not end as happily. Ernest, Mama Ruth's husband, came down with a sore throat. It hurt him terribly. By the next day, Ella could tell whatever it was, it was serious. "Oh, how I wish we had the plane so we could take Ernest to Firestone," she said to Harold that evening. "I'm really worried about him. He just seems to be getting worse by the hour."

On the third day, Ernest slipped into a coma and died. There was nothing any of them could do to prevent it.

When someone dies in Liberia, family and friends mourn for days, weeping and wailing. Visitors from other parts of the country, even a year later, will begin wailing some distance before they enter the village. Elaborate pagan rituals are performed by the witch doctors to give a proper burial.

All of the mourning, all of the rituals, have as their basis a fundamental lack of hope. For the average villager, there is nothing beyond death—certainly nothing good.

As Christians, Mama Ruth and her family were confident in the truth that, while Ernest was gone from this life and they would miss him, he was in heaven with the Lord. They were sad but not mournful. He was in a far better place and had merely gone on before them. They would see him again, in heaven.

Mama Ruth was able to use Ernest's death as a powerful illustration to share the Gospel with others in the village and the surrounding area.

Another thing Mama Ruth did was introduce the Landrus family to a young teenage Liberian girl named Maryann. Rather than returning to her family, Maryann stayed on at the mission station to assist the Landruses, particularly Ella with her work. It didn't matter what needed to be done, Maryann was there to help. From then on, for all the remaining years

Harold and Ella served in Liberia, at every mission station where they served, Maryann was there. She was Ella's interpreter, her companion and coworker, and one of her closest friends.

—◊—

Thomas was typical of the boys who were students at the mission. Ella provided his first pair of pants and a shirt. He wanted to learn to read and write, but there was no teacher in his entire tribe.

Thomas's father was a devil doctor and was showing Thomas how to do his witchcraft. Thomas spent his days learning to make devil jujus rather than to read or write.

Once he became a witch doctor, Thomas still wanted to learn how to read and write. He walked for several days to the mission station and begged the Landruses to become "one of their boys" and attend their mission school.

"We're so full here. I don't see how we can take you," Harold told him.

"But, Pa," he pleaded, "You don't have any boy from my tribe. And I walked four days to get here. Please, Pa. Please!" Harold thought for a moment and then said, "Well, I suppose we can afford one more."

Thomas became one of their hired helpers and a student in the school.

Years later, Ella wrote, "Thank the Lord we took Thomas in. He became one of our main preachers." Eventually, Thomas made his way to the central highlands, to the Konobo tribe, near Tchien, to preach and to build a church.

Rather than a traditional round building, Thomas was determined to build a square church as a means of demonstrating Christians had no reason to fear evil spirits hiding in the corners. Christ was far more powerful than any evil spirits were.

After much palaver, Thomas won the villagers over and built the first square building in the area. It was his testimony to the power of Christ in the lives of all believers.

—◊—

Nearly six months later, a runner arrived with word the engine for the plane had arrived back in Monrovia. Harold immediately made arrangements for Ed Mason to pick him up at Cape Palmas and fly him to Monrovia so he could put the plane back together again.

In less than a week, Harold was winging his way back to Palipo, delighted to be in the air again, and ready to resume his flying ministry with a vengeance.

Not many months later, he was skimming over the jungle treetops on his way to Feroka, about midway between Palipo and Neweka. It was a journey of one or two days on foot, less than an hour in his plane.

The mission station at Feroka was run by two dedicated, hardworking women missionaries. They had done their best at directing a team of native workers to carve the airstrip out of the thick, green jungle. But despite their efforts, the strip was, nonetheless, too narrow and far too short for any reasonable landing. It was probably the most difficult of the dozen airstrips for Harold to negotiate.

He circled the field once and then swung around to line up for landing. As he had to do for all of the short fields, he came in as low as he could over the surrounding jungle and then, just as he cleared the last of the towering trees at the end of the runway, he tried to immediately drop down and put the plane on the ground in the shortest possible distance. This would give him the maximum rollout space.

The airstrip was very uneven and as the plane touched down, it hit a rise in the undulating runway and was bounced airborne again. Harold knew immediately he was in trouble. Being thrown back into the air meant too much runway was being used up. By the time he regained control, he was approaching the end of the airstrip and traveling fast enough he knew he couldn't stop before slamming into the native huts crowded together at the end of the field.

His heart was pounding as he strained to maintain control, braking as hard as he could. Just before he reached the end of the runway, he swung the plane hard to the left and braced for the crash.

The plane swerved and then momentum flipped it onto its right wingtip, which dug into the ground and spun the plane around. Harold braced himself, anticipating the plane would cartwheel over on its back as it turned. Miraculously, it did not. The left wing rose almost perpendicular to the ground, throwing Harold against the side of the aircraft. It teetered for a moment but did not go over. It slammed down, righting itself and came to a stop. Harold sat dazed for several seconds and then reached forward to cut the engine.

The chaos of the landing had seemed so loud, so noisy. Now he just sat, rubbing his shoulder, in complete silence. Catching his breath, he prayed out loud, "Thank you, Lord. Thank you, Lord. But, Lord, please don't make the plane too bad!"

He slowly got out to survey the damage, dreading what he was sure was significant damage to his precious plane. Unbelievably, all he had done was tear the tip off the wing. Everything else was fine. His biggest concern, the flaps and controls, seemed to be untouched.

It would take a little time, but with a bedsheet and some airplane dope, a special hard finish paint, he could fix the wing and be back in the air in a few days.

⌇

Word of Harold's crash spread quickly through the village because, as always, when they'd first heard his plane coming, a crowd had gathered to watch him land. Unfortunately, one of the natives hearing the news left immediately for the daylong trek to Neweka, without really learning what had happened and that Harold was unhurt. Upon arrival, he reported Harold had crashed his plane.

Paul and Ruth, at the Neweka mission station for school, were devastated by the news. "What about Pa?" they asked repeatedly.

The villager could not tell them.

They were worried sick. "He had to have been hurt," Ruth stated emphatically.

"We don't know that for sure, Ruthie. He may be OK. The Lord's taking care of him," Paul responded, but without much conviction.

At fifteen and having grown up in the jungles of Liberia, Paul was more than a little independent. He decided he and Ruth should go to

Feroka to make sure their father wasn't hurt. "Come on, Ruth," he said quickly. "Get ready. We're going to find out about Daddy."

"But what about the Hixenbaughs? They won't just let us leave," Ruth answered.

"Just get ready. We're going."

Paul marched from the schoolyard to the house prepared to argue their case to Carl and Velma Hixenbaugh as forcefully as he could. To his surprise, they were both sympathetic, and Carl responded, "Paul, I know you are worried about your father. Mrs. Hixenbaugh and I have just been praying for him and asking the Lord what we can do. I believe you and Ruth should go, but you'll have to take a group of the boys with you, so you won't be alone on the trail. You can leave first thing in the morning. That will get you there by tomorrow night."

Paul's face lit up. "Thanks, Brother Hixenbaugh. And don't worry, I'll take care of Ruthie."

"I know you will, Paul," Carl responded and then added as Paul ran out the door, "Be sure to take your rifle with you." As if Paul would ever go anywhere without it.

They left at daybreak with three native boys from the mission school. Paul was anxious about his father, and he pushed the pace. He kept glancing back to see how Ruth was doing as they nearly jogged along the jungle trail. Ruth was four years younger than Paul and the journey was more difficult for her, but she was worried about her daddy, too, and was determined to keep up. As he watched her, Paul was proud of how intent she was at overcoming the miles and miles of jungle; the heat and humidity; and her own tired, aching muscles.

They arrived in Feroka late in the afternoon and ran immediately to the airstrip, where they found Harold so engrossed in fixing the wing of his plane, he didn't hear them coming.

"Daddy, Daddy," Ruth yelled as she ran to embrace him. "Are you OK?"

"Well, what are you doing here, Dollie?" Harold asked in return.

"We heard you crashed. We thought you might be hurt, even dead," she said with her hands on her hips, displaying a little anger at what he'd put her through, now she knew he was not seriously hurt. "Are you alright?" she asked.

"I'm fine. Just a few bumps and bruises," Harold said.

As Paul approached, he hugged his father, "We were worried about you, Daddy. Are you sure you're alright?"

"Yes. Yes, I really am. The Lord took care of me. It was quite a landing though!" Harold said. Then with a grin he added, "You should have seen it, Paul. That plane stood on its wing like you wouldn't believe. I thought I might be a goner for sure. Almost flipped it. But the Lord saved me! Can you beat that, son? Can you beat that!"

Back at Palipo, Ella had been told of Harold's mishap over the radio, but the word she received was Harold had been hurt. She quickly organized a team of boys from the mission school to act as porters and left with Esther for the two-day journey through the jungle to Feroka. They arrived tired and hungry the day after Ruth and Paul.

Assured Harold was unhurt, Ella, Esther, Paul, and Ruth stayed with him, helping with the wing repairs. Once they were complete, Harold flew Paul and Ruth to Neweka to resume their schooling there. He then returned to pick up Ella and Esther and fly them back to Palipo.

~

Not long after he returned to Palipo, Harold was once again in the jungles hunting. Elephants were back in country, and there was a rogue bull on a rampage tearing up the natives' farms and endangering their children. The local village chief had sent for Pa Landrus to rid them of this menace.

Harold and his hunting party had walked to the village and started following the giant beast from there. It hadn't been difficult to track him. He was leaving a path of destruction wherever he went.

Normally, elephants avoid confrontation with man. This particular animal, however, obviously had no such reservations. The small band of men passed several small family farms, where the elephant had mangled huts and trampled crops and then charged off into the jungle, leaving nothing but devastation in his wake. Fortunately, no one had been killed or injured.

They caught up with the elephant the afternoon of the second day. He was huge. When they found him, though, he was not thrashing about destroying a native farm. Instead, he was peacefully scratching himself against a large tree, which shuddered as he scraped his rough hide along the bark. Harold knew this rather tranquil scene could erupt in an instant to a level of fury they could not imagine if the elephant detected their presence.

He acted quickly. He would like to have gotten closer but knew the longer they took getting ready, the greater the chances the elephant would discover them. Harold would take his shot from there.

The hunting party spread out as silently as possible within the heavy jungle foliage as Harold picked out the best spot to shoot from. As he did so, he thought about what a good team he had—Moses the lead tracker, and Samuel and Joseph as gun bearers.

Once in position, Samuel handed Harold his elephant gun and slipped back into the trees. The elephant stopped scratching and raised its trunk in the air. A slight scent.

Its ears flapping, the giant animal turned slightly toward where the hunting party was hiding in the jungle. Aiming for the kill spot, where the bullet would pass through the elephant's thick skull and into its brain, made Harold's shot extremely difficult from this angle, but he couldn't risk moving to another location.

Taking careful aim, Harold gently pulled the trigger. The shot was true. The elephant stumbled once and then collapsed, dead by the time its enormous body settled to the ground.

The natives burst into shouts and cheers. Killing an elephant was a rare and dangerous event. They would all be greeted as heroes when they returned to their villages.

They immediately cut the tail off the elephant and sent a band of porters with it and a small amount of meat to Ella at the mission station. Upon seeing the tail, the villagers knew the team had, indeed, killed an elephant.

The porters reached Palipo at midnight and proceeded to announce their arrival by beating the largest drum in town, waking the entire village. As the sleepy natives heard the news and saw the tail, they began a celebration that lasted for the rest of the night. When morning came, nearly half of the village left, trekking twelve miles through the jungle to see the kill and to make certain they got a share of the meat.

They cut up the meat and distributed it among the local people and took some back to Ella. When they got to Palipo, they weighed the tusks and measured the ears. It had been an enormous elephant. Each tusk weighed fifty pounds and each ear measured fifty-six inches wide.

The meat would not only feed the village but would also provide a big portion of what they needed for the approaching annual convention.

Because he had been so busy flying, Harold had not hunted for almost a year. Paul had seen to most of their supply of fresh meat. However, for the convention, Harold shot not only the elephant but also three deer, a wild pig, and twenty monkeys. He decided that ought to be sufficient.

~

Paul loved their life in Africa. He understood the people. He had become fluent in many of the local dialects and often served as Harold and Ella's interpreter. But beyond interpreting, his gift for languages made it so he could go almost anywhere among the native tribes and communicate effectively. From the natives' standpoint, Paul was one of them. He hunted with them. He played with them. He thought like they did. He was as much at home in the jungle as they were.

Paul thinking much like the natives did was a matter of some concern for Harold and Ella. They wanted him to love and appreciate the natives and their culture. They wanted him to understand the Africans, but they worried he might be becoming "too native"—and that he would feel he belonged in Africa more than he did in America. They wondered, was this really fair to him? Was their life in Africa making it so he would never be able to live a normal life, away from Africa, when he became an adult and was off on his own?

They didn't know the answers and didn't know what to do, but the issue was troubling to them.

As far as Paul was concerned, he was happiest when he was out of school and hunting with Peter and his other African friends.

Over their years at Palipo, he had acquired a small zoo of creatures from the jungle as pets. One of their first chimps they named Big Boy. They had purchased him from a native passing through Palipo on their prior term. When they went to America on furlough, Florence Basset had reluctantly agreed to keep him until their return. Now, as they neared the end of their term again, they decided to sell Big Boy to a man who worked at the Firestone rubber plantation.

Other chimps included Small Boy and Little Boy. They had been captured as babies by Paul and his friends after the chimps' mothers had been killed by hunters.

Paul's favorite pets were his large collection of snakes. Ella, Ruth, and Esther hated them and dreaded the days he would free them on the lawn in front of the house for "exercise" before returning them to their cages.

As the end of 1949 approached, they began preparing to return to the United States for furlough. When they departed, Harold was passing his plane on to Cleo Crabaugh, another Assemblies of God missionary, whom they only addressed as "Brother Crabaugh". He, along with his wife and three daughters, was serving at Pleebo. Harold had taught Brother Crabaugh to fly, so the air ministry Harold had started could continue in his absence.

After so long in the bush, they were looking forward to going to America—except Paul, who would rather have just stayed in Africa. It was very difficult for all of them to leave the people they had cared for and loved so much.

They fretted about the fact there were no missionaries to take their place. No one to hold clinic. No one to conduct the mission school. No one to help Pastor Try and the other Christians to spread the Good News of Jesus to the rest of the Palipo tribe. They had now spent a total of nearly eight years toiling to make a difference in these peoples' lives. Had their efforts been sufficient for the work to go on once they had departed? They simply did not know, but they had done what they believed God wanted them to do.

That was their responsibility. That was all they could do. The results were His responsibility.

The entire town turned out to see them off as Harold flew out with Ella and Esther. They headed for Neweka to meet Paul and Ruth. From there, they went on to Cape Palmas to arrange for passage on a ship bound for Europe.

They reached Cape Palmas on October 9, 1949, and learned from Mr. Frey, the local merchant, that a ship would be stopping soon to take on three hundred tons of rubber. He would try to book passage for them.

Two weeks later, they were rowed out by surfboats and boarded the SS *Templar*. For Harold, the hardest part of leaving was giving up his treasured airplane. During the term, he had logged almost a thousand hours in the air and survived two crashes, one at Feroka and another similar one, damaging a wingtip on the short field at Sinoe on the coast. He had hauled missionaries and their supplies all over the country.

As the ship weighed anchor and began to steam off, Brother Crabaugh flew over in Harold's beloved plane, tipping its wings in a final salute good-bye.

They were leaving home in Africa for America, a place that would be like a foreign country to them now.

Chapter 11
Bwah

As they returned to America and to their family and friends in Southern California, Ella wondered how they would all fit into the small, one-bedroom apartment over the garage behind her parents' house in Alhambra. It had been crowded at the end of their last furlough after Esther was born, but it hadn't lasted long because soon they'd left for Liberia. Now, Esther was approaching four and somehow seemed to require a lot more space.

Ella needn't have been concerned. Dr. Britton and their friends at Bethany Church had other plans in mind.

During the Landruses' term, the church had acquired two small houses adjacent to the church property. One was to provide housing for the church's custodian and his family. The other, they decided, was to be a mission house. It would be a home for missionary families on furlough. Dr. Britton and his congregation intended the Landrus family would be their first guests.

Upon arrival, Harold and Ella were presented with the keys to the house. "We want this to be yours while you're here," Dr. Britton said. "Welcome home!"

There was food in the cupboards and a new set of clothes for each of them, including the children, in the closets. Neither Harold nor Ella knew what to say. They were grateful beyond words to these faithful, caring supporters, to Dr. Britton, and to the Lord for His generous provision for them.

~

As with all furloughs, this was a time for the family to rest and recuperate and for them to renew contact with their supporters, both in Southern California and in Colorado.

This furlough was also time for them to deal with the troubling issue of what to do about Paul. They couldn't allow him to become too African. He needed to be able to fit into life in America as well. They were convinced he was losing that ability, if he hadn't already lost it completely.

They didn't mind him loving Africa, but they wanted him to have a choice when he was older. If he continued on his current path, they believed life in the United States would not be a realistic alternative for him, and they wanted him to at least have the option.

For his part, Paul didn't see any problem. He wasn't interested in being able to adapt to life in the United States. All he wanted to do was to live in Africa.

After a great deal of thought, prayer, and seemingly endless discussions, Harold and Ella decided, when they returned to Africa for their next term, Paul should stay in Alhambra with his grandparents or with his Aunt Lillian and her family and attend high school. This, they felt, would help initiate him into American society. When he was older, he would be able to choose—Africa or America.

Paul didn't want anything to do with Harold and Ella's plans for him. When they returned to Africa, he wanted to return with them, period.

"Paul," Ella reasoned, "You have to get an education here in America. After that, you can decide where you want to be."

"Mother, I don't want to stay in America at all. Liberia is my home. All of my friends are there. That's where I belong!" Paul countered.

Harold responded, "That's the point, Paul. All of your friends are in Africa. You need to make friends here. You need to at least be able to live here. The way you're going, you won't even have that alternative before long. You'll be too African. You will never be able to fit in here."

"That's just fine with me! I don't want to fit in here. I fit in in Liberia."

The battle of wills continued for a number of months until Harold finally said, "Paul, your mother and I have prayed about this, and we believe this is what the Lord wants us to do. You will have to stay here."

That ended further discussion, except for Paul's angry response as he walked out of the house and slammed the door, "Maybe you and Mother didn't hear Him right!"

The issue of Paul was settled as far as Harold and Ella were concerned. Ruth and Esther were just glad they could return to Liberia when the time came. They didn't have to face this battle. Not yet. Not on this furlough. What they really were was very grateful there wouldn't be any more heated discussions about it.

If the matter was decided for Harold and Ella, it most definitely was not for Paul. He couldn't argue with them directly anymore. They were convinced the decision was the one the Lord wanted them to make and, therefore, it was no longer open to debate.

What he needed to do was convince them leaving him in America wasn't what the Lord wanted them to do. They had misread God's intentions for him. He really was supposed to return to Africa with them.

As he thought about his problem, Paul recognized he couldn't change their minds on his own, but a potential ally came to mind who just might. He would have to set his strategy well and to present his case as forcefully as he could if he was to win the ally's support.

Not many days later, after a fitful night and many hours of fervent prayer, Paul approached Dr. Britton's office door. Taking a deep breath and squaring his shoulders, he knocked. It sounded too timid, and he wasn't sure if Dr. Britton even heard it, so he knocked again more forcefully, just as Dr. Britton opened the door.

The sudden movement of the door startled Paul, and he jumped back slightly.

Dr. Britton smiled, immediately recognizing how nervous Paul was. He loved this tall, slender sixteen-year-old. He patted Paul on the shoulder and said, "Come in, Paul. Come in. Have a seat and tell me what I can do for you."

As he slipped into a chair opposite Dr. Britton, Paul realized he didn't know where to begin. After all of his discussions and arguments with his parents, he couldn't state his case. "I … I … I'm not sure how to say this, Dr. Britton … I … uh … I …"

"Let me help you, Paul," Dr. Britton said gently. "I know you and your parents have not been seeing eye to eye on you going back to Africa."

"That's it, Dr. Britton. That's it." Then the words came rushing out, and the tears came, too. "Dr. Britton, I know Mother and Daddy are doing what they think is best for me, and what they think the Lord wants them to do. But I can't stay here. I hate it here. Africa is my home.

He paused and then plunged on, "Besides, they need me more than they think. I do a lot of their interpreting for them."

As Paul explained, Dr. Britton sat quietly, nodding his understanding.

"And Daddy … Daddy is even teaching me to fly his plane. This next term I can even be a bigger help to them." Then he quickly added to strengthen his point, "You know, carrying out the Lord's work among the heathens and all."

With Paul's last comment, it took considerable effort for Dr. Britton to stifle a broad grin. He looked quickly down at his desk. He didn't want this earnest young man to think he wasn't taking him seriously, but he was chuckling inside at the lengths to which Paul was willing to take the argument in an effort to win him over.

"And there's my sisters, too. I really have to look after them. I can protect them. I've already killed a leopard." As he warmed to his subject, Paul grew more and more enthusiastic, speaking with increasing speed and fervor and adding emphasis with flailing hands and arms. It was as if he thought he could gain Dr. Britton's support by the sheer weight of how much he said and how fast he said it.

Finally, spent and out of breath, Paul gave it one last shot. "Dr. Britton, I think God really wants me back in Africa!"

"Well, Paul," the gentle pastor chuckled, "you certainly feel strongly about this don't you?" Then he paused and leaned back in his chair.

Paul could hardly stand the silence or the wait, but he wasn't willing to say anything. He felt his fate was being decided. What if Dr. Britton said his parents were right? *Oh, please no, God!* he thought. But, if he did, Paul knew he would have to accept it. There would be no appeal.

After what seemed to Paul like hours, but in reality was only a few moments, Dr. Britton sat forward and said, "You know, Paul, I've talked with your parents about this matter at some length. And you're right. They are trying to do what is best for you. They love you, and they believe this is what the Lord has for you now."

He paused to let his words sink in and could see Paul's hopes fading. Then he continued, "But as I've prayed about it with them and alone, I believe you are right again. I think you belong back in Africa, too. What's more important, I believe that's what the Lord wants for you as well!"

Paul could hardly comprehend the words. *Is he saying what I think he's saying?*

Dr. Britton went on, "I'll speak with your folks, son, and I'll argue on your behalf. But remember, the final decision must be theirs, and you must agree right now to abide by it." He paused briefly once more and added with a smile, "With a willing spirit! Agreed?"

Paul was at a complete loss for words. Finally, he stammered, "Yes, Dr. Britton. Yes! Thank you. Thank you."

True to his word, Dr. Britton spoke with Harold and Ella. And as he had expected, he was able to persuade them to change their minds. Paul could return with them to Africa.

They spent much of the rest of their furlough visiting many of the churches that were supporting them. After their first term, when Bethany had been their only real source of financial backing, they had gradually added other churches, and the list now numbered nearly thirty, many of them in Colorado. However, as was to be the case for their entire missionary career, Bethany Church remained their greatest and most faithful base of prayer, encouragement, and financial support.

Harold's biggest concern was to be able to raise enough money to take another airplane back with him. Bethany had bought his first one, and he wasn't comfortable asking them to pay for another—although he would if he couldn't get the money somewhere else.

He met with Mr. L. L. Layne, the man whose wife he had driven for when he was a Bible school student years before.

While not a Christian, Mr. Layne was, nonetheless, interested in helping Harold and Ella and asked, "Just what do you think you will need to take back with you, Harold?"

Harold hesitated and then quickly listed the most expensive items he wanted to have when they returned to Africa. "Well, sir, we need one airplane, one kerosene refrigerator, one stove, and a light plant."

"I'd say that's a pretty costly list," the old gentleman commented and then added, "I'll tell you what. If you can find ways to buy the stove, the refrigerator, and the generator, I'll buy the airplane for you, but not until you have enough for the other three."

"That's fine with me, sir. That's mighty fine with me. Thank you."

It took most of the rest of their furlough for Harold and Ella to raise the funds necessary to purchase the other items. In fact, Harold had begun to doubt whether they could make it, though he never said anything about it.

Ella was beginning to think, if they could get the stove, refrigerator, and generator, she'd be almost as happy if they didn't get the plane. At least Harold would be safe, and he'd be with her all the time, not out flying all over the country facing who knew what dangers.

As time for their departure for Liberia grew near, they had money for the stove and refrigerator, but didn't have enough for the light plant, which meant Mr. Layne wouldn't buy the airplane. Harold started wondering if maybe God didn't want him to fly this term. *Please, Lord! Let us have the plane!* That prayer filled his thoughts almost continually.

One Sunday, after the morning service, Dr. Britton called them aside and said quietly, "Bethany will buy the light plant for you, Harold."

Harold was elated. "Dr. Britton, we don't know how to thank you. You're not only buying our light plant, but it means we get our airplane, too!"

"A little birdie told me that might be the case," the diminutive pastor responded with a wink.

Early the next morning, Harold presented himself at the Layne household. "Well, Mr. Layne," Harold said with a great deal of satisfaction, "the Lord has provided the stove, the refrigerator, and our light plant."

"I imagine you're here for the fourth piece then, aren't you?" the elderly man replied.

"Yes, sir. I am."

With a broad smile, he presented Harold with a check for $4,000 to buy a four-place Piper Pacer 135 aircraft. It had a cruising speed of 125 miles per hour and used only about seven gallons of fuel per hour. Harold was delighted.

Now they could go back to Africa.

~

On November 18, 1950, the Landrus family boarded the freighter *African Sun*, bound for Liberia out of New York Harbor.

The freighter *African Sun*.

Paul was sixteen years old, tall, and lanky like his father. He had broken his leg playing ball with some of the boys in the neighborhood during their furlough and had to make his way around the ship on crutches. At twelve, Ruth was becoming a young lady. She was the student in the family, and Ella would be challenged to keep enough school material in Ruth's hands during the coming four years in the jungle. Esther was an exuberant, happy four-and-a-half-year-old and the apple of her daddy's eye, though he often had difficulty showing it.

Harold and Ella anticipated being in "the bush" again, so in addition to the three children and the airplane, which was carefully stowed in a crate lashed to the ship's deck, they had four hens, two roosters, three geese, and two dogs along with them. The chickens and geese were kept in cages, but the captain allowed the dogs to run free on the deck. Ruth and Esther put blankets in boxes for the dogs to sleep in.

The family and their menagerie were an interesting diversion for the ship's crew during the tedious days at sea. When Harold and Paul went on deck to feed the animals, the crew would tease them by singing "Old MacDonald Had a Farm."

It was a good voyage, and they were looking forward to being in Africa again. They all felt they were heading home. As she and Harold stood together on the deck enjoying the warm tropical sun, cooled by a gentle sea breeze, and watching the children play with the dogs, Ella thought she was about as content as she'd ever been. She thought, *how can I ever thank God enough for blessing us this way?*

She might have savored it even more had she known this, their fourth term, was to be their last together as a family.

        ~

When they arrived in Liberia, Harold quickly assembled the plane and, making a number of trips, flew the family, all their supplies and equipment, and their animals to Pleebo, where they stayed until they could decide where they were to serve.

The natural choice was Palipo again. They were needed there, and it was "home" to them. They just weren't sure that was where the Lord wanted them to go. They stayed at Pleebo until He made it clear to them.

The mission house at Pleebo was large, and it was a good thing it was. Two other missionary families were living there as well.

The Crabaughs were there, with three children, Bobby, Carol, and Janis. Janis was four. She made a perfect playmate for Esther.

The Kornelsen family was there as well. Walt Kornelsen was an airplane mechanic and was able to keep Harold's new plane, as well as the one he had left for Brother Crabaugh to fly at the end of their last term, in top running condition.

It was a major challenge for the three families to live together in a five-room, one-bathroom house, but they managed.

Pleebo was at the end of the twenty-five-mile road running inland from Cape Palmas to the giant Firestone rubber plantation. While there, the Landruses held evangelistic services throughout the plantation. There were more than thirty camps for the native workers. Many of the camps had more than a thousand workers each.

As Christmas was approaching, almost every evening they would drive to a different camp in a borrowed jeep, set up a kerosene projector, and show a slide story of the birth of Jesus. The slideshow amazed the people and ensured there were always large crowds. Paul, off his crutches now, interpreted and frequently did the preaching. The natives could not believe this white boy spoke their languages.

The Bwah tribe finally convinced the Landruses their tribe was in most need and most deserving of having missionaries in their town. The tribal elders had sent several delegations to present their case and had promised to send porters to carry all of the Landruses' supplies and equipment. As an indication of their desire and sincerity, the tribe had already cut an airfield in the jungle for Harold's new airplane.

What had settled the matter for Harold and Ella was the Bwah tribe was much larger than Palipo and would, therefore, give them many more souls to hear the message of Jesus. As Ella wrote later, "If you want to fish, you go where the fish are!"

Like Palipo, Bwah was remote and primitive. A mission house existed, but there was little else the Landruses could use.

They immediately set about making the mission compound functional. This meant repairing and cleaning the house thoroughly and arranging their few furnishings in it. It meant building coops for the geese and chickens and planting a garden. It meant organizing morning clinic and a Bible school.

The children helped as much as they could. Esther was still too young to do anything significant, but she always thought she was helping. Ruth was anxious to get started with her schoolwork. During the next three years, she completed her eighth grade, as well as all of high school by correspondence.

She would spend much of her time in the upstairs attic room studying. When she finished the schoolbook she had, while she was waiting for the next one to arrive from America, she would beg Harold to fly her to Monrovia to visit some of her African and missionary friends who lived there.

Paul was the biggest help. He was nearly a man now and could work almost as long and as hard as Harold. He communicated with the natives like none of the rest of the family could. Paul, not Harold, was often the one issuing directions to their work crews.

There was also time for fun. All three children loved to swim in the nearby river. Esther learned how to swim there. They particularly enjoyed swimming when it was raining. It seemed to be even more exciting in the rain.

Ella was concerned about the dangers involved; crocodiles were never far away. A more likely threat were the various disease-carrying bacteria in the water. She knew, though, she couldn't protect them from everything. They were missionary kids, growing up in the remote jungles of Africa. There were dangers everywhere. She had committed each of them to the Lord, trusting Him for their safety and well-being, and that was where she left the matter—in the secure, loving hands of God.

Hunting remained Paul's passion. At every opportunity, he would take his rifle and head into the bush with a small band of his friends, returning hours later with a deer or gazelle for supper.

Paul providing fresh meat for the family.

Paul also began catching small animals and snakes again. At first, he intended to keep them only as pets. However, when he accompanied Harold on a flight to Monrovia for supplies, he learned there was a lucrative market for his animals. He could sell them to agents in Monrovia for zoos located all around the world. From that point forward, Paul began capturing animals for zoos as a means of raising money for his longer-range plan—his plan to bring his own airplane to Africa on their next term.

Ruth and Esther enjoyed some of Paul's creatures, like the two leopard cubs whose mother had been killed. The cubs chased and romped through the house all day. They would crouch behind doors and pounce upon any unsuspecting human who walked by. Eventually, they became too big and too dangerous to keep, but while they were there, they were a source of endless fun.

As at Palipo, what the girls and Ella didn't like was Paul's snakes. He had dozens of them and delighted in letting them loose on the grass. He said it was to give them "exercise." The family's female contingent was convinced it was only to frighten them!

Harold spent much of his time flying in supplies; transporting missionaries; and, occasionally, flying businessmen and government officials.

On one flight to Monrovia, Harold was asked by a government official for a ride. Harold gladly obliged. Such flights helped supplement his budget for flying. When they landed, Harold walked around to the passenger side of the plane to open the door for the official. After the man had climbed out, Harold reached under the seat and withdrew a "gunny" sack.

Curious, the official asked, "What is in there, Reverend Landrus?"

Harold said nothing but lifted the sack toward him, holding the top open. The official leaned over and looked into the sack. Instantly, he jumped back and away from it as if he'd been struck in the face.

He was a big man and clearly frightened. His eyes narrowed, and his fright began to turn to anger. "What in the world ..."

Harold, who had been standing straight-faced looking at him, interrupted what the man was about to say with a snicker. The man looked at him, even a little angrier now that he was being laughed at. Then Harold's grin took the anger out of him. He, too, began to grin.

Then they both began to laugh. The more they looked at each other, the more they laughed. The man laughed so hard tears ran down his cheeks.

"That'll teach me to trust a missionary! How could you do that to me?' he asked through the laughs.

"Well, sir," Harold began, "if I'd told you there was a snake on board my plane and it was under your seat, you'd still be back in the jungle wishing you had a ride. I got you here, safe and sound. Now you can't beat that, can ya?"

"No, no, I guess I can't. Well, thank you Reverend Landrus for a most educational ride. I now know to check before I ride next time!"

⌐∾⌐

The African or Cape buffalo is considered one of Africa's most dangerous animals. Weighing up to 1,700 pounds and standing nearly six feet high at the shoulders, these powerful beasts are known for their mean dispositions and their unpredictable behavior.

Late one morning as they hunted, Harold and Paul encountered a rare lone buffalo. They had come upon it grazing in a small open spot in the jungle forest. Fortunately, it had not heard them, and they ducked quickly into the undergrowth to plot their plan of attack. Beyond what they needed for the family and to care for the students at the Bible school, this giant animal would provide food for the entire village for several weeks.

Harold instructed Paul and the native hunting party to remain where they were while he maneuvered to get a good shot. Slowly, he moved forward and to the left, selecting a spot downwind where he would have a clear, unobstructed field of fire.

As he settled into position, Harold could see the animal more fully. It was huge, and its horns were enormous. His shot would have to be well placed if it was to bring the beast down. He was close, perhaps only seventy feet, so he knew he could do it.

Harold braced his left leg against a tree root and lifted his rifle. Aiming carefully, he began to gently squeeze the trigger. The root supporting him broke just as he fired. The shot went wide. It struck the buffalo in the shoulder, causing significant damage but not coming close to killing it.

The stricken animal reacted instantly. It bellowed, charging off into the jungle at a startling speed.

"I can't believe I missed," Harold said in disgust as Paul and the hunting party ran up to him.

"It wasn't your fault, Daddy. The tree broke. You had him. Let's go. We can still catch up to him," Paul urged.

Moses, the native leader of the hunting party, spoke, "It not be good to go after the buffalo. He mean. He will kill us. We jus' go home now. Leave him."

"I don't like to do it," Harold responded, "but I think you're right, Moses. He's going to be real mad about now, and I don't want to get any of us killed. We'll leave him."

Discouraged and unhappy, the hunting party began working its way back through the jungle toward the Bwah mission station. There was little conversation. Each man was licking the wounds to his ego at having failed to bring home such a prize—none more so than Harold.

They were not following the same path they had when they had run across the buffalo. They were cutting their way through the jungle on a more direct route. It would still take them the better part of two days to reach home.

The going was difficult, but instead of adding to their gloom, it seemed to provide a means of letting out their frustration as they hacked their way through the dense jungle foliage. Besides, they might still encounter some worthwhile game before they made it back to Bwah.

They were traveling light, a total of only six in the hunting party. Moses, the chief tracker, was in the lead, with Harold about fifteen paces back. Paul was immediately behind him. Following Paul were two gun bearers and a porter.

They had just crossed a small stream and were rounding a large rock outcropping. Moses was temporarily out of sight ahead of Harold. As Harold cleared the last large boulder, he sensed something before he saw anything. Then, out of the corner of his eye, he saw the huge black animal standing motionless, waiting for its prey—waiting for Harold.

Harold turned quickly, instinctively facing the danger. Suddenly, the buffalo was no longer motionless. It was crossing the short distance between them like a locomotive traveling at full speed.

There was no time for Harold to grab for his rifle. The animal was upon him. He yelled for everyone to run and then, at the last instant, jumped to the side, narrowly avoiding the animal's deadly giant horns as the buffalo's charge missed and carried it past him. With remarkable agility, the enraged beast turned and was bearing down on him again.

The rest of the team had scattered at Harold's first yell, not knowing what was happening. Now, as they sought a place to escape, they were beginning to understand the wounded buffalo had, unbelievably, circled back on them and was attacking them hours after their first encounter. It was a hunter's worst nightmare come true.

As he fled in panic, one of the gun bearers had dropped Harold's rifle. Paul was able to scoop it up as he ran by and frantically began trying to figure out how he could get a shot before the buffalo killed his father.

Behind him, Harold dove again and again to avoid the buffalo's repeated charges, but he knew it was only a matter of time before the animal caught him.

Harold dove once more, and a shot rang out as the black beast flashed past. Paul had worked his way back along the trail, and though he was off balance and still moving, he had managed to take a shot. It wounded the animal a second time. Paul feared for a moment the buffalo would only become even more enraged, but instead, it stopped pursuing Harold and crashed off through the forest.

Running to Harold, who was gathering himself together off the ground, Paul asked, "Are you alright, Daddy? I thought he was going to get you."

"So did I, son. So did I," Harold answered, catching his breath.

The others were returning now, picking up the gear strewn along the path, grateful they had all survived. Moses said solemnly, "Pa, now we mus' kill dis animal. If we do not, it will kill many, many people before it dies."

"I agree, Moses. Now we have to get him. But we have to be careful. There's no telling where he'll be or what he's going to try to do. And we sure don't want to run into any of his friends."

It took them two days until they tracked down the wounded buffalo. For two days and one very long night, none of them relaxed for an instant. This time Harold's shot was true. The buffalo died where it stood and collapsed to the ground.

It hadn't happened as they'd anticipated, but they had their buffalo—a huge prize. It would provide food for everyone for weeks to come. And it had come as the result of a titanic struggle, which, at times, they were not at all sure they would win.

~

As Harold and Ella carried out their ministry in the clinic, the Bible school, and evangelistic meetings among the Bwah tribe, many of the people became Christians. They placed their faith in Christ as God's son and the loving Savior of all who believe.

In the village outside the mission compound, those who were Christian wanted to separate themselves from many of the traditional tribal rituals and superstitions that were so much a part of everyday life in the village. Like the Bwebo and Palipo people had done during the Landruses' earlier terms, the native Christians in Bwah developed a "Christian" town at the edge of the village. Here, they could live with fellow believers and did not have to submit to the laws of the devil doctors who ruled the rest of the village, which they referred to as "Heathen" town.

It was always a great joy for Harold and Ella to see the Christian town, with the number of its square huts growing, and the Heathen town shrinking. The contrast and the conflict between good and evil were evident. The devil doctors were constantly trying to maintain the influence they had once held over the Christians, while the Christians were striving to put aside the superstitions of their past and to trust and rely fully on Christ. It was not an easy struggle. Each day presented challenges to their new Christianity.

~

Alice had become a Christian as the result of one of Ella's first Bible studies at Bwah. From then on, she had been both a faithful, committed

Christian and a devoted friend and helper to Ella. She helped around the house and went with Ella when she preached in the villages.

When several of the clan chief's cattle died, the entire village was in an uproar. Everyone wanted to know who had placed a curse or as they said "witched" the cows. For them there was no natural explanation. As far as the people of Bwah were concerned, everything was caused by evil spirits which, in this case, had been directed to kill the chief's cattle.

A number of people were accused of the treachery, including Alice, though she vigorously protested her innocence. Harold and Ella were never sure why Alice was accused, but believed it was because she was a Christian and because she was very outspoken in her condemnation of the witch doctors and their practices.

The chief, at the insistence of the witch doctors, decreed they would conduct a "hot cutlass" ordeal to determine the guilty party. He ordered all the people, including those in Christian town, to assemble in the center of the village for the ritual.

The ritual involved placing a native cutlass into a burning fire and heating it until the blade glowed white with the heat. Those accused of a crime would be brought forward and the broad flat side of the cutlass blade would be drawn down the skin of their bare legs. The natives believed, if the accused was innocent, they would not be burned by the knife. If they were guilty, they would be burned. In their view, the hot cutlass was a simple, very effective "lie detector."

As the "trial" began, the witch doctor didn't realize Alice was not standing among the villagers. In fact, she was not in the village. She had left a few days earlier to visit relatives in another village and was not even aware the ordeal was being held.

It began with the witch doctor pulling one of the accused from the crowd and standing him in front of the fire. The man was trembling but stood bravely erect, head high as the cutlass was withdrawn from the flames.

The witch doctor examined the glowing blade and, satisfied it was as hot as he could get it, bent down beside the accused man, who gasped and held his breath. With a relatively quick motion, the witch doctor placed the cutlass against the back of the man's leg just below the knee and drew it downward. The man tensed but did not move. When the blade was removed, the man took a deep breath of air. The knife had not really hurt, and it certainly didn't feel like it had burned.

The witch doctor, dressed in a dirty cape with trinkets and jujus adorning it, examined the man's leg and then rose, faced the silent crowd, and pronounced with as much solemnity as he could muster, "Dis man, he not guilty." Then he thrust the cutlass back into the fire.

The ritual continued, with the witch doctor searching the crowd, looking for the next accused man or woman, usually found cowering among the assembled throng, hoping beyond hope they might be overlooked and forgotten. When he spotted each new candidate for the ordeal, he would grab them, yanking them out from their family and other villagers, to undergo the same trial as the first man.

Each time, the witch doctor would declare, "Not guilty." He was saving Alice for last. She was a troublesome woman, intent on making Christians of the other women in the village. She reduced his power and influence over their lives, and he would do everything he could to prevent that.

Alice would be found guilty. Of that, he was sure. He had been conducting the cutlass ordeal for many years. He knew exactly how to maneuver the knife, how to, ever so slightly, alter the speed with which he moved the blade. The difference meant burnt flesh. He had decided she was guilty. His knife would prove it. Guilty. The spirits would confirm his power, and everyone would believe it.

As he declared the last of the accused "Not guilty!", the witch doctor began looking for Alice. He didn't see her. He searched the crowd again. She wasn't there. He began asking individual villagers where she was. They didn't know.

Realizing he could not prove her guilty, he became livid. He screamed and yelled at the crowd, which stood in stunned silence.

Pacing back and forth hurling epithets, he reached out and snatched the hand of a teenage girl, pulling her toward him. She shrieked in terror and tried to pull away, but his grip was firm. "You will take her place. The spirits will use you to tell us she is guilty of this crime against our chief."

Trembling with fear, the young girl stood in the center of the crowd, tears running down her cheeks as the witch doctor stoked the fire with the cutlass, pulling it out several times and then pushing it back into the coals, tormenting her with the time and pleasure he was taking with the process.

Once again, he withdrew the knife from the fire. He ran it down her slender leg. She screamed in pain. The smell of burned flesh filled the air. Blisters formed almost instantly. The crowd gasped collectively.

"She is guilty. She is guilty," the witch doctor exalted, waving the cutlass over his head.

Fear and anger etched on her face, the girl's mother ran forward to tend her wounds and to carry her away.

The chief then said, "Alice is to be found. She is to be arrested and taken to the government prison."

When she returned to the village a few days later, Alice was told what had occurred and was apprehended. She couldn't believe this was happening to her. She was innocent. She was frightened.

Harold and Ella tried to intervene on Alice's behalf but were told very forcefully by the chief they had no say in the matter and they should not interfere.

Ella came to talk with her and to comfort her. "Remember, Alice," Ella assured her, "the Lord will take care of you. Be strong no matter what happens. We will be praying for you, and we will come visit you."

True to her word, Harold and Ella visited Alice several times at the government prison in Neweka where she had been transported. Each time they came, they tried to discuss Alice's case with the prison officials, but to no avail.

After several months, Alice was simply released. Just as there had been no real basis for her imprisonment, there seemed to be no basis for her release. Harold and Ella suspected, however, the prison warden had agreed to hold Alice in the hopes the Landruses could be coaxed into paying a fine, in reality a bribe, to free her. When it became apparent they would never do so, it was not worthwhile for the warden to keep her.

Throughout the entire time, as Ella said later, "Alice stayed strong in the Lord and kept the victory!"

On returning to Bwah and until the Landruses' term ended, Alice remained Ella's faithful helper and friend.

~

Because he spoke so many of the native languages, about a dozen by then, and had killed his first leopard in Palipo when he was only twelve years old, Paul was something of a celebrity among the Africans. Though he didn't want it, the term in Bwah served to elevate his status to near legend when he hunted and killed his first elephant at age seventeen.

When Paul and Harold and the native hunting party returned to the village with word of his feat, the dancing and celebration lasted for days.

Over the course of the next two years and the first three years of their next term, Paul shot and killed a total of six elephants with just seven shots. A remarkable testimony to his skill and abilities as a hunter.

Paul wasn't the only hunter in the family; after all he had learned to hunt from his daddy. When he wasn't flying or preaching or fixing something on the mission compound, Harold still loved to hunt, and like Paul, he did it whenever he could. The best times for him were when he and Paul could hunt together, though that was not often enough.

Harold had been out with his native hunting team. They had been successful and were returning to Bwah with several monkeys and a small deer to help feed the Landrus family and the Bible school students and their families. Paul had not been with his daddy on this particular hunt.

One of the practices Harold tried to follow when they were out on the trail was to never be away from camp, or the mission compound, after nightfall. It was simply too dangerous. Negotiating the jungle during the day was difficult enough. In the dark, it was almost impossible. Night was also the time for predators to be out, particularly leopards.

The hunting had taken longer than Harold had anticipated. Now, they were returning home in the dark, following behind Harold's big four-battery flashlight, trying to avoid the tangled roots and vines that cluttered their path.

They were silent for the most part as they carefully picked their way. Harold led; the long barrel of his flashlight thrust out in front of him.

Behind him were his gun bearer and Moses, who was bringing up the rear, since Harold knew the way back as well as Moses did.

Suddenly, a large leopard leapt onto the path directly in front of Harold, mouth open, fangs showing. The big cat was close enough Harold could smell its breath. Harold was so startled he almost dropped the flashlight, but managed to maintain a grip. There was little sound. It seemed as though the entire jungle was silently holding its breath.

The leopard let out a low growl but did nothing. It sat on its haunches in the pathway, yellow eyes gleaming, looking straight at Harold and his flashlight. Harold was equally still, looking at the leopard. It was as if each was trying to determine who was the hunter and who was the hunted, each poised, but waiting for the other to make the first move.

Harold made the first move, ever so slowly. With one hand holding the flashlight steady on the leopard, he reached back with his free hand fully expecting his gun bearer to place his loaded rifle in his hand. Nothing happened. He reached back further, waving his arm as he did so, trying to reach his gun. Still nothing.

This was clearly not as it should be. Over years of hunting together, his gun bearers knew they were to always be just a step or two behind Harold. If he stopped and reached back, even without looking, the loaded weapon was to be placed in his hand, ready for him to shoot. That way, he could keep his eyes on the game he had spotted.

Where is that guy? Where is my gun? Harold thought. *I have to have that gun. This leopard isn't going to stay like this for long.*

Harold realized the leopard had apparently been mesmerized by the light from the flashlight as they had worked their way through the jungle. Its curiosity had caused it to confront this unfamiliar shiny thing.

Reluctant as he was to do so, Harold decided he needed to risk the consequences of taking the light off the leopard just long enough to see if he could locate his gun.

Slowly, he panned the light off the leopard, swinging it around 180 degrees to shine back down the path he and his team had just traveled. When he did so, he later said, "All I could see was the bottoms of their feet, going in the opposite direction as fast as they could."

Knowing he could not get his rifle, Harold again swung the light forward, where the leopard remained motionless still staring up at him. The animal's snout was almost touching the end of the flashlight.

Harold saw the pupils in the leopard's eyes narrow. Then it began to growl again. This time, a long, low rumble that grew to an angry snarl.

At that instant, Harold brought the flashlight back and slammed it down across the bridge of the leopard's nose. Startled, the leopard screamed and bounded away into the jungle.

Harold stood in silence for a moment, shaking his head. "Thank you, Lord," he mumbled. "No one will ever believe this!"

Confident the leopard was gone and no longer a threat, he headed back down the trail to find Moses and the gun bearer. He found them cowering a couple hundred yards down the path.

"Pa, you are not killed," Moses said with great relief.

"No thanks to you fellas," Harold responded. Turning to his gun bearer he asked, "Where were you, man? I needed you."

Eyes downcast, the gun bearer answered quietly, "Pa, my heart she was strong. But my feet, they were weak."

The close of 1953 saw the family preparing to leave once more on furlough. They desperately wanted to stay. Again, there were no missionaries to take their place, and they did not want their dear Bwah Christians to feel they were being abandoned.

Harold and Ella took heart though in what they had accomplished and how well the Christian community was doing. Bethany had provided $600 to pay for material to build a school building on the mission station. A wonderful native by the name of Ralph Pompom was serving as teacher and doing an excellent job.

In Christian town, the natives had built a small church all on their own, and had even raised the money to pay for the materials. They had appointed a native pastor. Both the church and the pastor served as symbols of the community's strength and vitality. Harold and Ella would leave knowing the native Christians could continue their walk with the Lord without them.

The most difficult departure was for Ruth. It had been decided, when they went on furlough, she would not return to Africa, but would remain in the United States to go to college. She would live with her Aunt Lillian and her family. The decision devastated her. She cried and cried, certain she would never see Africa and all of her friends again. She begged her parents to change their minds as they had with Paul but knew they would not.

On October 19, 1953, the family sailed from Monrovia for Europe on the Delta Lines freighter *Del Campo*. All were sad to leave Liberia behind. Harold, Ella, Paul, and Esther knew they would be returning. For Ruth, leaving was final. She knew in her heart she would never again see the land of her birth, the only home she had ever known and loved.

She stood at the stern of the ship, straining to see every last bit of Liberia she could, until it faded and finally disappeared into the distance. She thought her heart would break.

Chapter 12
Heartache

Furlough passed quickly, and all too soon, another round of good-byes was at hand. This time, saying good-bye was especially difficult because they were no longer going to be together as a family. Harold and Ella, along with Paul and Esther, were once more returning to their beloved Africa. Ruth was staying in America with her Aunt Lillian, Lillian's husband, John, and their two sons, Harold and Glenn.

At twenty, Paul didn't have to fight the battle to return to Liberia he had at the close of their last furlough. He was a man now and could make the decision for himself. No one was trying to tell him he should stay in America and further his education. Everyone knew Africa was his home. Africa was where he, more than any of the others, belonged.

He had earned money in Africa selling animals to zoos and he had worked the entire year on furlough to earn enough to buy his own airplane. He decided to remain in Alhambra to earn the last bit he needed while Harold, Ella, and Esther began driving to New York to catch the freighter for Liberia.

They departed Alhambra on November 22, 1954, and spent Thanksgiving in Denver, where Esther thoroughly enjoyed her first encounter with snow. From there, they drove to Beaumont, Texas, where they stayed with E. L. Mason and his family and where Paul caught up with them.

Paul's plane was waiting for them in Texas. He had wired Mason money to purchase the plane, and his new three-seat Piper Cruiser was there when he arrived.

Paul, Mason, and Harold spent a few days checking it out and then crating it for the long journey to Africa.

The day after Christmas, the Landruses left Texas in a new, bright yellow jeep truck with a stake bed body, towing an equally bright yellow trailer with all their gear and Paul's plane securely tied down. They shipped out on the freighter MV *Del Oro* on December 29, 1954, truck, trailer, gear, and plane included.

They were excited to be bound for Africa again, completely unaware of the heartache and heartbreak that lay ahead.

⁓

As they steamed across the Atlantic, Harold was already anxious to get in the air again. As a bush pilot, he had logged nearly two thousand hours flying over the jungles of Liberia, and he longed to be at the controls again.

When the *Del Oro* pulled into the newly constructed harbor at Monrovia, they were delighted to be "home", in Africa. They stayed on board while cargo was being off-loaded, watching with particular care as their truck, trailer, and Paul's precious plane were lifted from the deck and placed on the wharf below.

As they were about to disembark, they returned to their cabin to gather the last of their belongings when they were met by one of the missionaries who had come to welcome the ship and who had come on board to talk with them. He carried with him a letter for Harold and Ella.

Visibly uncomfortable, he mumbled a greeting to them and thrust out his hand with the envelope.

Somewhat puzzled, Harold reached for the letter and opened it. He glanced through it quickly as Ella, Paul, and Esther stood by, patiently waiting to learn what this unexpected document had to say.

Ella watched Harold closely. She knew him, probably better than he knew himself, and she knew very little affected him, but she could tell what was in this letter clearly had. She said nothing but nodded to the children to sit down in their small cabin as Harold, too, sat down and read the letter for a second time. This time much more slowly.

When he had finished, he looked up at the missionary, who could only stare at the cabin floor. Still looking at the missionary, Harold silently handed the letter to Ella.

Ella read it and then put her head down, shaking it slowly from side to side. "I can't believe this. You don't mean it. You don't mean it," she said to no one in particular. Then she fell silent.

By then Esther, who was not yet eight years old, had been about as patient as she was going to be. She didn't understand what was going on, and she couldn't wait any longer to find out. Turning to Paul, sitting next to her, she asked quietly but very insistently, "What's happening? What's wrong?" She knew something was definitely wrong. She could not remember ever having seen her daddy cry, but there were tears in his eyes now; she was sure of it.

In slow, deliberate words, Ella answered Esther's questions. "This letter is from the Assemblies of God district superintendent's office. It says your daddy can't fly his plane anymore."

The words had barely left her mouth when Paul erupted. Leaping from his seat, he yelled, "What are you talking about?" Then, directing his anger toward the missionary messenger, he added, "What's the matter with you people? Why can't my daddy fly? That's what he does. Everybody knows that. Besides, all the missionaries need him."

Still seated, Harold held up his hand, bringing an end to Paul's outburst. "It seems the field council objects to the fact there were times last term when I flew outside the mission. I occasionally flew people who were not missionaries."

"They can't be serious," Paul jumped back in. "You flew a few businesspeople to Monrovia, and they paid you for it. What's wrong with that? All that did was help pay for maintenance and gas for the plane so you could keep helping the missionaries."

"Brother Landrus," the missionary interrupted, "I'm really sorry about this. We didn't even know you were on your way until after you had left the States. Brother King wanted to stop you from coming because of this problem."

"Mister," Harold responded, an edge in his voice, "let's understand something. The Lord called me to be a missionary to Africa. It would take a much bigger man than Brother King or even the whole field council to stop me from doing what God called me to do. Now, I think you'd better leave us alone. We need some time to figure this out."

The missionary quickly withdrew from the cabin and disappeared. The family remained stunned and silent. Harold's mind was racing, *Lord, I can't believe this is happening. How do I fight this, Lord?* Then, as the family sat quietly around him, a sense of peace came to him. *I don't understand this, Lord! And I surely don't like it, but if this is Your will for us—for me—then grant me the courage and faith to accept it.*

Finally, he stood and said, "Well, I guess we'd better go get our things and check on your plane, Paul. They sure can't keep you from flying!" And the family filed out the cabin door to go collect their belongings on the wharf.

They stayed for a few days at the mission house in Monrovia trying to decide what they were going to do. They felt angry about how they had been treated. It was unfair and unwarranted. They wanted to fight for what they knew was right, meaning Harold flying again, serving all the missionaries, helping them better carry out their ministries.

In the end, however, Harold made the final decision. "We have to keep a sweet spirit about this and keep the victory," he said. "That's the only way to truly honor Jesus. If we try to serve Him but have a bad attitude, our service doesn't mean anything. Just because these people are out of order doesn't mean we have to be." Then he added, "What we have to do now is figure out where we're going to serve this term."

They wanted to return to Bwah. The problem was they were reluctant to go to a remote village without the plane. They had done that. It was just too difficult and dangerous, and their lack of transportation would limit their ministry too much. The plane made it so much easier and was their lifeline in times of medical or other emergencies.

When they had left to go on furlough, Harold had parked his plane in the hangar he'd built on the airfield he'd constructed at Pleebo. The plane was secure there and would be easy to get to once they arrived back in country.

They decided they would ferry what they could of their supplies to Pleebo using Paul's plane. Harold would bring the rest of their gear in the truck, driving to Pleebo down the government road that ran up through the highlands to Tchien and then cut south for the long haul to Cape Palmas. The road was little more than a rugged dirt path covering most of the length of the country. It was a treacherous journey, but like so much of what they faced as missionaries in Liberia, Harold knew he really had no choice, so he simply set about doing it.

In a few days, the four of them were safely reunited at Pleebo, where they lived in the hangar, under the wings of Harold's grounded airplane. Paul became the flier for the family and the rest of the missionaries in Liberia, hauling supplies, delivering mail, and providing transportation.

Harold and Ella immediately began holding evangelistic services in the workers' camps in the giant Firestone rubber plantation located near Pleebo.

They drove their yellow flatbed jeep to the various towns and villages using a kerosene projector to show Bible films and a portable public address system to preach the Gospel. When he wasn't flying, Paul served as their interpreter. Over the course of the next several months, they ministered in fifty-three camps and villages spread throughout the giant plantation.

As disappointed as he was at not being able to fly, Harold was excited they were reaching far more people in just a few months at Firestone than they could in a year back in the interior.

While they worked the camps, two issues were of concern to Ella. The first had to do with Esther, the second, with Harold.

During their previous terms, Ruth and Paul had gone to either Neweka or Pleebo, where the Hixenbaughs and the Crabaughs taught school for them and the other Assemblies of God missionary children in country. Harold and Ella had assumed, this term, Esther could be schooled the same way.

However, when they arrived at Pleebo, they learned Esther was the only school-aged missionary child in the area, and the Hixenbaughs and Crabaughs had been assigned other duties now the other children were gone. Ella did not feel she could teach Esther properly, so providing for

Esther's education was rapidly becoming a very difficult challenge. For a brief period, they sent Esther to Sinoe, a village along the coast, where a missionary was willing to be her teacher. However, this arrangement was only intended to be for a few months until Harold and Ella could figure out another way to provide Esther's education.

Ella's other concern was for Harold. She knew he enjoyed their ministry around Pleebo, but she also knew they couldn't stay there long. It was just too hard on Harold to have the plane sitting idle in the hangar. She could see the look in his eyes as he ducked under its wing and patted it each time he walked past. She couldn't stand having him hurt so much.

There was nothing she could do but encourage him to get out of there, away from the plane, back to the bush where his heart could mend, and they could be about the Lord's work. After all, Paul had an airplane, and he was willing to provide transportation when they needed it. Though his availability was limited because he was frequently off on his own, flying businesspeople between Monrovia and various jungle airstrips or capturing animals for zoos around the world or working for R.J. LaTourneau, the giant American construction company that built huge earthmoving equipment for massive development projects in the wilds.

～

During this time, Harold and Ella were approached by Florence Steidel, the fellow Assemblies of God missionary who had preceded them at Palipo and who had been forced to leave because of the problem with the Que. After leaving Palipo, and after teaching at Neweka, she had founded a new mission work deep in the heart of the jungle some distance to the north and east of Cape Palmas. It was a leper colony she called "New Hope Town." She wanted Harold and Ella to join her in the work there.

She and two American nurses were endeavoring to help hundreds of lepers and their families, but were overwhelmed by the magnitude of the task and desperately needed additional help. With Harold's ability to build things and to hunt for food for the natives who could not provide for themselves, and with Ella's ability to preach, teach, and raise crops, they were just what Ma Steidel and her nurses needed.

As they thought and prayed about it, Harold and Ella began to feel New Hope Town might be just the spot for them. Ella would enjoy working with other missionaries for a change, and Harold could make an enormous difference in what they were able to accomplish there.

"But we can't take Esther to a leper colony," Ella said as they discussed their plans one evening. "No one even knows how leprosy is transmitted. It's all right for us to take the risk and go, but we can't put her at risk. What if she got leprosy? And what about her schooling? We have to do something about that, and we have to do it soon!"

"I know, Ella. I know," Harold replied. "Let's write the boarding school we heard about in Nigeria. Maybe we could send her there."

"But that's so far away. How can we send our baby halfway across Africa? She's only eight years old."

"Well, let's just see what they have to say. Then we can decide. I don't know what else we can do. We just need to trust the Lord in this," Harold urged.

The next morning, Ella wrote to Hillcrest Academy in Jos, Nigeria, inquiring about their school and the possibility of Esther being enrolled.

Not many weeks later, a response arrived from the school. Yes, they were a boarding school for missionary children, from first grade through high school. Yes, Esther could be enrolled at any time.

Harold hated the idea of sending Esther away. Though he rarely showed outward affection, he loved her dearly and enjoyed the happy childhood enthusiasm she brought to their lives. After much thought and prayer, he concluded sending her to Hillcrest was what the Lord would have them do.

He spoke with Ella about it. "I don't know what else we can do," he said. "I believe that's what the Lord wants."

Ella bowed her head and responded quietly, "Well, then, I guess its settled. We need to send her right away. But let's not tell her for a few days, until we can at least arrange for her to get there."

Making the arrangements took almost a month. The journey was nearly two thousand miles and would take more than a week. First,

Esther would have to fly from Monrovia to Accra, Ghana. Ella wrote to a missionary couple there asking them to meet Esther's plane and keep her for a couple of days until they could put her on a flight from Accra to Lagos, Nigeria. There, still another missionary couple would meet her; keep her for a day or two; and then put her on a plane to Jos, in north central Nigeria, along the southern edges of the great Sahara Desert.

Harold and Ella had never met any of the people who were to take care of Esther. In fact, when they put her on the plane in Monrovia, they hadn't received word back from the missionaries in Accra. They could only trust they had gotten Ella's letter and they would, indeed, meet Esther at the airport and care for her.

When Harold and Ella told Esther of their decision and that she would be departing in just a few days, Esther was devastated. She burst into tears. "Paul and Ruth didn't have to go away," she sobbed. "Why do I have to? This isn't fair."

Ella held her in her arms as Esther cried and cried. "I'll miss you," Ella whispered.

Paul was almost as upset as Esther. He was twelve years older than she was, and he enjoyed being her big brother. Of course, he seldom told her so, but he loved having her around. He loved teasing her and harassing her with his pet snakes. He loved scaring the daylights out of her when he would take her flying and do aerobatics. He loved knowing she looked up to him and thought he was wonderful, even if he did things to make her angry.

The days until Esther's departure went by quickly. All too soon, she was standing on the tarmac beside a West African Airways DC-3. After a wave and one last picture, she boarded and was off. The plane was nearly full, but once the stewardess had buckled her into her seat, Esther felt she'd never been so alone in all her life. She buried her face in the angel doll Ella had given her to carry and wept.

As a child, Esther never played with dolls. But Ella had insisted she carry the doll her Grandma Pratt had given her as a means of identification for the missionaries they hoped would be waiting for her in Accra and elsewhere along her route—as if there would be any other eight-year-old white girl flying alone halfway across Africa!

Esther about to board her flight for the first leg of her weeklong journey to Hillcrest Academy in Jos, Nigeria.

Harold, Ella, and Paul watched as the DC-3 took off, gained altitude, and disappeared in the distance. Lost in their own thoughts, they silently turned and walked toward Paul's plane to fly back to Pleebo and their lives, which now seemed so much emptier without both Ruth and Esther.

In July 1955, three months after Esther left for school in Nigeria, Harold and Ella joined Florence Steidel in her work among the lepers at New Hope Town. Paul flew them to the small airstrip Harold had made at Neweka when he was flying Paul and Ruth to school. From there, they could walk less than a mile to the leper colony.

Arriving there, they began to understand the magnitude of the work Ma Steidel had undertaken.

The nature of their disease makes lepers society's outcasts. From biblical times, leprosy has been considered one of the worst of all diseases, and one of the most feared. Leprosy, brought on by Hansen's bacilli, often causes scaly white or red ulcerous blotches to appear on the skin and creates numbness around the sores. This numbness allows minor cuts and injuries to go unnoticed because they cannot be felt. Infection sets in, and the victims frequently suffer terribly as a result. Internally, leprosy causes the victim's bones to begin to dissolve, often resulting in horrible disfigurement. Frequently, fingers and toes shrink back to useless, disabled stubs.

At that time, when a Liberian was found to have leprosy, the person was banned from the village and forced to flee into the jungle. Sometimes, those who had been banned fled alone. More often, the leper's entire family was forced out at the same time, because they were suspected of having the disease as well.

Florence Steidel first encountered lepers when she worked in the girls' school at Neweka, after she had left Palipo. Several lepers had come begging for food at the mission station and had then retreated back into the jungle. Her heart had immediately been touched by their plight and their misery.

She persuaded the local tribal chiefs to grant her 350 acres of land, where she could build a haven for these helpless, hopeless, wretched outcasts. The land was isolated, virtually inaccessible, and covered with dense tropical jungle, but it was land. It was land she could use to establish a place where lepers could obtain medical treatment and try to create new, worthwhile, meaningful lives for themselves. It was where she could tell them about Jesus.

The enormity of the task Miss Steidel had undertaken was staggering. As word of her project spread, new families of lepers arrived almost daily. From a mere handful at the beginning, by the time Harold and Ella arrived, there were well over two hundred, with the number growing daily.

Miss Steidel had to develop ways to house them, feed them, and treat them. When she learned Harold and Ella Landrus and their son, Paul, were coming to help, she could not stop telling God how grateful she was.

Ellen McCormick and Lois Lemm, the two American nurses, were already working with Florence when Harold, Ella, and Paul arrived. Two more nurses, Eloise Collier and Lettie Lewis, joined them shortly afterward. The addition of Harold and Paul, two strong, able-bodied men, to the team made a huge difference. Because the other women were nurses and heavily involved in treating the natives with leprosy, Ella spearheaded caring for the natives' spiritual needs. It was an effective, dedicated team. The Lord blessed their work, and New Hope grew rapidly.

They first began by tackling the housing problem. Miss Steidel and Harold taught the leper families how to make mud bricks and directed them in cutting and clearing more of the land. They built houses for the natives and for the missionaries, a clinic, a school, and a carpenters' shop, as well as, most importantly, a church.

With the airstrip at Neweka, Paul could fly limited amounts of supplies in, but Harold knew immediately they could never fly in enough to make New Hope what it needed to be. They would have to build their own road out to the government road eighteen miles away. If they could do that, they would be able to bring supplies in by truck all the way from Cape Palmas. He said little about it and knew other things had to take priority for a while, but he began planning how to build the road within a few days after their arrival.

Even with missing toes and fingers, the lepers were hard and willing workers. Once they had Harold to provide hands-on direction and encouragement, they began transforming the jungle into a settlement. Slowly, painfully slowly, a true community began to emerge. As the work moved forward though, Harold knew even more what they really needed was the road he'd already been thinking about.

Though they were extremely busy with the other work of the mission station, Harold and Paul went hunting as often as possible. This was the way they could provide meat for the missionaries and for the natives. It was also something they enjoyed as much as they did flying.

At New Hope, Harold didn't have the hunting team headed by Moses he had had at Bwebo, Palipo, and Bwah. He missed them. It wasn't so much that he really needed them. He was more than capable on his own. They had just become part of his life as a hunter, and it always seemed something was missing without them.

Not many months after their arrival at New Hope, Harold and Paul decided to go elephant hunting. It was a little early for the giant beasts to be migrating into the eastern portion of the country, but they had heard from some of the natives elephants had been spotted. The news was all the encouragement they needed. They were ready to go almost immediately.

Shooting an elephant would mean the entire New Hope community would have meat for several weeks, even months.

They selected eight or nine of the men in town to make up their hunting party. As they were about to leave, a young teenage boy named James ran up to Harold and asked, "Pa, can I go? Can I go? Please, Pa. I never been on a elephant hunt before."

"No, I don't think so, James. I don't think your mama would like that," Harold responded.

"Please, Pa," James pleaded. "Pa, if my mama say I can go, I can go?"

Recognizing James was not going to be put off easily, Harold said, "All right, James. Let's see what your mama has to say."

They found James's mother in front of her mud house pounding palm nuts in a wooden mortar with a long stub-end pole, preparing them for making palm butter.

"Mama, Mama. Tell Pa Landrus I can go hunting with him," James called to her as they approached.

James's mother paused in her backbreaking work and smiled at her young son. He was her only living child, and she loved him with all her heart. Out of eleven children she had given birth to, all but James had died before they reached the age of two.

She knew how badly James wanted to go and what a grand adventure it would be for him. She also knew hunting wild animals in the jungle was dangerous. Many natives, young and old, were killed each year doing so.

She was a small woman and looked up at Harold, studying his face for a moment. Then she said, "Pa, you take good care of my boy? You bring him back to me safe?"

Harold smiled. "Yes, Mama. I will bring him back to you safe." Turning to James he added, "Well, James. I guess you can come along with us. Let's go!"

It took them three days to reach the area where they expected to find elephants. Paul and two of his native friends were leading, with Harold, James, and the others behind.

Paul was the first to hear it, the low rumbling, like a stomach growl, by which the elephants communicate with one another. He instantly signaled for them to stop as he listened more closely, trying to determine which direction it had come from and how far away the elephants might be.

He concluded they were off to the left and close. He and Harold crept towards the sound.

They almost missed the first elephant. A medium-sized female, she was pulling tender leaves from low-hanging tree branches with her trunk. The vegetation was so thick, she was nearly invisible.

Beyond her, in a slight break in the jungle, was a second—also a female. She was massive, with large tusks, her giant ears flapping to cool her in the tropical heat.

Harold whispered to Paul they would try to take the larger of the two, hoping the smaller, younger one would run off at the sound of the gunshot.

As they maneuvered to get into a good shooting position, James crawled forward to see what was happening. Harold grabbed him and whispered strongly, "James, I don't want you getting any closer. If either of those elephants charges toward us, I want you to run into the jungle as fast as you can. Don't stop. Don't look back. Do you understand me?"

James, his eyes wide with excitement, answered, "Yes, Pa. I will run. Fast, Pa. Fast."

"Good boy," Harold said as he moved to get a closer shot.

Paul was slightly to Harold's left as they both set up for the kill. Harold nodded to Paul, indicating he would take the shot.

The sound was deafening as the gun fired. The giant elephant went down immediately. It was a clean shot, entering the animal's brain from the hole in its skull directly behind its ear.

The reaction of the other elephant was completely unexpected. Instead of dashing off through the jungle in panic, it turned toward them in full charge. Harold did not have time to reload. Paul, to Harold's right could not get a clear shot through the dense trees and bush. He yelled, "Run! Run! Get out!"

The natives were running at full speed as Harold and Paul cut through the jungle and caught up with them. Glancing over his shoulder to see where the elephant was, Harold gasped in horror.

James had not run. He had stopped to climb a tree. The elephant ran directly into the tree, knocking James to the ground where the elephant stomped and gored him.

Harold stopped instantly, dropped to his knee and fired toward the elephant. He didn't have a hope of killing it at this angle. He wasn't even sure he'd hit it, but the giant beast bellowed and thrashed off into the jungle, splintering trees and shredding vines as it ran off into the distance.

Harold and Paul ran to James. His body was a bloody mess. "James, James. Why didn't you run, man?" Harold asked.

"I'm sorry, Pa. I'm sorry," he whispered. "I see Jesus coming, Pa. He's coming for me. It's beautiful, Pa. It's beautiful." James closed his eyes and was gone.

They returned to New Hope carrying as much of the elephant meat as they could, but there would be no celebrating this time. As badly as the meat was needed, they had paid a terribly high price for it.

The hunting party walked slowly into town; eyes downcast. Harold and Paul were in the lead, with Harold carrying James' body.

They walked to James's house, where his mother sat silently rocking gently back and forth, tears running down her face. Laying the body before her, Harold knelt. He, too, was crying. "Mama, I am so sorry. I'm so sorry."

The two of them stayed there for a long time unable to give words to their hurt and grief but comforted by each other's presence.

In the moment, Ella wasn't sure which of them she felt sorriest for. She had never seen Harold as hurt. And how could a mother ever live through the death of her son?

Harold was a great storyteller and reveled in sharing tales of their lives and adventures in Africa with friends and family back in America. But in all their years together, Ella could only remember a handful of times when Harold told the story of that hunt and James's death. It remained forever too painful.

The next few months were busy for them, which was good for Harold, taking his mind off what had happened to James. Ella was helping at the morning clinic, teaching Bible study and sewing classes, and getting a garden started so they would have fresh vegetables. Harold was directing most of the construction work on houses for the lepers and their families and additional housing for the missionaries.

They missed Ruth and Esther, but the work helped keep their minds occupied. Letters from Ruth and from Ella's sister, Lillian, came often enough that they knew Ruth was alright.

As for Esther, they rarely heard from her, so they were left to wonder. They had received a seven-word telegram, delivered by a runner from Cape Palmas telling them Esther had at least made it to Hillcrest. It read, "Esther arrived safely and with a big smile." That was all.

Another project keeping Harold and Ella busy was construction of their own home on the mission station. The American Leprosy Society donated money to help pay for the materials, and the Landruses set about planning and building with excitement and enthusiasm.

Ella was elated at being able to build her own house. She selected a wonderful setting on a small rise near the edge of the mission compound. They could clear the jungle around it, leaving open grass to the dirt road in front and grass on the right side and rear for about fifty feet before reaching the edge of the thick green jungle forest.

On the left, they created a large field of gently sloping grass, which the native boys kept trimmed with their cutlasses so they could play soccer.

The house had a wide covered porch across the front and down the left side, perfect for sitting and talking during the heat of the day. It was constructed like an American house, with two-by-four stud walls, plastered inside and out. The wood used, however, even for the studs, was mahogany so the termites wouldn't eat it. The roof was of galvanized, corrugated steel which, when it rained each day, generated a roar so loud virtually all conversation ceased.

Constructing Harold and Ella's New Hope Town house.

The first floor had a living room with a dining area; two bedrooms; the kitchen, with its wood-burning stove and oven; and, wonder of wonders, an indoor bathroom. Upstairs was a large attic with room for plenty of storage; Harold's shortwave radio gear, its antennae sticking up outside above the roof; and a table with chairs where they could read, write letters home, or even play games at night. Ella loved to play games.

As part of the construction, Harold rigged gutters to collect rainwater off the roof and channel it into four fifty-five-gallon drums on stilts at the back of the house.

These were high enough off the ground to supply running water to the kitchen and to a shower in the bathroom and to make a flush toilet operate. "Nothing like living in the Ritz," Harold grinned as he demonstrated his handiwork to Ella. It was the first flush toilet they had ever had in the bush. On special occasions, they even asked Cook Daniel to heat some water on the stove and then pour it into the drums so they could have a warm shower. Ella couldn't believe the luxury. It was almost decadent.

They also had lots of visitors, all anxious to see what was happening out there in the middle of the jungle. For Harold and Ella, the most important of these visitors was their dear friend and pastor, Dr. Britton.

When he had learned the Assemblies of God had grounded Harold, Dr. Britton knew what a devastating blow it had to be, both to Harold and to Ella. He decided he needed to travel to Liberia to talk with them and to encourage them. Besides, it would give him an opportunity to see their work firsthand and to better know how the folks at Bethany could further support their ministry.

Dr. Britton arrived on the Pan Am flight from America, via Dakar, Senegal, and was met by Harold, Ella, and Paul at Roberts Field. They took a small boat from there up the river, in a torrential downpour, to the mission station at Owens Grove. Dr. Britton was drenched but enjoyed every minute of it.

Owens Grove was a beautiful mission compound. Miss Mildred Dunklee and Miss Opal Poag, the missionaries there, had built a wonderful Bible school complex to train native pastors. They were joined by Bob and Olga Renfroe who had helped with the construction.

A couple of days later, Paul flew Dr. Britton to Neweka, where Harold met them with the jeep and drove them to New Hope.

Dr. Britton was amazed at what Ma Steidel and her team, including the Landruses, had accomplished. He wanted to see it all, to visit every house, to walk to the entrance of the colony so he would know where Harold's Road would begin, and to hear their plans for expanding the ministry.

One evening as they sat talking quietly around the dinner table in Harold and Ella's newly completed house, Dr. Britton asked, "Harold, I don't want to open an old wound, but I want to say I know how disappointed you are about not being allowed to fly."

The subject was one Harold and Ella seldom discussed, and Harold was taken aback to have it before them once again. Dr. Britton was correct, it was an old wound—and really not all that old. It still hurt to think about it and to talk about it. "I appreciate that, Dr. Britton. But I've tried to put it behind me as best I can."

"I know, Harold," Dr. Britton responded gently. "The only reason I've brought it up is I want you to know, if you want to fly, you have our blessing to do so. Bethany will stand behind you. If you want to withdraw from the Assemblies of God and go back to flying, we will continue to support you in every way we can, both financially and with our prayers. We think that much of you and believe in your ministry."

Harold and Ella were both dumbfounded. They simply hadn't expected Dr. Britton to say anything like this. They hadn't expected the subject to even be addressed.

After a long pause, Harold replied, "Dr. Britton, I can't tell you how much it means to Ella and me for you to stand behind us in this way." Then he went on. "I don't understand why the Lord has allowed this to happen to us. Flying is about the greatest thing in the world to me. But we came out here under the Assemblies of God, and I figure we need to stay under their authority, as much as I'd like to take you up on your offer."

"Well, I wasn't encouraging you to do so. I just wanted to assure you that, if you did, we'd be with you. I think you've made the right decision, and I'm sure the Lord will honor you for it." Then he added with a grin and a twinkle in his eye, "We'll just have to keep an eye out to see how and when He does so, won't we?"

Chapter 13
Heartbreak

In early 1956, Harold began exploring the possibility of building the New Hope road in earnest. But as he met with other missionaries when he was in Pleebo or Cape Palmas or Monrovia and explained what he intended to do, they told him he was out of his mind. He could never get through the jungle or over the steep, muddy mountains and then construct bridges that would survive the ravages of the rivers.

He knew it would be difficult, but he also knew it was essential to making New Hope what all of them wanted it to be and, more importantly to Harold, what he believed the Lord wanted it to be.

He already had a good work crew headed by one of the lepers whose name was Sunday. What he needed to do was establish a path for the road to follow through the jungle eighteen miles from the entrance of New Hope Town all the way to the government road.

He and Paul, along with Sunday and a few members of the crew, left early one morning, crossed the big river at the edge of town, and began hacking their way toward the government road. Initially, their intent was only to mark a trail. Once they had set the route they would begin clearing and building.

The going was extremely difficult. Some of the route was through what they called "low bush," meaning a massed tangle of jungle vines and vegetation so thick they could see no more than a few yards ahead of them. The "low bush" rose perhaps thirty to forty feet in height.

Other areas along the path Harold was selecting were covered with "high bush," trees seventy-five to more than a hundred feet high, with vines spreading across their canopy, creating an almost tunnel-like feeling. Here they didn't have to hack and cut their way through because the vegetation was above them. The growth overhead made it dark enough on the ground that very little vegetation could grow there. However, in these areas, they would have to remove many more trees in order to make the trail into a road wide enough for trucks to pass.

Cutting the trees would provide them with the timber necessary to construct more than twenty-five bridges they would need to build over the streams and rivers crisscrossing the route. One of those bridges would have to be more than 140 feet long, reaching across the river at the entrance to New Hope Town.

Once he had marked out the path, Harold launched the project by dividing the route into seven segments, one for each of the tribes represented in the population at New Hope Town. He marked a tree with his cutlass at each end of the segment and then explained to the work team from that tribe they were responsible for clearing a fifteen- to twenty-foot-wide roadway through their segment along the path he had marked. He and his more skilled crew would focus on the bridges and the removal of the larger trees and stumps the crews could not handle.

What they were attempting to do was difficult under the best of conditions and with the best of equipment. They were a crew of partially disabled lepers, led by a missionary who had a four-wheel drive jeep with a wench. The only other equipment they had was their cutlasses and a few primitive handsaws and shovels.

The heat; the virtually daily rain; the raging streams and rivers; the gooey, sticky mud; and the mosquitoes made the project a nightmare.

After several months, with little progress to show for their efforts, Harold was beginning to question whether they could do this. But he was not about to give up. He believed the road was necessary, and he believed God wanted it. He would press on no matter how impossible it seemed.

In mid-1956, Paul Boyer and his wife, Elmira, arrived at New Hope. They were missionaries but were there only on a short-term basis specifically for Boyer to lend a hand with Harold's road. His help and encouragement were an enormous boost to Harold's spirits and to the project.

Boyer also brought chainsaws and other hand tools to help speed the work. He was astonished at how little Harold and his crew had to work with and amazed at what they had already accomplished. In October, he wrote home, "It is unbelievable that 300 lepers, many of them crippled, are building this road."

Over the course of the next dozen years or so, the Boyers made numerous trips to New Hope Town, and raised thousands of dollars in the United States to pay for materials and equipment to complete and then maintain the road.

Some months after Dr. Britton's visit, Harold and Ella had another visitor. A new superintendent had been appointed over the Liberian field. His last name was Phillips, and he wanted to spend a few days seeing firsthand what was going on at New Hope Town.

He was impressed with the progress on the road. About eight miles of the road was open, with a dozen or so bridges.

In a letter home, Ella described the road at this point as "pretty good," which, for her, meant they didn't have to get out to walk or to push the jeep. She did acknowledge it took more than an hour to drive the eight miles Harold and his crew had made at least passable. If he worked at it, Harold could now take the jeep through almost all the way to the government road, but there was still a lot of work to be done before his "road" could be called a real road.

At the house one evening Brother Phillips and Harold were talking about how important the road would be. "We'll really be able to bring supplies in here once the road is finished. It'll make all the difference in the world," Harold assured him. "But supplies and mail are sure a problem in the meantime!"

"What if you had a plane, at least until the road is finished?" Brother Phillips asked. "I understand you're a pilot."

Harold gave him a cold stare, not quite sure what the man was getting at, "Well, sir, you understand correctly. We have a plane, too! But it's gathering rust sitting in the hangar at Pleebo, thanks to the field council."

"So I hear, so I hear," the superintendent replied. "You're a good missionary, Brother Landrus, and you've accepted the authority of the council even though you didn't agree with their actions." He paused and then went on. "It seems to me the need to have you flying again is far greater than the need for someone to prove a point. I know you have more than enough work here, but I think it would help if you could fly when you need to. You'd better pull that plane out of the hangar and get in the air again."

Harold was stunned. He sat speechless. All he could do was grin. Then finally he called Ella. "Did you hear that, Ella? I'm a bush pilot again! Thank you, Lord!" Then he added, "Wait 'til Dr. Britton hears about this!"

In addition to his work on the road, Harold immediately began flying again. But his priority remained getting the road built.

~

Permission to fly again brought Harold more joy than he could imagine. Whenever the need arose, and occasionally when there was little need at all, he would taxi down the Neweka airstrip and then, dodging ruts and rocks, hurtle down the runway, managing to get airborne just in time to clear the giant trees that seemed to be rushing toward him from the jungle edge.

Flying with Harold was an adventure in itself. Taking off was a time to hold your breath. Landing was, if anything, more precarious. Frequently, Harold would have to buzz the field to signal he wanted to land and to allow time for the natives, or one of the missionary kids, to chase the cows off the landing strip.

Young Bob Renfroe incurred Harold's considerable displeasure by herding the cows off the strip but forgetting to keep them off. As Harold brought his plane down, he narrowly averted disaster when he nearly collided with a pair of cows ambling across his landing path, oblivious to their peril.

In the air, he often "treated" his passengers to a variety of dives, spins, and rolls. By then, he had logged nearly 2,500 hours flying over the rolling green jungles of Liberia.

~

As Christmas approached, they began preparing for special evangelistic meetings to be held at New Hope Town. Harold and Paul went elephant hunting, intent on providing meat for the visitors coming for the meetings and for the entire colony for the holiday season.

Their success was beyond anything they could have imagined. Paul understated the event considerably when he wrote to his Grandma Pratt, "Dad and I went elephant hunting to try to get some meat for the lepers' Christmas. He shot one elephant, and I shot three, so they ate a lot of meat. One ivory tusk measured a little over sixty inches. There is a lot of meat in four elephants."

The celebration over the success of the hunt lasted for days and added to the normal joy and excitement of the special meetings. Though they didn't want it and tried to avoid it, Harold and particularly Paul were hailed as heroes.

The people ate meat until they could eat no more, and then set about the task of drying and smoking the mounds of meat remaining. It seemed there was elephant meat hanging everywhere. The meat would last them for months and inject a much-needed boost of protein to what was normally a very low-protein diet.

⌒

Harold and Paul had been busy flying people in for the meetings, including the Melvin Petersens and their two daughters.

When the meetings were over, Harold told them he would fly them the short hop from New Hope, actually the Neweka airstrip, to their home at the mission station at Pleebo.

Harold carefully checked the plane, as he always did before taking off. Then the Petersens boarded. It was a tight fit for all of them and a little uncomfortable for Mrs. Petersen because she was pregnant. She asked if there were too many for the plane, but Harold assured her, since two of them were children, he wasn't worried about exceeding the aircraft's weight capacity as far as cargo was concerned.

The takeoff was remarkably smooth. At about four hundred feet altitude, Harold began a gentle turn, banking toward the coast and Cape Palmas, a path which would take them almost directly over Pleebo.

Suddenly, the engine coughed and sputtered. Harold checked the instruments. Everything seemed in order. The engine coughed again. The Petersens looked in worry at each other. Then the engine quit entirely.

After what had been a rather loud drone when the engine was running, the silence was stunning.

Harold hit the starter button. Nothing happened. He tried again. Same results. *Lord, we need your help here*, he prayed silently.

He put the nose down and began a slow glide, bringing the plane around in an attempt to return to the airstrip. The Petersens were frightened but remained calm. Harold wasn't afraid. He knew what he was doing. Besides, as always, he didn't think about what jeopardy he might be in. God had brought him there. God was responsible for their well-being. For Harold, there was no sense worrying about it.

The plane was gliding fairly well, straining to stay airborne and to make the distance they needed. However, it soon became apparent to Harold, they wouldn't make it to the airstrip. They simply hadn't been high enough when the engine quit.

"Tighten your seat belts, everybody," he said calmly. "We're going to crash."

～

Ella and nurse Ellen McCormick had seen Harold and the Petersens off at the airstrip and were leisurely walking past the girls' school at Neweka and back to New Hope a short distance away. As they walked and talked quietly, they were unaware of the drama unfolding in the air above them.

They could hear the drone of the plane's engine but were not paying any attention to it.

Then Ella stopped. Ellen looked at her quizzically, "What's the matter, Ella?"

"The plane. I don't hear the plane. Something is wrong. They're going to need help," and she took off running back toward the airstrip.

～

Above them about a mile away, Harold was trying to figure out how to put the plane down. With the trees and jungle, he knew it wasn't going to be pretty.

As they glided just above the treetops, he saw three tall trees looming ahead of them. Beyond them was a clearing not much bigger than the size of a large house. He would try to drop it in there. He later said he couldn't believe how the Lord gave him peace and calm through the ordeal.

He pulled back on the controls, and the plane simply quit flying. It dropped about forty feet, hit the ground, and then slammed into the trees. The propeller and the right wing took the brunt of the impact, but the entire plane was crumpled and broken. The plane came to rest on the ground, tangled in trees.

The impact threw Harold forward and smashed his face into the controls, breaking his front teeth. The Petersens were equally thrown about. All ended up with cuts and bruises, but none was seriously hurt.

Dazed and stunned, still strapped in their seats, they all began to stir. Grateful they had survived, Harold turned to Melvin sitting next to him, and said, "The Lord surely saved us. Let's get out of this thing."

~

Ella and Ellen arrived at the airstrip just as a young native girl emerged from the jungle running toward them sobbing. "Ma, Ma. They crashed, Ma," she yelled.

"I know," Ella said quietly, trying to calm her. "Now, tell us where they are." The girl did so, pointing in the direction of the crash.

Ella and Ellen jumped into the jeep and raced to the far end of the airstrip. The downed plane was several hundred yards into the jungle, but they couldn't see it.

In the plane, attempting to get out of his straps, Harold heard the jeep and began calling out to Ella.

At last, Ella heard him, and she and Ellen began working their way through the jungle. By the time they reached the plane, Harold and his passengers had managed to get out and were seated on the ground nursing their minor wounds.

Seeing Harold's bloody mouth gave Ella a start, but she was just glad he and the others weren't injured badly.

When Harold checked the plane later, he found water had worked into the carburetor, causing the problem. The plane was a total loss. It was well beyond repair.

Repairs to Harold's teeth came courtesy of an American dentist named Spencer, who made a partial to replace Harold's broken front teeth.

That was the last time Harold flew an airplane. He didn't have the money for a new one. Besides, he was far too busy with the road to be flying much anyway. He thought he might try raising money for another when they went home on furlough in a couple of years, but ended up not doing so.

Ella was just as glad Harold was staying on the ground. As far as she was concerned, it was far safer for him. Besides, another missionary couple had been killed when their plane crashed just off the Cape Palmas coast. No, she didn't mind at all that Harold wasn't flying any more. She still had Paul to worry about though. He seemed to be flying all the time.

❧

Half a world away, Ruth had graduated with the dental assistant class of 1955 at Pasadena City College and, as Christmas 1956 neared, was working in a dental office in Alhambra. Like most missionary kids plucked from the mission field and thrown into life in America, Ruth had struggled with the adjustment but was managing.

When she first arrived back in the United States, she didn't know anything American kids her age knew. The food, the clothing, the music, and even what people thought and cared about were all completely different from what she had known. She looked like them and talked like them, so they expected her to think and understand life the way they did. Of course, she did not.

After a while, she gave up trying to explain to her friends where and how she had grown up. They could never understand what her life had been, and in truth, they didn't really care. Over time, in order to better fit in, she spoke less and less about Africa. Because she missed her life in Africa so much, and it hurt so badly to remember it, it simply became less painful to get on with her new life in America and to let her life in Africa slip into a quiet, special memory in her mind and heart.

In Nigeria, Esther and most of her classmates at Hillcrest cried themselves to sleep every night. Hillcrest was an excellent school, and the staff and dorm parents were good and caring people. Yet there was no way they could fully understand or change the emotional pain these children were going through. It was just something the children had to endure.

It was particularly difficult for Esther. During the Christmas season and for summer recess, most of the other children got to go home to be with their families.

Because she had so far to travel, Esther only went home for Christmas. For summer break, she couldn't. If she was invited, she could go with one of the other students to their home. If not, she stayed with one of the staff families at Hillcrest.

The emotional and psychological trauma Esther had endured being sent away, on her own, at eight years of age was enormous. It was something that shaped who and what she was and would become. Through it all, the Lord was with her. He helped her cope. He made sure it didn't destroy her. By the time she left Africa at fifteen, she had grown to be a strong, resourceful, independent young woman.

***

Christmas 1956 was a happy time for Harold, Ella, and Paul. Esther was coming home from Nigeria. It had been nearly a year since she was last with them. They were anxiously anticipating having her home for the holidays.

With communication difficult between Liberia and Nigeria, they didn't know exactly when Esther would be coming. The Renfroes offered to drive in from Owens Grove to meet the sole daily Pan Am plane until she arrived. She could stay with them for a day or two, and then Paul could fly up to take her to New Hope.

Esther loved that Christmas. She was where she wanted to be, and they were having a great time. The family even took the little boat Paul had purchased and went fishing on the Cavalla River. Cruising down the river to its mouth at the Atlantic Ocean, Paul shot crocodiles lining the banks and then managed to catch a 145-pound tarpon out of the river.

For Esther, it was wonderful, but she knew it wouldn't last. On January 13, 1957, Paul flew her to Monrovia, terrorizing her with his aerobatics along the way. She was headed back to Jos and to the completely different world at Hillcrest Academy, unaware Harold and Ella's world was about to become completely different as well.

———

A few days later, Paul flew to Pleebo for supplies and to fill their empty five-gallon cans. They needed gas for Harold's jeep. They also wanted to have spare gas on hand at Neweka for Paul's plane. He planned to return in the afternoon so they could all celebrate Harold's fifty-second birthday together.

When he landed at Pleebo, he decided he needed to have his engine checked and flew to Cape Palmas to have it looked at by one of LaTourneau's mechanics. They were the best available. It meant he'd have to stay overnight in the mission house at Cape Palmas and would miss Harold's party, but he didn't want to risk any trouble with his plane.

The next morning, with the plane fully checked, Paul and a passenger were going to head back to Neweka. However, he had been asked to drop a letter for one of the priests at the Catholic mission at Grandcess, north along the coast.

Accustomed to such requests, he gladly obliged even though it would take him and his passenger significantly out of their way. Paul began their flight up the coast. It was a beautiful morning, and he was thoroughly enjoying himself, thinking, *What a great day. And here I am, doing what I most like to do. Well, what I like to do most after hunting,* he corrected himself. *Thanks, God!*

He easily located Grandcess and altered course to fly directly over the mission station.

Though it was on the coast, Grandcess was an isolated town, with no communication to the outside world except by jungle trail or from the air as Paul was providing.

There it is, he thought. He adjusted his speed slightly and dropped the plane to just above the treetops. Then he opened the window and set up for the drop. He had done it many times before, but timing a letter drop was always tricky because he never knew how the letter might float in the air. At just the right instant, he pushed the letter through the window and watched it quickly fall away. *That ought to do it. It should land right in the middle of their compound! I'll bank around just to make sure.*

He banked sharply to turn back over the mission. As he did so, a sudden gust of wind caught the plane and flipped it over. That close to the ground he didn't have a chance to regain control. The plane smashed, upside down, into some palm trees a few hundred feet from the compound.

In the mission, the priests had heard his plane coming and had gone out in time to see him drop the letter. Going to retrieve it, they watched in horror as, in midair, the plane was thrown over on its back and then plunged into the trees.

They ran to the crash site where they found Paul's passenger dazed, with cuts and bruises, but apparently not seriously hurt. Paul was a different story. He was still in the cockpit with obvious head wounds and lacerations.

Working quickly, they struggled to extricate him from the wreckage. He was unconscious, and they carried him to the mission. There, one of the priests who had some limited first aid training stitched his head and facial wounds. They also determined he had a broken leg. He remained alive but unconscious. A little later, Paul regained consciousness and was praying in the Palipo dialect and asking for his mother.

While they were able to bandage Paul's exterior wounds and splint his fractured leg, there was no way they could know about or treat the internal injuries he had suffered. Despite their efforts and their fervent prayers, Paul died four hours after the crash. As he died, he continued praying in a native language. It was January 22, 1957. He was twenty-two years old.

Paul's plane crash.

Grandcess is two days' walk from Cape Palmas and a day and a half from New Hope Town. Immediately following the crash, the priests dispatched a runner to carry the news to New Hope.

When the runner left, the news was Paul had crashed, but he was still clinging to life. It took eighteen hours for the runner to deliver the message to Harold and Ella.

Their response was to ask all the missionaries and the native Christians to be in prayer for Paul.

Ella's greatest fear when Harold and Paul were flying was they might crash and she would never see them again, never know what happened to them, never get to say good-bye. She prayed and prayed Paul would not die and, if he did, she would somehow be able to see him. She didn't hold out much hope for the latter. If Paul died, they would have to bury him immediately, in Grandcess, before his body began decaying in the blistering tropical heat and humidity. She and Harold could not get to Grandcess in time. "Please, Lord," she prayed that night, "let him be alive. If not, at least let me see him."

They sent a runner to Pleebo to tell the Crabaughs of the crash and to ask Brother Crabaugh, who was still flying Harold's original plane, to fly to Grandcess as quickly as possible to determine what had happened.

The runner arrived in Pleebo ten hours later. It was much too late for Crabaugh to attempt flying to Grandcess, as night was nearly upon them, but he did so anyway.

~

Several years before Paul's crash, one of the priests at Grandcess had become gravely ill. There appeared to be no hope of his survival, and the other priests had sent for embalming fluids in anticipation of his death.

Then the Lord provided a miracle; the man recovered. When the embalming fluids and other materials arrived, they were not needed and had been carefully stored away in a closet at the mission.

Now they were brought out, and the priests tenderly prepared Paul's body with them. It would mean his body could be returned to New Hope for burial. Ella and Harold could see his body and say their good-byes. The Lord had provided the answer to Ella's prayer, years before it was needed.

~

Crabaugh arrived at Grandcess safely, landing on the beach just as the last glow of sunset was disappearing. He spent the night with the priests, learning the details of Paul's death and sharing with them the worth and meaning of his life.

The next morning, he flew to Neweka with Paul's body. He landed at 10:00 a.m. and was met by Harold and Ella and the people from New Hope and Neweka. It was only then Harold and Ella learned Paul had died. Until then, they thought he might still be alive. The Lord, once again, had answered Ella's prayers. She and Harold got to see Paul one last time and to say good-bye.

Native carpenters prepared Paul's coffin out of mahogany. It was their finest work, a token of their love and respect, not only for Paul but also for Harold and Ella.

There were floral wreaths made of flowers from the area. The pallbearers were Paul's closest native friends. More than eight hundred attended his funeral. All the missionaries were there, as were the people of

New Hope Town and natives from throughout the country. They wanted to pay their respects—to say farewell, to remember one of their own. For Paul was one of them. He spoke their languages. He knew their ways. He was their friend, their brother.

Paul's grave at Newaka.

Harold and Ella were devastated by Paul's death, though they accepted it as they had so many other things. It was fundamental to all they believed that God was in charge. He alone controlled what happened to them and to everyone else. Their responsibility was to trust Him and to love Him.

Two days after Paul's death, Ella wrote to her parents and to Ruth, "It makes a big vacancy in our home, but Paul is with the Lord tonight. We're so glad we know he is with the Lord. Though we are bereaved by Paul's 'Homegoing,' we are comforted to know we'll see him again when we meet our Jesus face-to-face."

More than a decade later, an American friend of Paul's visited the Landruses and went deep into the bush hunting with Harold. As he met natives along the way, he discovered, among virtually every tribe he encountered, the natives sang a song about Paul, which included the words, "Don't cry, Ma. Don't cry, Pa. Paul was our friend. Now he is with the Lord."

In Nigeria, Esther was called from class and told the tragic news of Paul's death by one of her teachers, Miss Wimberly. Esther was beyond consolation.

She had just been with him at Christmas. He had flown her to Monrovia to catch her flight back to Nigeria. She could not believe he was gone. She could see his smile. How could God do this? She hadn't had the chance to say good-bye. She hadn't been able to say she loved him.

Alone and not yet eleven, Esther believed she couldn't stand the heartache she felt. It was more than she thought she could bear. But through the tears and pain, through the loneliness and broken heart, she did bear it.

Harold and Ella had sent a telegram to Dr. Britton telling him of Paul's death and asking him to break the news to Ruth.

When she answered her front door, Ruth was delighted to see Dr. Britton, but she could immediately tell by his face something was very wrong. When he told her about Paul, she burst into tears. All he could do was hold her gently and let her cry.

She and Paul had grown up together in the bush. Four years older than she was, he was her big brother. They had been separated since she'd come to the States, but Africa had bound them together in ways even they could not fully understand. She did not know how she was going to face him being gone.

Ruth and Esther loved Paul with all their hearts. He was their big brother. He teased them. He tormented them. He laughed with them. But they always knew he loved them and would be there for them no matter what. Not being able to see him, to tell him good-bye, to say they loved him, was one of the most difficult things both of them had to face.

A few days after Paul's funeral, as Harold and Ella began picking up the pieces of their lives, a native woman came to Ella in tears. "Ma, I will miss you so," she wailed.

"What do you mean?" Ella asked.

"Now Paul has died, we know you will be leaving us," the woman said.

"No, no," Ella assured her. "We aren't leaving. God called us to this place. Our ministry is here. We miss Paul terribly, but God doesn't make any mistakes. He gave Paul to us for a short time, and now He has taken him away. But the Bible tells us all things work together for good to those who love the Lord."

Less than a week later, Ella wrote a newsletter to their friends and supporters in America telling of Paul's death and pledging to them, "Harold and I have determined in our hearts to give more of ourselves than ever before for the cause of Christ. Life is short, and only what we do for Christ will last."

With that, they plunged into their work with even greater intensity. By April 1957, they reported they were "now treating six-hundred patients for leprosy, so have a big family and hundreds of others begging to come here. The Lord has been blessing New Hope and we had seventy-eight saved … in our last revival, for which we praise God."

On the construction front, work on the road was steadily progressing. By the time they were ready to return to the United States on furlough, they could drive all the way to the government road and on to Cape Palmas. The road wasn't really finished, but it was usable. More work on it would be waiting for Harold when they returned.

Stuck in the mud during work on the road to New Hope Town.

December 1957 was approaching, and Harold and Ella decided, when Esther returned from Nigeria for her holiday break, they would leave for furlough. This would allow them to have Christmas in America with Ella's family.

The three of them departed from Monrovia on December 16, flying for the first time all the way to Los Angeles. It would, however, be a very long journey. Their route took them to Lisbon, Portugal, and then on to Boston. From Boston, they flew to New York and then on to Los Angeles. The entire trip took forty hours.

Tired but grateful to be back, they were greeted at the airport in Los Angeles by Ruth and her husband and by Helen Bridges, their dear friend and encourager from Bethany. Ruth was pregnant with her first child. It would be a boy, and they would name him Paul.

It had been a grueling, difficult term. In addition to the day-to-day struggles and hardships, in three short years, they had suffered through their first term without Ruth, Harold's grounding, Esther being sent to Nigeria, James's death, Harold's crash, and Paul's death.

It had tested them to their limits. They returned with deep wounds to their hearts and spirits, wounds that would take a long, long while to heal. But there was no better place to begin recovery than in the arms of their family and their dear friends and supporters at Bethany.

Chapter 14
New Hope

After only eleven short months in America, Harold and Ella and Esther were once again packing their travel-worn suitcases. They were anxious to get "home" to Liberia. They enjoyed being with friends and family, but they didn't feel they belonged in California. There was purpose and meaning to their lives in Africa.

They traveled once again to New York and, following a few days of sightseeing, including a climb to the top of the Statue of Liberty, on November 1, 1958, they sailed aboard the luxury liner the SS *United States* bound for England.

They were shipping a Dodge Power Wagon with them. Harold had purchased it with money provided by Bethany. Its four-wheel drive, heavy-duty suspension, and rugged construction made it a perfect vehicle for them at New Hope Town and for helping him with his work on the road.

It was a particularly joyous voyage for them, not only because of the splendid accommodations of the ship, but also because they were being accompanied to England by fellow missionaries Janie and Billy Reames, a friend named Bernice van Antwerp, and by dear Helen Bridges. Helen was on her way around the world to visit missionaries in Europe, India, and the Far East.

They all stayed in England for a few days and then Harold, Ella, and Esther bid them farewell and flew to Liberia, via Lisbon, Portugal.

When they arrived in Liberia, they stayed a short time with Opal Poag and Mildred Dunklee at Owens Grove, outside of Monrovia. Leroy Ward was now flying as a missionary in Liberia and flew Esther to Sinoe and then on to Gedapo. She would be returning to boarding school in Nigeria in January, but Harold and Ella wanted Miss Cleft at Gedapo to help her with her studies until then. Esther would join them for Christmas at New Hope Town and then journey on to Nigeria from there.

A grand celebration awaited them as they returned to New Hope. They even managed to drive in using Harold's road, which they had decided to name the Paul Landrus Memorial Road.

On the drive in, Harold realized he still had a great deal of work to do, but the Dodge Power Wagon handled the road well. It sure beat walking!

⌐◡⌐

Ella was delighted to be back. She felt she belonged. With Cook Daniel humming merrily to himself as he baked bread in the small cast-iron wood-burning combination stove and oven in the kitchen, Ella felt totally content. She dearly loved her big house and their work at New Hope. She loved that Maryann had arrived to work beside her. After all the help she had been at Palipo and Bwah, Maryann had become like a member of the family.

Ella spent the bulk of her time teaching Bible studies to the women and to the children. She regularly had 150 bright-eyed children to teach and more than a hundred in her women's Bible study group. She also taught sewing and quilting to the women.

Because they occupied the "big house," they entertained most of the visitors to New Hope. After so many years of isolation in Bwebo, Palipo, and Bwah, Ella was particularly grateful for the companionship of other missionaries on the same station and the company of frequent guests.

Among those guests were Paul and Elmira Boyer. They were totally committed to the work at New Hope and gave generously of their time and resources to help make it succeed. On each return to the United States, Paul would raise financial support for the work on the road. He even raised funds to purchase and plant hundreds of rubber trees on the mission station grounds in the hope, over time, New Hope Town could become as financially independent as possible.

⌐◡⌐

While the Landruses were on furlough, Norm and Betty Backman and their three children had joined the work at New Hope. They were one of the first lay missionary couples ever appointed by the Assemblies of God.

Norm was a mechanic, and his ability to keep equipment up and running was a major factor in enabling New Hope Town to grow and develop. As the road project continued, more and more heavy equipment was required. Eventually, they had a grader, a dump truck, and even a tractor.

The tractor was a John Deere, trucked to New York by Harold's brother and shipped by freighter to Liberia. It became an invaluable help in further development of the road.

In addition to the road construction equipment, Norm maintained the ragged old jeep, the Dodge Power Wagon, the light plant, and much more. With little in the way of spare parts, Norm managed to keep it all working, helping to bring hope, help, and the life-changing Gospel to the people in the jungles of West Africa.

Later, Norm and Betty were ordained as ministers by the Assemblies of God and went on to serve just north of Liberia in the rather tiny nation of Sierra Leone. They had a long, effective ministry there among the people in the town of Sefadu in the eastern section of the country. By the time they retired, they had built four beautiful churches in Sierra Leone, testifying for the cause of Christ in the heart of this strongly Muslim country.

Harold continued hunting. But the truth was much of the joy had gone out of it for him, now that he could no longer share it with his son.

It was the same with flying. After his last crash and Paul's death, Harold was content to stay on the ground, much to Ella's relief. She did, though, frequently see him looking at planes flown by other missionaries, like Crabaugh and Mason and Ward, with a certain longing in his eyes.

Harold's big focus remained on the road. It was far from finished. And once it was, it would take most of his time and energy to maintain it as their lifeline for supplies from the outside world.

He had considerable incentive to get the road completed quickly. They learned William V. S. Tubman, President of the Republic of Liberia, was going to visit New Hope after the first of the year.

~

President's Tubman's visit was a time of unrivaled excitement at New Hope Town. In anticipation, work on the road went on at a feverish pace. All of the huts and buildings were newly whitewashed. Ella and Cook Daniel struggled with the task of preparing to feed the presidential party, more than thirty in all, as well as the large number of missionary guests who would be there.

On March 20, 1959, Paul Boyer escorted President Tubman and his entourage to New Hope Town, down the Paul Landrus Memorial Road. They crossed the final "big" bridge over the river at the entrance to the colony and drove through the main street, lined with cheering lepers and their families.

Ella standing on the "big bridge" at the entrance to New Hope Town.

They stopped at Harold and Ella's house pausing for introductions and pictures. Then the President stood on the porch and addressed the people.

When the President's speech was over, everyone sat down to the dinner Ella and Cook Daniel had waiting.

Ella and Daniel had prepared palm butter and rice, with chicken. This was considered to be a particularly special meal, and it helped that the ingredients were readily available at New Hope Town. Only after the president arrived did they learn he wouldn't eat chicken.

The witch doctor present at the future president's birth had prescribed a personal law for the little boy, which decreed he could not eat anything with feathers. Years later, though he was an educated, enlightened leader of his nation, President Tubman remained influenced by the superstitions and rituals of his native tribe. He would not eat chicken or meat from any other foul.

It would have been a significant breach of etiquette for Ella to serve the president chicken. Fortunately, she had some canned ham in the kerosene refrigerator and quickly substituted it for the chicken in the president's meal.

As the President and his group left the compound, the missionaries gathered to discuss the events of the day and to speculate as to whether he had been favorably impressed with their work. He had been most gracious in his remarks, and they felt the government would remain supportive of their efforts.

Little did they know how supportive President Tubman's government would become.

Not long after the president's visit, they received word he had granted New Hope nearly nine thousand additional acres of land. Paul Boyer had room to plant all the rubber trees he wanted to help finance the New Hope ministry.

⌒

Esther had left for school in Nigeria in January, before President Tubman's visit.

Much to her delight, in June, Harold and Ella drove more than two thousand miles from Liberia through Cote d'Ivoire, Gold Coast, and Dahomey all the way to Hillcrest Academy in Jos, Nigeria, to visit her. They stayed for several days, meeting her teachers and friends and then began the long journey back to Liberia.

As Christmas 1959 approached, Esther was looking forward to flying home to be with Harold and Ella for the holidays. When her plane landed at Roberts Field in Liberia, however, she encountered a significant problem.

When she had left Liberia, the paperwork for her return had all been in order. She had the documents necessary for her to re-enter the country. However, unknown to her, her parents, or any of the other missionaries, during the time she had been at school, the Liberian government had changed the papers required. When she arrived, her paperwork was not acceptable.

As Esther stood, tired and somewhat confused in the customs office, Jim Barnard, a missionary who had driven in from Owens Grove to meet her, pleaded with the customs officials. "That's Pa Landrus's daughter," he shouted. "You have to let her in."

Undaunted, one official simply shook his head. "I'm sorry. I know who she is, and I know Pa Landrus. He used to fly here all the time. Nonetheless, she cannot be admitted without the proper documents. She will have to fly on to New York and apply for the right papers there."

Unable to convince them to let her into the country, Jim looked on helplessly as Esther picked up her bags and turned to reboard her airplane for the next leg of the flight to New York, via a stop in Dakar, Senegal. As she did so, she called back to him, "Tell my daddy his globe-trotting daughter is off to Dakar."

When Jim reported the situation to Harold and Ella at New Hope Town over the shortwave radio, Ella exclaimed, "But she's only thirteen years old. How can they send her away?" Then she added shaking her head, "What will she do in New York? She doesn't even have a coat, and its winter there!"

On board the Pan Am plane, Esther was upset she couldn't stay and worried about what would happen to her in New York. But with all she had experienced in her short life, she was a very independent young girl and quickly concluded the Lord would take care of her. There was nothing she could do about the problem, so there wasn't much sense getting upset over it.

Fortunately, the Pan Am flight had to stop in Dakar before heading for America. There, a change of flight crews would take place. The flight had originated in Lagos, Nigeria, where Esther had boarded. The crew knew she was a young girl traveling alone, and she had been denied entry into Liberia.

Under the circumstances, when the crew left the plane, they elected to "adopt" Esther. They decided if the Senegalese authorities would allow her into the country, she could stay with them until her paperwork could be straightened out, and she could fly back to Liberia on another Pan Am flight.

The Lord worked it out exactly that way. Esther thoroughly enjoyed staying with the stewardesses while customs officials in Senegal and Liberia worked out the details. A week later, she was once again bound for Roberts Field, followed by an uneventful clearing through customs and a joyful reunion with Harold and Ella, who had flown up to meet her.

～

While Ella continued with her Bible studies and children's work, Harold concentrated on making the road a real road. The leper colony was growing, and his road was the only means of bringing in supplies. He and his crew labored six days a week, widening and smoothing the road, building new bridges, and strengthening old ones.

The work was difficult and often dangerous, but it was not without its lighter moments.

After Harold obtained a used dump truck, the crew would scamper into the back to ride as Harold drove to the day's worksite. They laughed and chattered with one another while Harold maneuvered the steep hills and sharp turns, dodging the larger ruts as much as he could.

As he approached a steep slope one morning, Harold pressed on the clutch pedal of the old truck and reached to shift to a lower gear to better take the hill. He was thinking about the repairs they were going to make on the bridge he was driving to and was not paying particular attention to what he was doing. Instead of the gear shift, he grabbed the lever to dump the truck.

Harold didn't notice the truck hadn't shifted gears. He simply gave it more gas and started up the hill, oblivious to the fact the truck bed was beginning to rise.

In the back, the road crew at first thought the increase in the incline of the truck bed was because they were going uphill. Then they realized the truck was dumping. They looked at one another, eyes and mouths wide open in disbelief. Screaming and yelling and laughing at the same time, they grabbed the sides and tried to hang on.

Because the old engine was loud, and the truck rattled and creaked a great deal, Harold didn't notice what he had done and didn't hear the chaos behind him.

One by one, as the truck bed rose higher and higher, members of the crew lost their grips and slid out of the back of the truck, bouncing unhurt onto the road below.

Eventually, as he drove up the hill, Harold happened to glance at his rearview mirror. As he described it later, "There was that truck bed pointin' upward like a homesick angel and my crew bouncing all over the road behind."

He quickly stopped and got out. His first concern was no one was hurt. Once satisfied they were not, all he could do was laugh. For months following, the crew had something they could tease Pa Landrus about unmercifully.

There were numerous steep grades on the road, each of which held its own particular peril, when the daily rains turned the roadway into a slippery, muddy mess.

The Dodge Power Wagon had been an invaluable help with work on the road and hauling people and supplies to and from New Hope. But by then, it had seen better days. Unfortunately, its brakes had seen better days as well.

It had rained a great deal, and Harold decided to stop work early. They weren't getting much accomplished anyway. He and the crew loaded into the Dodge and began the drive back to New Hope.

They had reached the crest of the "big hill," the highest and steepest point along the road. It was raining so heavily and the windshield wipers were working so poorly, Harold had to hang his head out the side window periodically to see as they began the long, treacherous, winding descent.

Gradually, the vehicle picked up speed and Harold downshifted and applied the brakes to slow them.

He negotiated the first tight turn to the right, fighting the slippery road and the rain all the way and then prepared for the next turn—a long, sweeping one to the left.

He applied the brakes again. Nothing happened. The Dodge didn't slow at all. The grade was getting steeper, and they were gathering momentum. He tried the brakes again. The pedal went to the floor. His brakes were completely gone. He pumped them. Nothing.

With the weight of the vehicle, the slippery road, and the ever-increasing slope, they were rapidly gaining speed.

They made it through the long left turn. But as they careened down the mountain, Harold didn't think they could make the next one. It was just too sharp.

Virtually completely out of control, Harold yelled to the crew jammed in the seats behind him, "Hang on. And pray!"

Harold tried to slow them by steering into the embankment along the uphill side of the road. As the vehicle brushed the hillside it seemed to slow slightly. Then they hit a protruding rock, and the Dodge caromed off the embankment and catapulted across the road. That side had no embankment. It was a sheer drop-off of more than a hundred feet. Fighting to keep the vehicle on the road, Harold decided not to try that again.

Entering the turn, Harold didn't believe they had a chance of making it. As they turned, slipping and sliding, the vehicle began tilting, its momentum threatening to overturn them at any instant. Just as they reached the point at which Harold was sure they were going to roll, the turn straightened, and the Dodge righted itself.

Thank you, Lord, flashed through Harold's mind, followed immediately by the realization they were still gaining speed and they had no way of making the next curve, which lay immediately ahead. *We're in trouble here, Lord!*

At that moment, Harold thought of something. At the entrance to the curve, off to the right was a giant tree stump. It was the remains of one of the hardwood trees they had felled to build a bridge. "Hold on," he yelled. "Hold on!"

Flying down the hill, he hoped he could steer the flailing vehicle well enough to do what he had in mind.

There it was. Just as he'd remembered. He judged the distance carefully, knowing, if he missed, they would crash. Then he realized, if he didn't miss, it would be one whale of a crash anyway!

The Dodge roared off the road, across a few brief feet of clearing and hit the tree stump dead center. The impact was horrendous. The sound was deafening. The tree stump quivered but held. The back end of the Dodge flew in the air and Harold thought it might flip over frontwards, but it didn't. With a tremendous crunch, it slammed back to earth.

Harold had been thrown forward into the steering wheel and knew he would have some sore ribs for a while. But as he felt himself gently, he didn't detect any blood or noticeably broken bones. He turned to see how his passengers had fared. They, too, were going to be pretty sore for a few days, but other than some minor cuts and bruises, they seemed to be all right.

He smiled. "Well can you beat that! Praise God, we made it!"

He opened his door and climbed out slowly, reluctant to see the damage done to his overworked Power Wagon. To his surprise and considerable delight, the only damage he could detect was right in the middle of the normally straight front bumper. It had a half-circle-shaped indentation about eighteen inches deep, reflecting the spot it had wrapped around the tree stump.

In 1960, the Assemblies of God sent a film crew to New Hope town and produced a sixteen-millimeter sound and color motion picture called

Steps to New Hope. The film documented the work and ministry at New Hope Town.

The missionaries were delighted the amazing story of New Hope was finally going to be told.

———

By mid-May 1961, it was time for Harold and Ella to return once again for furlough in the United States. They flew from Roberts Field in Liberia to Lisbon and then went by train to Munich, Germany. They bought a bright red Volkswagen Beetle and drove from there to Frankfurt. Rather than having met them in Liberia, Esther was flying in directly from Nigeria to meet them in Frankfurt.

Unfortunately, Esther did not receive word of Harold and Ella's plans until it was too late to purchase her airline ticket. She had to wait an extra day in Kano, in north central Nigeria, until she could catch the next flight that could get her to Frankfurt.

Harold and Ella met the plane the day they expected Esther, but she was not on board. Somewhat worried, they returned to the Bible school where they were staying in Frankfurt and decided they would go out the following day to see if she was on the flight.

Early the next morning, before they finished breakfast, Esther called from the airport to report she was there, waiting for them to come pick her up.

The three of them spent the next four weeks driving through Europe on vacation. Harold and Ella thoroughly enjoyed it. For Esther, the entire trip, and the upcoming furlough in America, were nothing but misery.

She knew she would not be returning to her beloved Africa and the only life she had ever known. Harold and Ella had decided she would stay in Southern California living with Ruth and her family so she could go to high school in America. They were convinced it was the only way Esther would ever have a chance of fitting in any place other than Africa.

As a fifteen-year-old teenager, facing other teenagers in an American high school was probably the most terrifying experience Esther could imagine. She might speak English like they did, but she knew nothing about them—nothing about their culture, nothing about the food they ate or the music they listened to. She knew nothing about America. In reality, she was a foreigner, but no one would know she was.

Through Europe, Esther sat in the back seat of the little VW and ate cheese and Ritz crackers, dreading what lay ahead for her.

One of their stops was Rome. Esther perked up a bit there. It was a fascinating city, with amazing sights.

As they headed back to their parked car after taking a bus tour of the city, Ella had a sudden sense of trouble. "Harold let's hurry. I'm afraid something's happened to the car."

Rounding the corner, her fears were confirmed. The car had been broken into, and all their belongings except one suitcase, with a few of Ella and Esther's old clothes, had been stolen. Other than the one suitcase and an extra suit Harold had with it, they had nothing.

Tired and discouraged, they returned to their hotel. They purchased a few things to travel in and then headed for Sweden to visit their friends the Paulssons before departing for America.

They left Gothenburg, Sweden, on the Swedish Chicago Lines freighter MS *Caroline Smith* on June 30, 1961, their Volkswagen cozily stowed below deck for the amazingly reasonable fee of $126.32. Their fares were equally reasonable, only $210 per person, full fare from Sweden to the United States, via a thousand-mile journey up the St. Lawrence River.

After dodging icebergs during their Atlantic crossing, they arrived in Canada on July 11th. They then drove along the US-Canadian border and down America's west coast to Alhambra. They were back in the United States once more.

~

Their furlough went by quickly, and in May 1962, Harold and Ella sailed once again for Africa.

As much as she hated the idea, Esther stayed in America. She lived with Ruth and her family. When she wasn't busy with homework, she worked at a local coffee shop in order to pay her expenses. Not long after, she began dating Blake Gibbs, a college student who had grown up attending Bethany Church, and knew the Landrus family were missionaries the church supported.

When Harold and Ella arrived back in Liberia, they were asked to minister to the laborers at the huge Goodrich rubber plantation outside of Monrovia at Brewerville. They lived in a travel trailer they parked on the Goodrich grounds. They had a very productive ministry among the hundreds of Goodrich workers, but both of them longed to be at the leper colony at New Hope Town. That was where their hearts were and where they felt they could be of most value. After several months, they were able to leave the rubber plantation and resume their ministry at New Hope. They were thrilled. They remained at New Hope until the end of their three-year term.

In March 1965, they left Liberia and returned to America on furlough. They wanted to be at Bethany Church when, on July 3, 1965, Esther and Blake were married. Dr. Britton, the Landrus family's dear friend and mentor, was there to perform the ceremony.

The year following the wedding was a difficult one for Esther. One month after she and Blake were married, he shipped out for Vietnam, where he spent more than a year serving with the US Army.

In June 1966, Harold and Ella returned to Africa for their eighth and final term as missionaries. They were able to spend the entire term at New Hope Town. They considered being able to serve their last term at New Hope a special gift from the Lord. This was their home in Africa. They had put their hearts and lives, their sweat and tears into this place. They had buried their son in this place. This was where they belonged.

In America, worrying if Blake would return safely from Vietnam, Esther was alone and on her own once again.

In August 1966, he did return, and they began their life together.

Before they were married, after they had been going together for about three years, Blake dutifully wrote a letter to Harold asking for Esther's hand in marriage. He had to wait almost six weeks for Harold's response to finally arrive through the mail. Much to Blake's relief, Harold granted his permission.

When he proposed to Esther, she said "yes." However, she did have a request for him. She asked him to promise he would take her home before Harold and Ella retired. Home, of course, meant Africa.

In spring 1969, Esther and Blake visited Harold and Ella at New Hope Town a few months before they retired. They brought a surprise with them, Ruth's son, Paul. He was eleven years old.

It was remarkable for Blake and Paul to experience Africa for the first time—to see what the Landruses' lives had been like for all those years in the bush. While Ella, Esther, and Paul flew from Monrovia to Cape Palmas, Blake got to drive with Harold from Monrovia the length of the country to the Paul Landrus Memorial Road and to drive the road into New Hope Town. While they were there, he and Paul even got to go out with Harold and Sunday and the road crew to repair a broken bridge. Their visit changed both Blake and Paul forever and placed a piece of Africa in their hearts for the rest of their lives.

For Blake, it was wonderful to better understand and appreciate how Esther had been raised, and how she had become the remarkable woman he had married.

For Esther, she simply loved being back in Africa again. She was home again—alive again. Everything was real again.

Chapter 15
Gifts from the Lord

Harold and Ella left Africa and came back to America to retire in August 1969. They had given their all to the Lord, to Africa, and to the people of Liberia.

They arrived just in time for the birth of Esther's first child, Tyler.

Retiring was really a gift from Harold to Ella. He would probably have spent the rest of their lives in Liberia. He was certainly far more at home there than in America. He knew, though, how much Ella had missed being home when Ruth's children, Paul and Pari, were born and while they were growing up. He knew how much she missed being there for their birthdays and for Thanksgiving and Christmas—how much she missed talking with them and hearing about their friends and time at school. Missing those kinds of things, not being able to build those kinds of memories was part of the price both she and Harold had willingly paid to serve the Lord as missionaries. Ella never complained about it.

Nevertheless, Harold wanted Ella to be able to enjoy all those family times with Paul and Pari as they grew older and also with Esther's new baby, from the very beginning, as well as any other children she might have in the future.

Retirement meant Ella could get to know and enjoy her grandchildren on an ongoing basis, not just for a short time every four years while they were on furlough.

After so many years in the jungles, even though they had been home on furloughs, adjusting to living permanently in America was not easy. It was more difficult for Harold than for Ella.

In addition to spending time with family and friends, they attended Bethany Church regularly. Ella cared for her ailing mother. She also began taking flower arrangements that decorated the platform at the church each Sunday and distributing them to elderly members of the congregation who were sick or shut in. Her visits brought encouragement and a happy break in their day. That was especially true a few years later when Ella began taking Tyler, probably six or seven years old, and his four- or five-year-old little sister, Kristin, with her. The children always added some extra joy to Ella's visits, and the people looked forward to them immensely.

~

Though they were off the mission field and retired, Harold always seemed to be working on a project.

Things just seemed to happen differently around Harold than they would have for anyone else. Some of the uniqueness of Harold's life can be summed up in an episode that occurred in America. It was a clear indication the Lord was still looking after him, even though he was no longer a missionary in Africa.

Harold had worked all day cutting some large, overhanging oleander bushes along the driveway at Ruth's house. As he cut, he loaded the branches into the bed of his mini pickup truck, piling them higher and higher. By the time he had finished, the branches towered above the truck and hung out both sides to nearly twice the normal width of the vehicle.

Recognizing it was too late to drive to the dump to get rid of the branches, Harold headed home with two of his grandchildren, Tyler and Kristin, bouncing along beside him in the front seat. (This was before the time of mandatory seat belts.)

The route home led down Huntington Drive, the main avenue through the very expensive, very proper community of San Marino, California.

With the load hanging out in all directions, Harold couldn't see anything in his rearview mirrors when a motorcycle policeman drove up behind him, red lights flashing. The officer followed what looked like a giant pile of brush for several blocks, wondering when this guy was going to pull over.

Eventually, Tyler, all of about seven years old, happened to see the red lights behind them. "Grandpa, Grandpa," he shouted. "There's a policeman behind us."

Harold quickly pulled to the right and stopped his truck. Then, in a fashion typical for him (but definitely not acceptable today), he jumped out of the truck, walked back to the motorcycle, and thrust out his hand just as the officer was climbing off.

Taken completely by surprise, the policeman nonetheless reached out to shake the hand being extended to him.

"Hello. I'm H. H. Landrus, missionary to Liberia, West Africa," Harold announced to him proudly. "What can I do for you, Mister?"

Shaking his head in disbelief, the policeman responded, "Don't you know you can't drive that thing on city streets? You can't see a thing behind you. And nobody can get around you. Besides, if you're a gardener in this town, you have to have a business license."

Harold explained what he had been doing and assured the officer he really didn't think he'd done anything wrong. After all, he could have driven that load down the road he'd built in Africa.

Not believing anyone could be so out of touch with how things were done in America, the officer gave Harold a traffic ticket and sent him on his way, warning him to get off the roads as quickly as possible and to rearrange the load before taking it to the dump the next morning.

At home two days later, Harold heard a knock at the front door and went to answer it. As he swung the door open, he recognized the man standing there as the policeman who had given him the ticket in San Marino.

Before Harold could say a word, the officer began, "Mr. Landrus, do you remember me?"

"Well, I surely do," Harold responded. "You're the fella who gave me a ticket the other day."

"Yes, sir, I am," the officer responded. Looking down and shuffling his feet slightly, the policeman went on. "I've been thinking about that ticket. It just doesn't seem right for me to give you a ticket, you bein' a missionary and all. So, if it's all right with you, just give the ticket back to me, and I'll take care of it. You just forget I ever gave it to you. Would that be OK?"

"Well, you know it would." Harold grinned. He ducked back into the house and emerged holding the ticket. Handing it to the policeman, he said, "I thank you for that. That's a fine thing for you to do. God bless you for it."

The officer smiled and walked away.

That was the way things happened with Harold. First, he would do something the rest of us would likely never do. He would do it in a way we would probably label unacceptable. And yet the job got done. The results were achieved. And God performed a little miracle to provide encouragement along the way!

That was the way Harold's life was in Africa. He did what needed to be done, the best he knew how to do it, with God providing a string of miracles, big and small, to keep it all on track, day by day, one day at a time.

～

Harold and Ella's life in Africa and the work and ministry they did there had an enormous impact on the individual lives of countless thousands of Liberians. Several months after they had retired, Ella received a wonderful letter from a grateful Liberian clearly illustrating that fact.

As a young boy, the letter writer had attended one of the Bible schools Harold and Ella had run deep in the Liberian jungle. After graduating, he had become a pastor. The letter was addressed "Dear Ma Landrus" and was a thank you note. In part, and in his own words, it read, "Thank you, Ma, for giving everything to us. You left your home in America and came far, far for to tell us about Jesus. Without you, we would not know he died for we. Thank you, Ma. Now we have Jesus in our heart. Our sins, they are gone. He make us new people, our lives, they are good now."

That was what Harold and Ella went to Africa for. That was why they did what they did—why they endured what they endured. They did it so native tribespeople could hear about Jesus and invite Him into their hearts. That's what gave the Landruses' lives purpose and worth. Their lives were demonstrations of their faithfulness to God's call, and of God's faithfulness to them, through it all, no matter what.

In 1979, after Harold had passed away, Ella had the unexpected opportunity to return to Africa again. Esther and Blake and their children had been asked to go to Sierra Leone to carry on Norm and Betty Backman's ministry for about six weeks, while the Backmans were in America for their son's wedding. Blake and Esther invited Ella to go with them.

At first, she was reluctant. She didn't know what she could do there. When Blake and Esther promised they would visit Liberia while they were there, she was sure no one would remember her. It took a great deal of discussion, but they were finally able to persuade her to join them.

In addition to Ella, Blake and Esther invited Steven Davis, a young family friend, to join them for the trip. It was the first trip to Africa for Steven, and for Tyler, and Kristin.

It was a wonderful trip. Ella had the time of her life preaching and leading Bible studies. One of the natives served as interpreter. Tyler and Kristin made friends with the children of a Lebanese diamond merchant who were about their same ages. They were in the town of Sefadu, about two hundred miles interior from Freetown, the capital. It was a remarkable adventure for all of them.

There wasn't the bush of Liberia. It was much dryer. The forests were not as dense and lush and they were broken by large areas of open arid grassland. Ella loved it anyway.

About a week before they were to head back to America, they drove south from Sefadu through the town of Kenema and on toward the Liberian border. It was a long, dusty drive on a definitely unimproved dirt road. The border crossing for their entry into Liberia was marked only by a stick across the roadway. The nearby checkpoint "office" was a mud hut with a thatched roof.

As Blake brought their vehicle to a stop, a border official stepped out of the hut and approached them. He asked to see their passports and Blake gave them to him. Then the man headed back into the hut.

Moments later, he emerged from the hut running back toward their vehicle. He was carrying one of the passports, pointing to the open picture page, and shouting, "Where is this woman? Where is this Landrus lady?"

In the vehicle, everyone was confused and concerned. What could possibly be wrong and what did this border official want? He had the power to make their entry into the country very difficult and time-consuming.

As the official approached the driver's side window, Blake said, "Mrs. Landrus is right here in the back seat. Is there a problem?"

Looking through the window and speaking directly to Ella, the man said, "Ma Landrus, I know you! Pa Landrus, he gave me my first ride in a vehicle. It is good you have come back to Liberia!"

Then speaking to everyone in the vehicle in his most "official" voice, he said, "The rules say, in order to be permitted to enter Liberia you have twenty-four hours to get from here to Monrovia and to report to the immigration office there. There will be much paperwork required."

Blake responded, "We'll go directly there."

Then the man said enthusiastically, "But I know you. Because I know Ma Landrus." He waved the passport with a broad smile. "You will not need to go to Monrovia. I will stamp your passports for you to stay in Liberia for as long as you wish."

He turned quickly, disappeared into the hut, and reemerged shortly with all their passports. Showing them, he said, "You see, they are all stamped for you. Welcome to Liberia." Then looking at Ella with a smile, he said gently, "Welcome home, Ma. Welcome home."

Ella needn't have worried about being remembered. The Lord graciously made that abundantly clear to her through the border official at a crossing between Sierra Leone and Liberia in the middle of nowhere a decade after she had left.

They did go to Monrovia for a reunion between Ella and Maryann. It was a special time for both of them, remembering when they had met at Palipo, their ministry at Bwah, and their many happy years serving together at New Hope.

While they were in Liberia, Ella also got to go back to New Hope Town one last time. It was a special gift from the Lord. As she walked into what had once been her home, there was an old Liberian man with failing eyesight sitting at the table with his back to her. She hadn't known if he was still alive or whether she would be able to find him if he was, but she knew immediately it was him. Her heart filled with joy and her eyes filled with tears as she stopped and said gently, "Do you know who I am?"

Dear, faithful Cook Daniel stood immediately, turned toward her, and said, "Ma Landrus, I could never forget you! You have come home!

⌒

Soon after Harold and Ella had retired, their friends at Bethany held a special welcome home banquet in their honor. Dr. Britton had retired by then as well but wouldn't miss being there for this special occasion.

Following Dr. Britton's leadership and vision, Bethany Church had made it possible for Harold and Ella to go to Liberia. Bethany had faithfully supported them for nearly thirty-five years while they were in the field. Bethany had bought Harold his first airplane. Bethany had bought their "light plant" and a sawmill and the Dodge Power Wagon when they were at New Hope Town.

Now, as Harold and Ella entered retirement, they had virtually no income. Bethany, again, stepped in to meet the need. The church committed to providing them with a retirement benefit for the rest of their lives. When Ella died, Bethany had generously and faithfully supported the Landruses for seventy years!

Over the course of those seven decades and under the leadership of five different pastors, the people of Bethany loved and encouraged and supported Harold and Ella continuously and without fail. This was a true testament to their hearts for the Lord and for those who have yet to hear the message of Jesus.

As the gala evening drew to a close, Reverend Kenneth Haystead, Bethany's pastor at the time, called Harold and Ella forward to present them with gifts and to express the church's love and appreciation for them. As he closed, he turned to Harold and asked, "Harold, if you had it to do all over again, what would you do?"

Without hesitating, Harold replied, "If I had a thousand lives to live, I'd choose to live every one of them as a missionary to Liberia."

Epilogue...

Harold passed away following a series of strokes in 1977. He had fought the good fight. He had finished the race.

I picture the scene no other way than that he was greeted at heaven's gate by Jesus, the Lord and Savior he had served for so many years in Africa.

I believe Christ's greeting must have been, "Welcome, Harold. You have been a good and faithful servant." Perhaps this was followed by, "Now I'd like you to meet a band of very exhausted guardian angels I've had looking after you for all those years."

Ella went to be with the Lord in December 2007. She was ninety-eight years old. She had led a long, remarkable, extraordinary life. I'm sure, like Harold, she was greeted in heaven by Christ himself, along with hundreds, if not thousands of Africans with whom she and Harold had shared the life-changing message of the Gospel.

Acknowledgements...

There is much I am thankful for in developing and writing this book.

I am grateful for the time the Lord enabled me to spend with Harold and Ella Landrus. They were remarkable people. Their commitment to serving the Lord and the courage with which they lived their lives are truly an inspiration to me.

It would not have been possible to write this book without countless hours of conversation with them. Particularly with Ella, after Harold passed away. As I began gathering information, Ella willingly shared their experiences as well as boxes and boxes of letters, documents, journals, and pictures chronicling their lives. Ella's mother, Anna Pratt, kept the letters Harold and Ella wrote home to her during their years in Africa. Those letters helped enormously in understanding the Landrus story and in putting the chronology of their lives together.

Thanks to Ruth Seifert, Harold and Ella's eldest daughter, who was born in Liberia, for her willingness to share her life and her first-hand knowledge of the family's life on the field.

Three of Harold and Ella's great-grandchildren contributed significantly to the project. Hollie Seifert spent hours editing and making it a "better read". Davy Seifert did an amazing job bringing decades old, faded, poor quality pictures to life so they could be included in the book. He also helped create the map. Ireland Walton made it a better book with her editing and content recommendations. I am grateful to them for their work and, as their Papa, immensely proud of them for the extraordinary people they are.

Thanks to Kris Gibbs, our amazing daughter-in-law, for her help with layout, content, and editing.

Thank you to Debra Perryman for her advice and recommendations.

Thanks to the team at WestBow Press for their efforts at making my dream of publishing this book a reality.

Special thanks to Esther, my wife, the love of my life. She is Harold and Ella's second daughter. I thank her for sharing her life and her perspective so freely and openly. For helping me understand "what it was like" for her and for the rest of the family.

To all who have encouraged me over the years to write this book, thank you. We want as many people as possible to know the Landrus family story because their story is a powerful testimony to the Lord's faithfulness, mercy, and especially to His guiding hand in and through every adventure, every experience they encountered as missionaries in Africa.

About the Author...

W. Blake Gibbs, a native of Pasadena, California, grew up in neighboring Arcadia. He earned his bachelor's degree from Claremont Men's College (now Claremont McKenna College).

After serving in the US Army in Vietnam, Blake began a nearly forty-year career in business and industry.

He married Esther Landrus, Harold and Ella's youngest daughter, in 1965. They have two children, five grandchildren, and two great-grandchildren (with another on the way).

Together, Blake and Esther have travelled extensively in Africa, Asia, and Europe.

When Blake turned sixty, He and Esther felt the Lord was leading them to become missionaries with Agape Children's Ministry. Agape rescues street children and other at-risk children in Kenya. The ministry's focus is to share the Gospel with the children and, after counseling and preparation, to reintegrate them back into their family or extended family. The Lord has granted Agape remarkable results with the children. Over the past decade, they have a success rate of nearly 80 percent. Blake and Esther retired from Agape in 2019.

They currently live in Modesto, California.

Visit the Jungle Courage web site at:
www.junglecourage.com

To learn more about Agape go to:
www.agapechildren.org

Printed in the United States
by Baker & Taylor Publisher Services